P9-CJZ-022

ED YOUNG

Been There. Done That. Now What?

The meaning of life may surprise you

BROADMAN
& HOLMAN
PUBLISHERS

Nashville, Tennessee

© 1994 by Ed Young
All rights reserved

Printed in the United States of America

4261-58
0-8054-6158-2

Dewey Decimal Classification: 128
Subject Heading: CHRISTIAN LIFE \ ETHICS
Library of Congress Card Catalog Number: 94-34952

Library of Congress Cataloging-in-Publication Data
Young, H. Edwin, 1936–
    Been there. Done that. Now what? : the meaning of life may surprise you / by Ed Young.
        p. cm.
    Includes bibliographical references.
    ISBN 0-8054-6158-2
    1. Bible. O.T. Ecclesiastes—Meditations.   2. Meaning
(Philosophy)—Biblical teaching.   I. Title.
    BS1475.4.Y68   1994
    223'.806—dc20
                                                        94-34952
                                                          CIP

This book is gratefully dedicated to seven wonderful friends and men of God who, in each church I have pastored, have consistently and faithfully introduced other people to the meaning of life whose name is Jesus:

Jimmy Spell: Woodland Hills Baptist Church
Jackson, Mississippi

Wally Dean: Fernwood Baptist Church
Spartanburg, South Carolina

Floyd Glover: First Baptist Church
Erwin, North Carolina

Jack Abbott: First Baptist Church
Canton, North Carolina

Wesley Neely: First Baptist Church
Taylors, South Carolina

Lud Milne: First Baptist Church
Columbia, South Carolina

Johnny Baker: Second Baptist Church
Houston, Texas

And to L. G. Gates, pastor of the First Baptist Church of Laurel, Mississippi, who for forty years prayed these words as a benediction each Sunday:

Now to Him who is able to keep you from stumbling, and to make you stand in the presence of His glory blameless with great joy, to the only God our Savior, through Jesus Christ our Lord, be glory, majesty, dominion and authority, before all time and now and forever. Amen. (Jude 23–24)

Contents

ACKNOWLEDGMENTS

L ET ME FIRST THANK Jerry Vines, pastor of First Baptist Church of Jacksonville, Florida, who convinced me of the timeliness of Ecclesiastes. This conversation led me to reread Charles Swindoll's excellent book, *On the Ragged Edge*, published in 1985. Coincidentally, I happened to be reading a book by Peter Kreeft, the Boston College apologist, and noticed that he also explored Ecclesiastes in a collection of essays entitled *The Three Philosophies of Life*. Suddenly, the search was on. Ecclesiastes began to come alive for me, and God was most definitely up to something. I decided to use Solomon's life as the basis of my quiet time study and, for several months, lived in his shoes.

"Through many dangers, toils and snares" (a reading of all the commentaries), "I have already come" (twenty-six sermons on Ecclesiastes preached to the Second Baptist family in Houston). Here is the finished product. How the Holy Spirit works in speaking to and through this pastor never ceases to amaze. Thank You, Lord.

After studying Solomon and seeking to understand his life, I am more convinced than ever that God gives enough reasons for our faith to be reasonable, but not enough reasons to live by reason alone. Solomon discovered this the hard way. We must not repeat his mistake. *Been There. Done That. Now What?* is written for those who struggle with their faith, as well as those who walk in faith. It is an argument for the *absolute* truth of God, written for the doubter and the skeptic, the agnostic and the atheist—those who have not yet met Him who visited us from above the sun. Ecclesiastes is also for the believer. Solomon's spiritual autobiography impels us to answer the basic questions of life, challenges us to go deeper with Him, and reminds us how easy it is to let the world's agenda squeeze us into its mold. Ecclesiastes forces us to think, examine, re-examine, question, and search. It calls us to doubt our doubts.

Without question, it is a word from God for such a time as this. Life does have meaning. Don't miss it.

Special thanks to Leigh McLeroy, my writing assistant, who takes my oral pronouncements and transforms them into the written word. Leigh is a most gifted writer and scholar whose contributions to this study are too numerous to detail. She has taken my creativity and brought it down to earth—and added to it her insightfulness and breadth of understanding. Her deep commitment and steady witness breathe life into any endeavor.

Also, let me thank Beverly Gambrell, my research assistant, for chasing down quotations, illustrations, articles, books, and authors I vaguely remember and sometimes only imagined! In addition to being a master of the one-liner and a CompuServe guru, you, Bev, are a faithful sister in Christ.

The church side of my life is managed by Linda Richard, my administrative assistant, who effectively helps me prioritize my time. Her skillful handling of my office and pastoral pressures makes preaching and publishing possible.

Also, thanks to Glenn Lucke, a young and gifted scholar who came off the bench in the fourth quarter to bring an added dose of practicality and real-world savvy to this manuscript.

Team '94—my personal prayer team of strong and faithful brothers in Christ—has held up my arms daily for the battle. Their commitment means more to me than I can say.

I am grateful to Chuck Wilson, vice-president of Trade and Retail Markets for Broadman & Holman Publishers, for his unfeigned support and encouragement of this project from its birth to completion. Thank you, dear brother, for every expression of friendship. Bucky Rosenbaum, Greg Wilson, Kirk Freeman, and Vicki Crumpton are valuable members of the Broadman & Holman team who are not only dedicated to their vocation but are solid servants of the King.

Thanks as always to dear Jo Beth, my wife and mother to our three sons, Ed, Ben, and Cliff, "mother-in-love" to Lisa and Elliott, and "Super Mimi" to our four grandchildren, LeeBeth, E. J., and twin girls Laurie and Landra. Thank you, Joby, for romancing our home for thirty-five wonderful years. The words of Browning that your Uncle Wilfred quoted at our wedding were indeed prophetic:

> Grow old along with me!
> The best is yet to be;
> The last of life for which the first was made;
> Our times are in His hand who saith,
> "A whole I planned.
> Youth shows but half;
> Trust God: See all, nor be afraid."

INTRODUCTION

WHEN MY FRIEND JERRY VINES told me that Ecclesiastes was an excellent book for gaining an understanding of today's "Boomers" and "Busters," I was skeptical. But after a casual study I understood the relevance. Not only that, its length was well-suited to a generation who wants everything *now*— all twelve chapters can be read in a leisurely forty minutes.

Ecclesiastes is pure philosophy written as a confessional autobiography. The book's composition style is meandering, and it is held together loosely by a series of suppositions about life and death. The unvarying theme, which revolves around man's foremost question, is treated in an amazing variety of ways. Ecclesiastes not only asks this one question repeatedly, but contains King Solomon's confession of how he spent his lifetime in search of its answer.

Ecclesiastes is the logical point from which to embark on a study of the entire Bible, because it asks the question the rest of the Scripture answers: "What is the meaning of life?" Tragically, most people today have no clue. Socrates said the unexamined life is not worth living—and he was absolutely right! "When you get where you are going, where will you be?" is certainly an important question, but even more important to consider is "Why are you going there in the first place?" Questions like "Where did you come from?" and "Where are you going?" have value for us only when "Why are you here?" is understood.

Solomon had the ability and resources to search everywhere under the sun for the answer. At the end of his life he was the quintessential pessimist. To life's foremost question, he could only answer, "Vanity . . . all is vanity." Or simply put, "Life is without meaning." (So Jean-Paul Sartre's "No Exit" is Ecclesiastes restated.)

Only one individual on this planet has ever been given a blank check by someone who could deliver, regardless of the sum. The Almighty had said to Solomon, "Name it and claim it." Solomon chose—and his choice pleased the Giver. He asked God for wisdom and he also received riches and honor in tremendous supply (1 Kings 3:4–13). What a gracious God! What an auspicious beginning!

Solomon, you will remember, wrote three books in the Bible. Song of Solomon was penned when he was young and hopelessly in love. Proverbs was the fertile ground of his middle years, when God was exalting his every endeavor. Ecclesiastes was written when he was old, confused, and empty—having discovered that the things of this world do not satisfy. Here is Horatio Alger in reverse: from riches to rags, from a tremendous beginning to a near-tragic end. That his was a gradual fall makes it no less dramatic.

In his early years, Solomon was a theologian. He was known as "Qoheleth," or "the preacher." (Theology pictures God searching for us.) In his later years, he became a philosopher. (Philosophy pictures our search for God.) What happened? I believe Solomon, like so many in our culture, began to sing the Frank Sinatra refrain: "I did it my way." "Thy will" gradually became "my will." As a result, God's man became his own man. Sound familiar?

The apostle Paul said it correctly: "The one who sows to his own flesh shall from the flesh reap corruption" (Gal. 6:8). Solomon was a great man, internationally acclaimed. He was the builder of history's most famous place of worship—the temple—and an "attender" every time the doors were opened, but he (of all people) broke off his relationship with Him who is above the sun to "do his own thing." Could there be a more accurate picture of us, as we rush headlong into the twenty-first century?

Study Solomon closely. Here was brilliance unsurpassed in all of history. Here was exhaustive pursuit of human wisdom, education, power, wealth, pleasure, religion, temperance, and longevity. It would have been no boast for him to have said of any place under the sun: "Been there." Or to have said of any lifestyle or activity under the sun: "Done that." This phenomenal personality worked the world's agenda, receiving every recognition and accolade imaginable. An authority no less than the Queen of Sheba, after observing Solomon's accomplishments first hand, said, "The half has not yet been told." Here is the ultimate twentieth-century secularist, who just happened to live four thousand years too soon! He had everything and still came up empty.

Here is the bottom line: Our arms *are* too short to box with God. Ask Marilyn Monroe or Janis Joplin or Michael Jackson—or march backward in history and inquire of the first Adam himself, "What does it profit a man if he gains the whole world and loses his soul?"

Scary? Modern? Challenging? You bet.

Ecclesiastes *is* the book for this generation. We, too, have been there. We, too, have done that. And for every honest searcher who has not stopped long enough to be found by the Searcher, this is the time to ask, "Now what?"

This book is divided into three sections. The first two chapters are under the heading "Been There." They set the stage for Solomon's search.

The next five are headed "Done That," and they chronicle the king's attempts to find meaning in five "under the sun" endeavors: hedonism, philosophy, intellectualism, materialism, and religion. Each subsequent chapter is followed by a brief application section entitled "An Above the Sun Postscript." Solomon, like many of us, did not always practice what he preached. These "Postscripts" are meant to serve as a practical bridge between *theology* and *application*. What we do is a direct result of who we are. "Postscripts" will help you translate your beliefs into action.

The final chapters are under the heading "Now What?" and each illustrates a directive by Solomon for the man or woman who is interested in an escape from "flatland living." They are a road map to true meaning and are meant to change lives. (Consider yourself warned!)

"An Appeal to the Open-Minded Skeptic" is a final word for all who have decided to live "under the sun." Our skeptical, humanistic culture implies that if a person cannot find meaning—or at least satisfaction—in this life, he is weak. Not so. Only the strong are willing to seek and ask the profound questions that cannot be easily answered. Be brave—examine life!

Scripture references are included at the end of each chapter that direct the reader to the corresponding text of Ecclesiastes. I believe that by reading the Scripture itself, you will be rewarded with a greater understanding of yourself, your world, and God.

Part I

Been There:
Under-the-Sun Living

1

Flatland Living

In the land of lobelias and tennis flannels
The rabbit shall burrow and the thorn revisit,
The nettle shall flourish on the gravel court,
And the wind shall say:
"Here were decent godless people:
Their only monument the asphalt road
And a thousand lost golf balls."

—T. S. Eliot

SERIOUS FANS OF BASKETBALL will remember October 6, 1993, as a significant date in the sport's history. Of course, the professional basketball season was not yet underway, but on this particular autumn day the man who was unarguably the game's finest player called a press conference—and retired at age thirty, after winning an unprecedented third world championship and seven consecutive NBA scoring titles. There was no injury, no indictments or shocking personal revelations, no contract dispute.

As he faced the assembled crowd of media representatives with their cameras, microphones, and notepads, Chicago Bulls superstar Michael Jeffrey Jordan told them the game offered no more challenges to motivate him. Having accomplished everything basketball could ask of him, he simply felt it was time to call it a career. This young man, whose God-given athletic ability revolutionized the way the game was played, retired with more money than he could possibly spend in a single lifetime, and at an age when many are only beginning to taste career success. Including endorsements that far exceeded his salary, his last season as a player netted him $40 million.

Why would a man with everything under the sun walk away? Jordan, whose father was murdered earlier in the year, hinted at the answer as he told reporters, "One thing about my father's death was that it reinforced how [life] can be taken away from you anytime." The "stuff" of life lost its meaning for Jordan when he considered the fragile transience of it. Basketball—and the fame, money, and excitement of being better at it than anyone else—no longer was enough for this superstar. And as he looked ahead to the prospect of another NBA season, in his heart he must have said, "Been there. Done that. Now what?"

> *"Why is this nation that marched so proudly into the twentieth century slouching so dejectedly toward the third millenium?"*

This sense of detached meaninglessness is not limited to burned-out, multi-million-dollar athletes. *Forbes* magazine devoted its seventy-fifth anniversary issue to a single topic: "Why we feel so bad when we have it so good." Noting that Americans live better than any other people on the planet, *Forbes* invited prominent observers of modern culture to speculate as to why we are "depressed," or in the words of editor James Michaels, "Why is this nation that marched so proudly into the twentieth century slouching so dejectedly toward the third millenium?" The articles included in this special issue chronicled an alarming loss of values, absolutes, and meaning in contemporary life.

Theologians and philosophers of the day have asked similar questions. "Now why are we bored?" queried philosopher and author Peter Kreeft. "Why this distinctively modern phenomenon? The very word for it did not exist in pre-modern languages! Above all, how do we explain the irony that the very society which for the first time in history has conquered nature by technology and turned the world into a giant fun-and-games factory, a rich kid's playroom, the very society which has the least reason to be bored, is the most bored?"[1]

If the word for "boredom" is a modern invention, the search for meaning in life is not. It is as old as time. In every man and woman, there is a gnawing desire to know what life is all about that goes beyond activity, intellectual prowess, fame, or wealth. "Who am I?" and "Why am I here?" are deeply profound questions that have perplexed great thinkers throughout the ages. From Augustine's *Confessions* and Aquinas's *Treatise on Happiness* to Pascal's *Penseés* and Aristotle's *Ethics*, we have probed for the "why" of our existence with a dogged determination.

The modern philosophers—Marx, Camus, Nietzsche, Kant, Rousseau—have been less direct, either edging around the questions or ignoring them altogether, because they have no answers. Kant would say that there is only one road—the path of duty. Rousseau believed that his purpose was to reflect his own nature, and he was egotistical enough to hold that he saw himself as God did. Marx preached that the value of anything was reflected by its "labor-time," that is, the time it took a worker to produce it. Nietzsche's assertion that God is dead (and man has killed him) meant that life is

> *We have probed for the "why" of our existence with a dogged determination.*

no longer undergirded by eternity and that no wisdom exists beyond man's own. Each struggled to understand the "what" of his world more than the "why."

Years ago, a man with more power, money, and fame than Michael Jordan also asked, "What is the meaning of life?"—and chronicled his search for the answer in a book. His name was Solomon and his book is called Ecclesiastes. This philosophical exploration of "flatland living"—life under the sun—is the only book of philosophy in the Bible. Because I believe the Bible is the greatest book in the world, I would argue that Ecclesiastes is the greatest book of philosophy in the world. In fact, if I were asked to teach the whole Bible, I would be tempted to start with Ecclesiastes—because it asks the questions the rest of the Bible answers in sixty-five more books of prophecy, poetry, history, and narrative.

The late C. S. Lewis said that people can ask only three basic ethical or philosophical questions. To describe them, he used the metaphor of ships at sea. When sailing ships leave port to embark on a journey, sailors must determine three things, according to Lewis. First, they must know how to keep from bumping into one another. This is a question of "social ethics." In other words, how do we get along with one another on this journey called life? Second, they must know how the individual ships remain seaworthy. This is "personal ethics," and it deals with the individual's vices and virtues—with character. Finally, sailors must decide where the ships are going. What is their mission and their destination? This last question is the ultimate one for us. What is the purpose of human life? Why are we here?

> *To understand Solomon's quest for meaning in Ecclesiastes, we have to know who he was.*

People are asking the same question today that they have asked for centuries. The honest search for its answer became Solomon's consuming quest. Michael Jordan has asked it as a young man, and presumably, his search is still underway. Solomon came to the end of his life before he had tasted all that the world had to offer, but as an old man, he arrived at the same conclusion Jordan reached: "Been there. Done that. Now what?" Or, in the language of the Old Testament, "Vanity of vanities, all is vanity." Solomon—with immeasurable wealth, power, and wisdom at his disposal—tried everything that life under the sun had to offer and came up empty. He tried pleasure. He tried philosophy. He tried materialism. He tried education. He tried religion. Nothing satisfied.

In the end, he rediscovered the God of his youth, and only then did the pieces fall into place. Contemporary society's boredom is an "under the sun" phenomenon as well. Our dilemma can be compared to that of a child with too many expensive toys: "Why is an American child playing with $10,000 of video equipment more bored than an Indian child playing with two sticks and a stone? The answer is inescapable. There is only one thing that never gets boring: God."[2] G. K. Chesterton concluded that when a man ceases to worship God he does not worship *nothing*, he worships *anything*, and, as Solomon would add, "[he] finds nothing worthy of his worship."

What about us? Where did we come from? Where are we going? What do our lives mean? When the hour of death comes and we are carried out, when they lower us into a waiting grave and toss

> *There is only one thing that never gets boring: God.*

the earth back in, what will it all amount to? At that moment each of us will be "as is"—without title or achievement, without cash or credit. We will be alone. Solomon knew that at death he would stand alone before the God of creation. What difference will it make that we lived and died? That is the mystery, the supreme question, in all of life lived under the sun.

What's It All About?

Ask a hundred people the meaning of life and be prepared for a hundred different answers—each of them given from a particular point of view. *Life* magazine queried a number of people on "why we are here" for its holiday issue several years ago, and the responses represent a medley of philosophies, both ancient and modern. Jose Martinez, a taxi driver, saw it this way:

> We're here to die, just live and die. I do some fishing, take my girl out, pay taxes, do a little reading, then get ready to drop dead. Life is a big fake. . . . You're rich or you're poor. You're here, you're gone. You're like the wind. After you're gone, other people will come. The only cure for the world's illness is nuclear war—wipe everything out and start over.

Jason Gaes, an eleven-year-old cancer victim, had a stronger sense of purpose, despite his grim circumstances:

I think God made each of us for a different reason. If God gives you a great voice, maybe he wants you to sing. Or else if God makes you seven feet tall, maybe he wants you to play for the Lakers or Celtics. When my friend Kim died from her cansur [sic] I asked my Mom if God was going to make Kim die when she was only six, why did he make her born at all? But my Mom said even thogh [sic] she was only six she changed people's lives. I used to wonder why did God pick on me and give me cansur. Maybe it was because he wanted me to be a dr who takes care of kids with cansur . . .

Ordinary people answered. Famous people gave it a shot. Writer and humorist Garrison Keillor offered this response:

To know and serve God, of course, is why we're here, a clear truth that, like the nose on your face, is near at hand and easily discernible but can make you dizzy if you try to focus on it too hard. But a little faith will see you through. What else will except faith in such a cynical, corrupt time? When the country goes temporarily to the dogs, cats must learn to be circumspect, walk on fences, sleep in trees and have faith that all this woofing is not the last word.[3]

To weigh the validity of anyone's answer about the meaning of life, it is important to know where he is coming from—what his perspective is. Jose observed life from the inside of a taxi cab. Jason saw it from the eyes of a child in a hospital cancer ward. Garrison Keillor's perspective combines a strict Plymouth Brethren midwestern upbringing with a keen sense of humor. To understand Solomon's quest for meaning in Ecclesiastes, we have to know who he was.

Who's Asking?

Ecclesiastes' author was Solomon, the son of David, king of Israel, and Bathsheba, the widow of Uriah—the general whose murder David ordered. Solomon ruled Israel during forty years of peace and prosperity. His heritage was a godly one. Although many remember his father David chiefly for his adulterous affair with Bathsheba, David was a man who loved God—and whose repentence was as intense as his sin had been.

On his deathbed, David ordered that Solomon be anointed king of Israel and offered this advice to his son:

I am going the way of all the earth. Be strong, therefore, and show yourself a man. And keep the charge of the Lord your God, to walk in His ways, to keep His statutes, His commandments, His ordinances, and His testimonies, according to what is written in the law of Moses, that you may succeed in all that you do and wherever you turn, so that the Lord may carry out His promise which he spoke concerning me, saying, "If your sons are careful of their way, to walk before Me in truth with all their heart and with all their soul, you shall not lack a man on the throne of Israel." (1 Kings 2:2–4)

Solomon began well. He had a godly heritage. He was wealthy, powerful, and wise. In fact, Solomon was blessed by God in a way that few men have ever been. His assets surpassed even the superstars of our day; he was "dressed for success" in every sense of the word. As a young king, God had made him an offer unlike any other recorded in all the Bible (see 1 Kings 3:12–15). Appearing to him in a dream at night, God said to Solomon, "Ask what you wish me to give you" (v. 5). Solomon humbly responded that God had already blessed him greatly by allowing him to follow his father, David, on the throne. He realized, however, that the task before him was enormous. "So," he responded, "give Thy servant an understanding heart to judge Thy people to discern between good and evil. For who is able to judge this great people of Thine?" (v. 9).

> *Solomon was blessed by God in a way that few men have ever been.*

Solomon's answer pleased God. No one else in history had ever been given such an open-ended offer. He had written Solomon a "blank check," and Solomon had chosen well. He could have asked for anything: long life, riches, continued prosperity, or good health. Instead he asked for the discernment to execute justice among the people of Israel. True to His word, God gave Solomon what he requested. And just as true to His character, He gave even more: "Behold, I have done according to your words. Behold, I have given you a wise and discerning heart, so that there has been no one like you before you, nor shall one like you arise after you. And I have also given you what you have not asked, both riches and honor, so that there will not be any among the kings like you all your days" (1 Kings 3:12–13).

God's great gifts of wisdom, discernment, riches, and honor elevated Solomon to a position no other individual has enjoyed, before or since. The world was at his fingertips. His future was bright. Then slowly, almost imperceptibly, an erosion process began that ended in his disillusioned benediction, "Vanity of vanities, all is vanity." Or "Been there. Done that. Now what?" His descent to "flatland living" can be observed in the books that he wrote. The Bible contains three of them, penned at different times in his life.

> *Proverbs is full of condensed wisdom, or "reality bites," that are contemporary and true.*

As a young man, King Solomon wrote Song of Songs, or the Song of Solomon. It is a love story—a passionate one—of one man and one woman, a bridegroom and his bride. It brims with romance and energy; in fact, in modern translations, the pages seem to sizzle! The story of his youth was one of deep passion and devotion for his true love. In the beginning, he knew how to romance the home.

Solomon chronicled his middle-aged years in Proverbs, a collection of profound, pithy sayings written by one who had observed life—and taken notes! Proverbs is full of condensed wisdom, or "reality bites," that are contemporary and true. His mid-life years were marked by their practicality.

The elderly Solomon wrote the Book of Ecclesiastes. The passion of youth was gone. The practicality of middle age deteriorated into the weathered, tired cynicism of old age. In Ecclesiastes this gifted leader, this man of wisdom and prestige with every talent and asset possible, said that he was empty. Actually, Ecclesiastes was a written address—and it is easy to imagine a graying monarch speaking to the gathered assembly from the portico of his palace. It takes forty minutes or so to read the book aloud—about the length of a sermon—but it is not a sermon. It is a testimony. Solomon observed, "I went down every path. I exhausted every extreme in life, because I had the talent and the means and the position to do so. And now that I'm old, I see that most of it was just so much chasing after wind. Life is meaningless."

Solomon's term was *vanity*—a word that literally means "vapor." The word *vanity* is left when a soap bubble pops. Vanity is when we have added everything up and the sum is zero, nothing, emptiness, meaninglessness. Old Solomon looked at all that he had done, built, conquered, and accomplished, and he simply said, "All is vanity." How did this happen? Where was the fire of youth or the practical wisdom of middle age? What became of this man who had everything under the sun?

Held by a Single Strand

A Danish philosopher tells the story of a spider who dropped a single strand down from the top rafter of an old barn and began to weave his web. Days, weeks, and months went by, and the web grew. It regularly provided the spider food as flies, mosquitoes, and other small insects were caught in its elaborate maze. The spider built his web larger and larger until it became the envy of all the other spiders. One day this productive spider was traveling across his beautifully woven web

> *God gave Solomon the gift of wisdom and the ability to discern.*

and noticed a single strand going up into the darkness of the rafters. *I wonder why this is here?* he thought. *It doesn't serve to catch me any dinner.* And saying that, the spider climbed as high as he could and severed the single strand that was his sustenance. When he did, the entire web slowly began to tumble to the floor of the barn, taking the spider with it. This is exactly what happened to Solomon.

As a young man, he asked God for the gift of discernment that would make him a good king, and God answered his prayer. Entering into a special relationship with Solomon, God gave him the gift of wisdom and the ability to discern. Somewhere along the way, however, Solomon clipped the strand that united him with God *above the sun* and decided to find meaning and satisfaction in a life lived strictly *under the sun.* In other words, he chose a life lived on his own terms, in a natural dimension with no reference to the divine.

A Downward Spiral

Solomon's downward spiral began as many do, with a simple rationalization. Although the children of Israel had been specifically warned against intermarriage, he took an Egyptian wife for political purposes. "Then Solomon formed a marriage alliance with Pharaoh, king of Egypt, and took Pharaoh's daughter and brought her to the city of David" (1 Kings 3:1). He rationalized that this act would protect Israel, but instead it imperiled them. Whenever we disobey a direct command of God, it is never to our benefit, no matter how we may try to rationalize it.

Solomon took his Egyptian wife to the city of Jerusalem, where construction was underway on the temple of God and on the wall around the city. Because there was no completed temple for the Lord, the people sacrificed as their neighbors did—on the high places of the pagan gods. Solomon sacrificed there, too, even though God commanded that Israel worship no other gods. His actions were easily justified, of course. Although these were pagan altars, he was sacrificing to Jehovah God, and only because God's temple was not complete. But that was Solomon's agenda—not God's. "Now Solomon loved the Lord, walking in the statutes of his father David, except he sacrificed and burned incense on the high places" (1 Kings 3:3). Solomon justified his disobedience by saying that he loved God in spite of it.

Solomon justified his disobedience by saying that he loved God in spite of it.

Solomon's spiritual erosion was also evidenced in his personal relationships (see 1 Kings 9:10–13). Hiram, king of Tyre, honored and helped Solomon because of his friendship with Solomon's father David. Hiram provided significant labor and materials for the construction of God's temple, and he himself fashioned all the bronze work contained in the temple. After twenty years of construction on both the temple and Solomon's palace—and after all the work and materials Hiram provided—

Solomon "paid" him with a gift of twenty cities in Galilee. When Hiram saw the cities he called Solomon's gift "Cabul"—which loosely translated means, "Baloney!" They were worthless, and Hiram knew it. A long-lasting relationship was damaged, and, as far as we know, Solomon never resolved his conflict with Hiram.

Exhorbitant living marked Solomon's days, too, as he began to drift farther and farther from the single strand of relationship with God. He became greater than all the kings of the earth, and people began to pay him costly tributes for his wisdom:

> And all the earth was seeking the presence of Solomon, to hear his wisdom which God had put in his heart. And they brought every man his gift, articles of silver and gold, garments, weapons, spices, horses and mules, so much year by year. Now Solomon gathered chariots and horsemen; and he had 1,400 chariots and 12,000 horsemen, and he stationed them in the chariot cities and with the king in Jerusalem. (1 Kings 10:24–26)

Finally, Solomon amassed a harem of foreign women that surpassed even his riches. Once more, against the commands of God, he took for himself seven hundred wives and three hundred concubines. (Can you imagine that many mothers-in-law?) The wives were a mistake, though, for the very reasons God warned:

> "You shall not associate with them, neither shall they associate with you, for they will surely turn your heart away after their gods." Solomon held fast to these in love . . . . And his heart was not wholly devoted to the Lord his God, as the heart of his father David had been . . . . And Solomon did what was evil in the sight of the Lord, and did not follow the Lord fully, as David his father had done. (1 Kings 11:2, 4, 6)

Five Candidates for Meaning in Life

Solomon's descent illustrates the five major candidates for meaning in life. No matter how we stretch and dance around it, there are really only five avenues that we have traditionally pursued to give life meaning. Other minor candidates may exist, but these are the chief ways we go about trying to make sense of our lives. Of course, there are always those who pin their significance on a single, peak experience (I know one fellow who went to the Chicago World's Fair and still wears a lapel pin that says so) or a record they hold or a university they attended. But these are lesser candidates. The five major ones, I believe, have gone unchanged since the time of Solomon.

> *There are only five avenues man has pursued to give his life meaning. . . wisdom, ethics, hedonism, materialism, and religion.*

Most of us want enough *wisdom* to satisfy the mind, enough *ethics* or philosophy to satisfy the conscience, enough *hedonism* or pleasure to satisfy the body, enough *materialism* to satisfy the pocketbook, and enough *religion* to satisfy the spirit. Wisdom, ethics, hedonism, materialism, and religion—in his quest for better living under the sun, Solomon explored them all. They are contemporary, are they not? There are those today who give themselves to wisdom, those who give themselves to pleasure, and those who give themselves to wealth and power. There are those who give themselves to sex, those who give themselves to political reform, and those who give themselves to the New Age or spiritual understanding—so called "man-made" religions.

If you think that this is not so, consider the appeal of an ad that ran in a Houston paper recently:

> Most people in my generation see religion as too much of a hassle. We're finally starting lives of our own—beginning our careers, entering relationships, building our families—and we're not looking for any more burdens or responsibilities. That's how I saw religion, until I learned more about [name of congregation]. Here was a religion that gave me room to breathe. They offer services that are relevant to my life. Their philosophy encourages me to explore my inner spirituality. And their belief in activism and social justice inspires me to look outward. [4]

Some in our day, as in Solomon's, attempt to give life meaning through a general, nebulous, non-challenging belief in God—a God that makes no requirements on the way that we live.

Conventional Wisdom

My favorite feature in *Newsweek* magazine is a little column called "Conventional Wisdom." One glance at "Conventional Wisdom" can tell you who's up, who's down, and who's just holding his own. The Secretary of State travels to the Middle East and his arrow points up for the week. The chief of staff juggles the crisis du jour in the White House, and his arrow points down. "Conventional Wisdom" might show any public figure from the first lady to the pope or the mayor of Los Angeles holding steady.

Solomon—the son of a man after God's heart, a man given discernment by God—lived out his life by "conventional wisdom." He assessed his performance on a one-dimensional plane and measured his worth by totally subjective standards: conventional wisdom. And at the end of his life, he concluded "it all amounts to nothing." His "bottom line" is found in Ecclesiastes 1:3: "What advantage does man have in all his work which he does under the sun?" That little phrase "under the sun" appears twenty-nine times in the book of Ecclesiastes. It describes Solomon's perspective perfectly: He said he could see no "advantage" or profit in a life lived out under the sun—and he was right.

We never begin to understand life by viewing it from the flatlands. It simply has no meaning without faith in God. Faith in a living, holy, knowable God is enough to give our lives meaning. Faith gives us reason enough to live and reason enough to die. So many of us never see that truth until it is too late. Presbyterian minister Robert McAfee Brown illustrated this in a euology delivered for a friend:

> Ralph Sumner died the other day, full of years (80-plus) and wisdom (dairy farmer, cabinetmaker, churchgoer, member of the local road crew, dowser). When we laid him in the ground there were some tears, but there was also a lot of gratitude for the joy he had spread around the folk of Heath, MA 01346. I believe we are placed here to be companions—a wonderful word that comes from *cum panis* ("with bread"). We are here to share bread with one another. There are many names for such sharing: utopia, the beloved community, the Kingdom of God, the communion of saints. And . . . it is still our task to create foretastes of it on this planet—living glimpses of what life is meant to be . . . but I expect Ralph Sumner now sees it more clearly than I do. [5]

What life is meant to be is a life-long love affair with Almighty God, but many of us never discover our true purpose. Solomon's search is like a mirror that reflects our own attempts at wringing meaning from flatland existence. Looking at it honestly can lead us to the truth, too. So lean in, Michael Jordan, and all the "been there/done that's" of this generation. Watch as Solomon spins his web, and learn.

(Eccles. 1:1-2)

2

Going Nowhere Fast

Row, row, row your boat, gently down the stream
Merrily, merrily, merrily, merrily, life is but a dream.
—Unknown

HAVE YOU BEEN TO THE GYM LATELY? Every time I work out, I am astounded at the array of exercise machinery—stationary bikes, recumbent bikes, treadmills, and stairclimbers—all designed to enhance fitness. You get on them, and you go . . . nowhere. In fact, going nowhere is part of their design. The point is not to get somewhere—the point is to expend as much energy as possible for as long as possible *while* you are going nowhere. Every time you step off the treadmill or the bike, you are in the same place you began. Some new-fangled exercise bikes can even be wired into a VCR; your thirty-minute workout could then take you through the mountains of Colorado or the fall foliage of the New England countryside. But a quick reality check will confirm that you are, in fact, still in the gym!

We are dedicated to getting nowhere fast, are we not? We want to know "how" to do things—how to get fit, lose weight, achieve financial success, find the love of a lifetime—and, naturally, we want to do them all in the quickest possible way. The most frequently asked questions in this life under the sun are "how" questions. How was the world made? How was the solar system put into place? How are addictions overcome? How is grief processed? How? How? How? How? But the real question about life isn't "how?"—it's "why?" Why be successful? Why strive for power? Why spend your life searching for prestige?

Any parent can attest that children are full of questions. If you have children, you have answered your share of puzzlers. We have seen the commercials with the children in the back seat of the family car repeatedly asking, "Are we there yet? Are we there yet? Are we there yet?" But the questions that set a parent's heart racing are not the "when," or even the "how" questions. With a little research or a well-placed phone call, "Hi, mom. I was wondering . . . " those questions are easily handled. The tough ones are the "why" questions. Children are unaware that they are not supposed to ask them—and so they do, with great regularity. And quite often, Mom and Dad are stumped. They simply do not know "why."

A Limited Search

Solomon dared to ask the big questions: Is life really worth living? And if it is, why? But although he asked the right questions, he arrived at the wrong answers, because he limited his search to a single, flat dimension. First, he limited his search in terms of space. He only looked under the sun. He searched the observable world for his answers. Second, he limited his search in terms of time. He examined his own experience from birth to death and explored no further. Solomon had no concept of life after death since no one he knew had ever experienced death and lived to tell about it! He sought meaning in this life only. And his eventual conclusion was that for the secular person, life is meaningless. And if we were bound by time and space—by what we could observe and by how long we live—we would be forced to agree with him.

Life is pointless, Solomon argued, because it is always moving in circles but going nowhere. Then he supported his thesis by observing patterns in nature—and noting that they are all cyclical. Generations come and go. People are born, they die, and another generation is born. The sun rises, sets, and then rises again. The wind blows south, and then turns to the north. Rivers flow to the sea, but never fill it. They just keep flowing seaward.

Life is pointless, Solomon argued, because it is always moving in circles but going nowhere.

"A generation goes and a generation comes," Solomon wrote, "but the earth remains forever" (Eccles. 1:4). I remember as a boy going to county fairs in my hometown, where there was usually a fellow with gaming machines who would say something like this: "Around and around and around she goes . . . and where she stops, nobody knows." I believe Solomon would have said, "That's exactly the way it is with life lived strictly under the sun!" We are born. We die. Others are born. They die. Have you noticed that the average person has his or her name in the paper twice? When they're born . . . and when they die. One generation comes and goes, and another does the same, but the earth as Solomon said, remains. Humans were created to rule and subdue the earth, but instead it is humans who disappear and the earth that remains.

There is truth in his observation. We all die. And from one perspective, our lives are a lot like the round most of us learned as children: "Row, row, row your boat, gently down the stream. Merrily, merrily, merrily, merrily, life is but a dream." I never stopped to think how depressing that sounded as a child, did you? Life is but a dream lived out under the sun. It is absolutely void—and everyone dies. As each new year begins, there are usually several books and magazines that publish a retrospective of the previous twelve months, including who was born during that time, and who died. Death is universal and democratic. Everybody dies. Tough people die—Sonny Liston is dead. Athletic people die—Jim Valvano and Don Drysdale are dead. Country and western singers die—Conway Twitty and Patsy Cline are dead. Famous politicians die—John F. Kennedy and Richard Nixon are dead. Funny people die—Jack Benny and Lucille Ball are dead. So are John Belushi and John Candy. People from all walks of life die. Their lives are remembered by some, but forgotten by most, and others take their place. Or as Shakespeare said, we occupy our brief time on life's stage, and then we are gone.

Solomon did not only look at humankind. He observed the heavens as well: "Also, the sun rises and the sun sets; and hastening in its pace it rises there again" (v. 5). Each day, Solomon watched the sun come up, travel its path from horizon to horizon, and slip out of sight. Sunrise. Sunset. Sunrise. Sunset. For six years I lived in the foothills of the Smoky Mountains. The view out my front door was of Mount Pisgah, and it was beautiful. The seasons changed in explosions of magnificent color. But after the first or second year, I did not seem to notice the splendor of the view anymore. I have been on some beautiful seashores, too—the Atlantic, Pacific, Mediterranean, even the Sea of Galilee—but after a while, what was breathtaking at first became merely background.

Then Solomon became an amateur meteorologist, paying particular attention to the wind. It blows toward the south, he said, then turns north and continues whirling on its circular course. I was recently between two hurricanes, one going by on one side while another one came up on the opposite side. As my wife Jo Beth and I watched, the wind stirred up, swerved off, then came roaring up again. I have never seen anything like it.

Finally, Solomon observed a river flowing and saw yet another cycle. "All the rivers flow into the sea," he said, "yet the sea is not full. To the place where the rivers flow, there they will flow again" (v. 7). Water is evaporated into the clouds, falls as rain, feeds the rivers that feed the ocean . . . then the whole process repeats itself.

Are you depressed yet? Feeling defeated? Overwhelmed by the meaninglessness of life under the sun? Solomon was. Then he concluded that life is so meaningless there are no words to describe it. "The eye is not satisfied with seeing," he wrote, "nor is the ear filled with hearing" (v. 8). His assessment would be tough to debate. No matter what we see, we continue to look for things more pleasing to the eye. I read recently that in the future there will be five-hundred-plus cable television channels available in our homes. Five hundred channels! (Grab the remote control, men, and get ready!) Rocker Bruce Springsteen's song "57 Channels and Nothin' On" is very close to the truth. But we will scan those channels, all the same, just to be sure we are not missing anything—because the eye is not satisfied, no matter where it looks.

Certainly if ears were filled with hearing, teenagers would be full. I saw a teenager in a truck once that had speakers in the back bigger than its tires! The sound was cranked up so loud that the whole truck was rocking back and forth. I thought his ears must be bleeding from the sound—mine almost were! But when we like what we are hearing we cannot get enough of it, can we? There is not enough sound to fill us.

Solomon summarizes his thoughts with these words: "That which has been is that which will be. And that which has been done is that which will be done. So, there is nothing new under the sun" (v. 9). Do you believe there is anything new in our world today? What about space stations? Pacemakers? Sub-notebook computers? Laser surgery? Actually the elements of these inventions have always been with us; we have just learned how to combine them into different forms. But how far have we really come? The seven deadly sins are as deadly as ever, every single one of them. People are still at war with one another, and no less inclined to fight than before. There is no less greed, no less immorality, and no less dishonesty, as far as I can see. Is our world getting better?

The optimistic humanists say that it is. We are moving toward our ultimate potential, they tell us. It is just a matter of time before we make right all that has been wrong. But Solomon would disagree. "Is there anything of which one might say 'See this, it is new'? Already it has existed for ages," he wrote (v. 10). Our nature is the same. And even the events of history have a remarkable sameness about them. Leon Uris, the author of *Exodus* and *The Haj* has written a book on the history of Ireland, called *Trinity*. At the conclusion of this book that chronicles over three hundred years of Gaelic history, he states,

> *The seven deadly sins are as deadly as ever, every single one of them.*

"There is no future for Ireland, only the past happening over and over again."[1] Even though history tends to repeat itself—we do not remember it. Solomon observed this too, and said, "There is no remembrance of earlier things; and also of the later things which will occur, there will be for them no remembrance among those who will come later still" (v. 11). How quickly we forget!

Weighing his evidence alone, most of us would have to agree with Solomon's conclusion that life is empty, would we not? In fact, I believe that even the best life lived out under the sun, and under the sun alone, is meaningless, boring, and empty. Listen to the words of a modern-day Solomon if you are not sure. Alexander Curry is a thirty-something Wall Street trader for a large brokerage house. His hefty six-figure income affords him a well-appointed Upper East Side apartment filled with high-tech toys. He planned to quit the Wall Street rat race at thirty, but he is still there. In his more introspective moments, he wonders what it is all about.

> I've always felt that there was something that I could do and feel I was doing something of real tangible benefit. Trading, arbitraging futures markets, does not have any real tangible benefit, in my opinion. I mean, it serves a purpose for the economy, but I don't think of myself as really doing a lot for society. I'm really doing more for myself. I would have to say that I feel that there is a lack of purpose in my being. I don't understand why I'm here. I don't really try to understand why I'm here because I think it would probably be futile. It does provide a real hole in my existence.[2]

Is there a way off the treadmill? Can we step off the stairclimber? Is there an alternative? Saint Augustine suggested there is when he said, "He who has God has everything. He who does not have God has nothing. He who has God and everything has no more than he who has God alone." You see, God never meant for us to have a circular existence. From our beginning in Genesis, we were built for linear living.

God never meant for us to have a circular existence. We were created to go somewhere— with purpose.

We were created to go somewhere—with purpose. Solomon said

life is pointless. God says life is full of purpose. We were meant for linear living, but sin has forced us into a circular pattern. We are meant to live in relationship, but our sin has forced us into isolation.

A Historic Example of Treadmill Living

The Bible records in Genesis that God chose a people for Himself by initiating a relationship with one man, Abram. In His call to Abram, God offered fellowship and blessing and even a purpose that future generations might fulfill:

> Now the LORD said to Abram, "Go forth from your country, and from your relatives and from your father's house, to the land which I will show you; and I will make you a great nation, and I will bless you, and make your name great; and so you shall be a blessing; and I will bless those who bless you, and the one who curses you I will curse. And in you all the families of the earth shall be blessed" (Gen. 12:1–3). Although Abram and his wife Sarai were old and had no children, God gave them further hope with these words: "Now look toward the heavens, and count the stars if you are able to count them. . . . So shall your descendants be." (Gen. 15:5)

Abram and Sarai obeyed God and believed Him, and He did as He had promised. They had a son Isaac, who married Rebekah. Isaac and Rebekah were the parents of Jacob, and Jacob the father of Joseph. Through Joseph, God's people came to live in Egypt, and eventually became slaves there, as God had predicted to Abraham that they would: "Know for certain that your descendants will be strangers in a land that is not theirs, where they will be enslaved and oppressed four hundred years. But I will also judge the nation whom they will serve; and afterward they will come out with many possessions" (Gen. 15:13–14).

Again, God did for His people what He promised He would, and He raised an unlikely general named Moses to lead them out of Egypt into the promised land of Canaan. In His faithfulness He restated His covenant with Israel to Moses, with all its magnificent promises:

> "I am the LORD, and I will bring you out from under the burdens of the Egyptians, and I will deliver you from their bondage. I will also redeem you with an outstretched arm and with great judg-

ments. Then I will take you for My people, and I will be your God; and you shall know that I am the LORD your God, who brought you out from under the burdens of the Egyptians. And I will bring you to the land which I swore to give Abraham, Isaac, and Jacob, and I will give it to you for a possession; I am the LORD." (Ex. 6:6–8)

So God's people embarked on a trip that should have taken just a few days—but forty years later Israel was still wandering in the wilderness of Sinai! Why? They were disobedient. They disobeyed God's chief command to them to have no other gods and worshiped ones of their own invention. They lost their hearts to other things. Each time they sinned, Moses interceded for them; they renewed their covenant with God; and they went on. But they abandoned their original sense of calling, commitment, and purpose as they drifted further and further into disobedience. Finally, they stood on the brink of the promised land, and a majority saw it and said, "No, thanks."

Instead of Canaan being their destination, Sinai became their home. They lived between two worlds: They were out of Egypt, but not yet in the promised land. An entire generation was lost during those wandering years, and many on the journey probably never knew *why* they were traveling at all. They were born nomads, who knew nothing else beyond their flatland perspective! Their relationship with God was a "borrowed" faith at best, and they never knew that Canaan was where they were headed. God was present, to be sure. He led them by a cloud and a pillar of fire; He provided manna each day for food; and He indwelt the tabernacle they built for Him—but He was no longer *personal*. They had moved away from His purpose and His plan.

What About Us?

"Well, that's an old story," you might say. "It doesn't have much to do with me today." Yes, it is an old story, but it is a true one. And if history does repeat itself, it is one from which we can learn much. You see, Israel was once under the hand of God—but they moved. It is a wonderful thing to be under the hand of God, experiencing His blessing. Tragically, too often we do not recognize or choose to acknowledge His grace. When we no longer experience these good things, we cry out that God is judging us—and certainly there are times when He deals with His children in judgment. But more often we have simply moved from under His protective hand and have chosen to live our lives in our own strength.

You say you bought your house as an investment and paid on it for ten years, and now it is worth less than when you bought it? You worked hard at your job and a lazy coworker received the promotion you deserved? Your ship did not come in, but instead it sank at sea? Is it the judgment of God? Or have we simply moved away from the One who is the author of life and begun to write our own story? Consciously or unconsciously, we have moved. And when we do, we move out of His linear life of purpose, promise, and significance into a cyclical, "under the sun" existence. Our lives look very much like the lives of those who never knew Him at all, until our joy is at the mercy of this capricious world, and our lives are stripped of meaning.

A Paradigm Shift

What about you? Are you experiencing life—or pedaling the stationary bicycle? Are you on a track or a treadmill? Are you climbing a staircase or laboring away on the stairclimber? If you are on the fast track to nowhere, take heart. Change is possible. It begins with what contemporary thinkers call a "paradigm shift." Instead of viewing life as Solomon did, "under the sun," try looking at it from God's perspective—"above the sun." Move from your flatland outpost to a higher lookout—and consider life from there. As the following story illustrates, the effects can be remarkable.

Are you on a track or a treadmill? Are you climbing a staircase or laboring away on the stairclimber?

Two men were walking down the sidewalks of Manhattan—one a native American Indian, the other a born-and-bred New Yorker. The noise was incredible—cars, buses, horns, sirens, people talking loudly as they moved down the street, jammed shoulder to shoulder in the chaos. Suddenly, the Indian said, "Listen. I hear a cricket. Do you hear it?"

The New Yorker was incredulous. "No way! You couldn't possibly hear a cricket on a Manhattan sidewalk during rush hour."

"I'm serious," his friend countered. And to prove it, he stopped, bent down, and retrieved a chirping cricket from between a crack in the sidewalk.

"How could you hear it?" the New Yorker asked.

"Easy," said his friend. "I've lived outdoors all my life. I can hear a cricket over any other kind of noise. That's not amazing. If you want to see amazing, watch this!" And with those words he reached in his pocket, pulled out a quarter, and dropped it on the concrete.

As soon as he did, heads began to turn. It seemed as if every Manhattanite for blocks heard the coin as it hit the sidewalk. He had proved his point: You hear what you are listening for. Our ears pick up the sounds to which they are tuned. If it is the sound of a cricket for which we are listening, we hear it—no matter how much "background noise" exists. If it is money to which our ears are tuned, we can hear the clinking of a coin above any clamor.

What are we listening for? Is it the din of the world or the voice of God? Does our life have meaning, or is it just "around and around and around she goes"? Too many of us get up in the morning, go to work, come home, and go to bed—and then repeat the cycle, day in and day out. Get up, go to work, come home, go to bed. Get up, go to work, come home, go to bed. Before we know it, we are trapped. But that is not what God intended, and that is not what truly satisfies our soul. We are bigger than that. We must reach above the sun and above this life for meaning—and when we do, we will come to the conclusion God has known from the beginning: we are too big for this world. We were never intended to camp here anymore than the Israelites were meant to live out a generation in the wilderness.

> *What are we listening for? Is it the din of the world or the voice of God?*

Living under the sun is not enough. Under-the-sun living has meaning only when we know the Son who comes from above the sun. Consider these words from a preacher who had seen it all and lived to tell: "If then you have been raised up with Christ, keep seeking the things above, where Christ is, seated at the right hand of God. Set your mind on the things above, not on the things that are on earth. For you have died and your life is hidden with Christ in God. When Christ, who is our life, is revealed, then you also will be revealed with Him in glory" (Col. 3:1–4).

Solomon looked at nature within the limits of time and space, and he said, "It is meaningless, repetitive, boring." The apostle Paul looked at life through heaven's eyes and said instead: "I count all things to be loss in view of the surpassing value of knowing Christ Jesus my Lord, for whom I have suffered the loss of all things, and count them but rubbish in order that I may gain Christ" (Phil. 3:8).

Paul was asked to sum up everything he had achieved and he called it dung! Do you get that? Dung! Does it need defining? Waste! Excrement! He was a wealthy Roman citizen, an aristocrat, a member of the privileged class. He was educated by the finest teachers and held positions of power in the courts. He had the highest moral ethics. He had been everywhere, done everything, . . . and seen it all. He had covered every base in life, and looking back, he described it all with one word: dung. It is a waste, he said, just a dream. Sunrise. Sunset. What was true of Paul is true for us: When we are through with life and look back at our accomplishments "under the sun," we too will have to say it was dung—a waste.

Oh, but above-the-sun living—now that is a different story. To know Him is real life. Listen to Augustine's words again: "He who has God has everything. He who does not have God has nothing. He who has God and everything has no more than he who has God and nothing."

I am ready for a lot of above-the-sun living under the sun. What about you?

(Eccles. 1:3–11)

Part II

Done That: Under-the-Sun Searching

3

A Hedonist's Solution: Party Harder

Living for his own pleasure is the least
pleasurable thing a man can do;
if his neighbors don't kill him in disgust,
he will die slowly of boredom and
powerlessness.

—Joy Davidman[1]

HER PARENTS CHRISTENED HER Madonna Louise Veronica Ciccone—but the world has been on a first-name basis with Madonna since she took the record industry by storm in the early 1980s. She has become the icon of the outrageous, parlaying what industry experts call only average talent into extraordinary profit and shocking as many people as she can along the way. Her record lyrics, explicit MTV videos, and sexually suggestive concert antics fall somewhere beyond good taste and just shy of censorship.

The self-proclaimed "boy toy" and "material girl" pursues the pleasures of life in the fast lane as if there is no tomorrow. *Forbes* magazine called her "the smartest business woman in America" on a recent cover, and, since her I.Q. is nearly 150, many think she is. In five years she made $125 million through music, acting, merchandising, and endorsements. (Pepsi Cola paid a reported $5 million for three soft drink commercials featuring the star; they received so much negative response after the first was aired they never shot the remaining spots—but she kept the $5 million.)

I can think of few modern personalities who seem to live for pleasure more than Madonna. If a hedonist is one who lives by the creed, "If it pleases me, I'll do it," then Madonna is the rightful queen of hedonism. Yet in personal interviews she has said that she is not happy, that she doesn't know anyone who is, and that her only goal in life is to "be somebody." When asked what she considers her greatest gift, she states confidently that it is the ability to manipulate people. Over five hundred thousand people were "manipulated" to purchase her book, *Sex*—a collection of erotic photographs (mostly of herself) that retailed for fifty dollars or more.

Certainly Madonna is not alone in her pursuit of pleasure as a way to give life meaning. That pastime is centuries old. The author of Ecclesiastes spent years in pleasure-seeking, expending tremendous energy and resources in his quest. Although he entered into a special relationship with God early in life, somewhere along the way Solomon abandoned Him and sought satisfaction in life only in human terms. Having "clipped the strand" that united him with his above-the-sun God, Solomon tried to find meaning in life under the sun, and ultimately concluded that there was none. The path of wisdom was a dead end. Education, erudition, and intellect were vanity. Even the pursuit of pleasure was eventually numbing.

> *Constantly pushing the edge of the envelope marked "pleasure" is lethal.*

If joy and meaning could be found in the "If it pleases me, I'll do it" approach, shouldn't Madonna be a happy woman? She has done whatever she pleased. Shouldn't Solomon, with seven hundred wives and three hundred concubines, have been a satisfied man? He certainly denied himself nothing. But what happens to the hedonist is just the opposite. Constantly pushing the edge of the envelope marked "pleasure" is lethal. It alienates, deadens, and eventually it kills. Consider the contemporary evidence that a lifestyle devoted to pleasure is empty at best, deadly at worst: Kurt Cobain, River Phoenix, Elvis Presley, Jim Morrison, Janis Joplin, Jimmy Hendrix. All sought pleasure; all died young.

"I Said to Myself . . . "

Who advised Solomon to pursue a pleasure-seeking lifestyle? No one. He simply listened to his own desires. "I said to myself," he wrote, "Come now, I will test you with pleasure. So enjoy yourself" (Eccles. 2:1). As much as we might like to blame a hedonistic bent on the encouragement of others, no one else is responsible. The truth is that the rush to gratify our desires is simply an outgrowth of who we are in our hearts. Jesus understood this well: "For from within," He said, "out of the heart of men proceed the evil thoughts, fornication, thefts, murders, adulteries, deeds of coveting and wickedness, as well as deceit, sensuality, envy, slander, pride and foolishness. All these evil things proceed from within and defile the man" (Mark 7:21–22).

Solomon "suggested" to himself that he seek meaning through pleasure. He thought it would be a good idea. His search began with "I said to myself . . . ." He could have sought the wisdom of other counselors—but he did not. He knew better. He had already written in Proverbs 11:14 that "in abundance of counselors there is victory." He said, "I'll make up my own mind," and he decided pleasure was the ticket to a fulfilling life. Thoughtful friends could have shown him the error of his ways, but he never consulted them. Even a fleeting consideration of his father David's life could have warned him that hedonism was a dead end. But the pleasure Solomon decided to pursue eventually convinced him: "And behold, it too was futility"(v. 16).

What happens when we listen only to ourselves? When I was growing up, we listened to music on phonographs and then on "record players." We enjoyed it. There was no noise reduction then, no "surround sound," or complex system to balance the treble and bass, but our ignorance was bliss! We enjoyed what we heard. Now those in my generation have developed a more "sophisticated" ear. Phonographs and record players are obsolete; records—of any speed—are obsolete, too. The "flat" sound we listened to as teenagers and young adults has been given a whole new dimension by compact discs, digital recording, and stereos with complicated instrument panels.

> *Solomon heard his own voice and lived by its flat sound. He passed up the symphony in favor of the solo.*

The sound is better, enhanced by "other voices" of modern technology. Solomon heard his own voice and lived by its flat sound. There was more to life, but he never fully grasped it because he passed up the symphony in favor of the solo. He said, "I'll make up my own mind." And he decided in favor of hedonism. When we seek and receive counsel only from ourselves, we are in trouble from the outset. Once again Solomon had forgotten—or failed to heed—the words of advice he wrote in his middle years: "Trust in the LORD with all your heart, and do not lean on your own understanding. In all your ways acknowledge Him, and He will make your paths straight" (Prov. 3:5–6). Instead, Solomon lived and died by the slogan that is so popular today: "I did it my way."

"Little Islands of Relief"

How contemporary is Solomon's self-styled "pleasure safari"? Consider the words of comedian and television star Jerry Seinfeld: "Everybody's looking for good sex, good food, and a good laugh. They're little islands of relief in what's often a painful existence."[2] Solomon said this:

> "Come now, I will test you with pleasure. So enjoy yourself." And behold, it too was futility. I said of laughter, "It is madness," and of pleasure, "What does it accomplish?" (Eccles. 2:1–2)

He said first of all, "I'll try laughter. I'm going to have a good time." So he brought in the stand-up comedians of his day—the jesters, the magicians, the acrobats. He wanted to have fun and enjoy life—to provide a little "island of relief" against the pressures of the monarchy.

Today's pleasure-seeker goes to comedy clubs, watches the comedy cable network, and lines up for movies that provide a brief escape from life's grim realities. But no matter how many hit comedies we sit through, we emerge from the theater and life is still there, waiting. No combined dose of fun, pranks, humor, cynicism, or sarcasm can change that. Then Solomon said, "I explored with my mind how to stimulate my body with wine while my mind was guiding me wisely, and how to take hold of folly . . . " (v. 3). In other words, he wanted to experiment with pleasure, but keep his wits about him. He wanted to dance close to the edge of consciousness, but not fall off. He wanted to be a connoisseur of epicurean delight, not a pleasure-addict. But the line between temperance and temptation is a fine one, and many never see it until they have crossed over.

No one starts drinking with the goal of becoming an alcoholic. No one glances at pornography hoping to become addicted to it. No one enters into an extramarital affair longing for it to completely upset his or her life. But social drinkers sometimes do become alcoholics, and the curious can develop sexual addictions. And harmless affairs destroy marriages and homes. Every day. The trouble with pursuing these little "islands of relief" is that we have more faith in our own ability to say no than we really should.

Solomon's intentions were not evil. He was not a bad man. In fact, he did manage to do all of his pleasure-seeking with a measure of temperance. He became a "controlled" party animal, but it didn't make him happy. Instead, he experienced the immutable law of diminishing returns. "And all that my eyes desired," said Solomon, "I did not refuse them. I did not withhold my heart from any pleasure, for my heart was pleased because of all my labor and this was a reward for all of my labor. Thus I considered all my activities which my hands had done and the labor which I had exerted, and behold, all was vanity and striving after wind and there was no profit under the sun" (Eccles. 2:10–11).

> *The line between temperance and temptation is a fine one, and many never see it until they have crossed over.*

He did not withhold anything from himself. He did not tell himself no. And soon, what used to satisfy became ho-hum, commonplace, boring. So he allowed himself a little more—a little more wine, a little more food, another concubine—or two, or ten. Maybe you do not have a wine cellar like Solomon's—or a team of chefs ready to tickle your palate with the latest culinary delights—but the law of diminishing returns is easily illustrated in other ways. It could apply to golf, for example. Do not misunderstand. I like golf. I like being outdoors and moving around. I like competition, even if it is just competing with myself to improve last week's score. But one of the first things I learned when I began to play was that there are golfers, and then there are *golfers*. Some people out there are passionately committed to the game. I recently saw a needlepoint pillow which stated: "Life is a game—golf is serious." They probably started as I did—borrowed clubs, any course I could get on, make-shift attire—but now they have gone far beyond that first stage.

"Hacking" isn't fun anymore, so they succumb to the theory of escalation: "If you look good, you feel good. If you feel good, you play good. If you play good, you win." The time comes when only Ping™ irons will do. And Callaway™ woods. Graphite shafts become essential. Without these "necessities" the game just isn't fun anymore. (Of course, a swing helps, too—but according to Lee Trevino, you can get one of those from your local PGA professional.) These "escalation" golfers cannot get excited about a 7 A.M. tee time at the city course. But just watch their eyes light up when they tell you they have played the Masters, Pebble Beach—or better yet, the Plantation on Maui, Hawaii. Or that they are members of the most exclusive club in their state. Get the picture? The law of diminishing returns says the same effort produces less satisfaction. So we put more into our passion—whatever it may be—just to enjoy it as much as we did yesterday.

All for Myself

From partying, Solomon the pleasure-seeker moved on to projects. "I enlarged my works," he said. "I built houses for myself, I planted vineyards for myself; I made gardens and parks for myself, and I planted in them all kinds of fruit trees; I made ponds of water for myself from which to irrigate a forest of growing trees" (vv. 4–6). If there is a phrase in Solomon's project diary that stands out, it is the phrase "for myself." All that he did, he did for himself. Amazingly enough, when he listed his architectural enterprises, he failed to mention the biggest, most historically significant thing that he built—the Temple. It was, after all, the foremost architectural feat of that day, and perhaps of any day. The Bible records in 1 Kings that it took him seven years to build the Temple—but it took him almost twice as long to build his own palace. The temple was built for the glory of God—but the palace was built for the glory of Solomon!

Solomon built houses for the daughters of Pharaoh, too—the pagan women that he married. He built houses, homes, offices—his portfolio of construction projects would make Donald Trump's operation look small-time. And he planted vineyards—for himself—which perhaps provided him with the wine he also enjoyed. But he did not stop there. Oh no. There were gardens and parks designed as a virtual paradise, with trees of all shapes and sizes, many of them bearing fruit. Then he built lakes and ponds to water his trees, surrounding himself with as much horticultural "eye candy" as he could manage.

> *If there is a phrase in Solomon's project diary that stands out, it is the phrase "for myself."*

Does this sound unusual? Excessive? Have you ever seen Bleinham Palace, the birthplace and ancestral home of Winston Churchill? Or the Mellon or Rockefeller estates? Or San Simeon, the California castle of William Randoph Hearst? Wealthy men and women through the ages have undertaken building projects, leaving behind colossal monuments to their wealth and creativity. They have built great retreats, study centers, libraries, and gardens—for themselves. The projects are beautiful, but they probably did not satisfy their builders' tastes for pleasure any more than Solomon's did.

When partying and projects were not enough, Solomon focused his hedonistic efforts on the accumulation of possessions.

"I bought male and female slaves," he said, "and I had homeborn slaves. Also I possessed flocks and herds larger than all who preceded me in Jerusalem. Also, I collected for myself silver and gold, and the treasure of kings and provinces. I provided for myself male and female singers and the pleasures of men— many concubines. Then I became great and increased more than all who preceded me in Jerusalem. My wisdom also stood by me. And all that my eyes desired, I did not refuse them" (vv. 7–10). Solomon's desire for self-gratification was so intense that he took his own people, the Jews, and made them slaves for the first time in history. He acquired slaves, livestock, and gold as quickly as he could, and he knew the exact moment when he became "the richest man in the history of Jerusalem." Twice he mentions that he accumulated more possessions than his father David who had immediately preceded him. Like many men today, he was compelled by pride to "do better" than his dad, and could not resist letting the world know when he had reached that milestone.

Happiness comes not from having, but from being. It is a condition of the heart.

He collected gold. Historians estimate that he received 666 talents of gold each year from taxes. That amount is equal to twenty-five tons of gold annually, which he used primarily "for himself." With this fortune, he funded his party machine, his projects, and his insatiable need to acquire. I know quite a few folks with money. And I know some genuinely happy and contented people. But I cannot say that the richest people I know are necessarily the happiest, although some of them are certainly content. To the contrary, what Solomon discovered was that happiness does not come from possessing—from having things. Happiness comes not from having, but from being. It is a condition of the heart, and "the heart," said George MacDonald, "cannot hoard. Only the hand can hoard."

Perhaps the most destructive thing that Solomon acquired "for himself" was a palace filled with concubines. The Bible says that his relationship with them turned his heart away from God, illustrating a simple but profound truth: You cannot mean business for God and live in the flesh at the same time. Jesus articulated this principle clearly when He told His disciples, "No one can serve two masters; for either he will hate the one and love the other, or he will hold to one and despise the other. You cannot serve God and mammon" (Matt. 6:24). Perhaps one of the biggest lies of our day is that you can have it both ways—that you can be Executive of the Year and Parent of the Year. That you can love God and worship the dollar, or sex, or yourself. It is a dangerous deception.

Englishman Malcolm Muggeridge was the editor of the British magazine *Punch* for many years and a respected journalist both nationally and internationally. Muggeridge tells a story in his autobiography *The Wasted Years* that beautifully illustrates a Biblical truth. Muggeridge had been faithful to his wife for the length of their marriage, but he carried the thought in the back of his mind that if the right opportunity ever presented itself, he would be intimate with another woman, just for the experience.

That opportunity seemed to present itself when he was in India, teaching journalism far away from his wife and family. Muggeridge said that early each morning, he rose and went swimming in the Ganges River. On one such morning, he saw a woman bathing herself in the river, quite a distance away. "This is my moment," he told himself. "I am a wealthy Englishman. She is a poor Indian. What could it hurt? Who will know?" As he began to swim upstream to her, he struggled, not just against the water, but against the current of his conscience: "Malcolm," a voice inside him said, "don't do it." But then another voice countered, "This is your chance. It's now or never."

He continued to swim toward her, staying underneath the water until he was only a few feet away. When he surfaced, it was he, not she, who experienced the shock of a lifetime. He came up out of the water and looked into the eyes of a woman who was . . . a leper. Her nose, he said, was eaten away. There were sores and white blotches all over her skin, and the ends of her fingers were gone. She looked more like an animal than a human being. Immediately he thought, "What a wretched woman she is," but almost at the same moment he was overwhelmed with the devastating truth: "What a wretched man I am!" Though he never expressed it in his autobiography, he probably came to understand a basic principle: Physical leprosy is crippling and terminal, but spiritual leprosy is deadly and eternal.

> *When we walk away from the plan of God, we walk right into disease—the disease of sin.*

Muggeridge's graphic, real-life experience illustrates an unalterable truth: When we walk away from the plan of God, we walk right into disease—the disease of sin. Solomon, in his insistence on marrying pagan women and acquiring others as concubines, disobeyed the direct command of God. He opened his arms to embrace sin. In doing so, he cut the strand between himself and God and opted instead for a one-dimensional life. He became a party animal, seeking after possessions and engaging in projects that he hoped would soothe a conscience that would not be quieted.

"Party on, Dude!"

We live in a culture that encourages the exploration of hedonism. Are you a teenager who is curious about sex? Your school nurse's office has free condoms just waiting for you. Interested in a "non-committal" arrangement in which you try on a potential spouse like a pair of shoes? By all means, our society would say, live together. Would you like to experience the sensation of free-falling through life? There are legal and illegal substances available to assist you in your descent.

In a much-quoted 1987 commencement speech to Duke University seniors, newsman Ted Koppel hit the bull's eye:

> We have actually convinced ourselves that slogans will save us. Shoot up if you must; but use a clean needle. Enjoy sex whenever and with whomever you wish; but wear a condom. In the place of Truth we have discovered facts; for moral absolutes we have substituted moral ambiguity. Our society finds Truth too strong a medicine to digest undiluted. In its purest form Truth is not a polite tap on the shoulder; it's a howling reproach. What Moses brought down from Mount Sinai were not the Ten Suggestions . . . they are Commandments. Are—not were.

These are powerful words, unexpected words. But we have become a nation of people who excuse our pleasure-driven behavior with the disclaimer, "I'm just the kind of guy who. . . has to say what I think, or can't say no, or needs a lift now and then." Writer George A. Tobin describes these people as "Large Bobs,"[3] and suggested that they base their choices on a three-step rationale. First, they conclude that they are the product of their nature. They simply cannot help or change how they feel. And heaven forbid that they should go against their natural impulses! Second, they acknowledge that lots of people share their particular addiction or compulsion or craving so it must be okay. Finally, "Large Bobs" reason that denying themselves the pleasure they desire would betray their very nature. Surely they could not chance so injuring their psyches.

Such a perspective leaves us little to live by but the proverbial wisdom of Wayne and Garth, the two garage musicians and self-styled talk show hosts of "Saturday Night Live" fame, whose motto is echoed by millions: "Party on, dude!"

Two Pleasure Myths

I believe there are two big lies or myths related to pleasure seeking. Christians tend to tell one; non-Christians espouse the other. Both are untrue. In an effort to curb what they view as harmful and ungodly behavior, some Christians have tried to convince the world that sin is not pleasurable. (I see this as the equivalent of trying to push a two-ton rock up a hill—and estimate the odds for moving the rock are better.) Sin is pleasurable. Otherwise, what would temptation be? Satan tempted Eve with a beautiful piece of fruit and promised that ingesting it would have wonderful side effects. Since she did not spit it out, we can only surmise that it did, in fact, taste good. And the side effects were more serious than she was first led to believe.

Sin does feel good sometimes. There are moments of gratification and pleasure and laughter and fun. But there are two things that we should know about the pleasures of sin. First, they are temporary. They do not last—and they never completely satisfy. If they did, everyone would sin only once and be done with it! Second, the consequences of sin are inevitable—and deadly. This fact contradicts the second big myth about pleasure seeking: That as long as you do not intentionally hurt another person, whatever you choose to do with your body and your life is fine. But God's Word clearly states that sin—falling short of God's standard—is a death sentence: "Therefore what benefit were you then deriving from the things of which you are now ashamed? For the outcome of those things is death . . . for the wages of sin is death, but the free gift of God is eternal life in Christ Jesus our Lord" (Rom. 6:21,23). Sin always pays, and it pays what the one who works it has earned—death. The inevitability of its ultimate consequence is a law of the universe in which we live, and not simply the empty threat of a preacher or a parent.

The reason this truth is hard for many to see is that sin's consequences are not always immediate. Solomon, for example, enjoyed worldly wealth and fame and wisdom, even in his disobedience. "Then I became great," he wrote, "and increased more than all who preceded me in Jerusalem. My wisdom also stood by me" (Eccles. 2:9). Who can argue with that in one-dimensional living? Solomon was a mover and a shaker in Jerusalem. He pursued pleasure with a vengeance, and he never lost his name or his mind doing it. He maintained control of his life. He lived like a kid in a candy store, wanting one of everything he saw. And because he had the means to get it, there was nothing he did not try. He did not withhold any pleasure from his heart, because he considered pleasure the rightful return for his labor.

> *Solomon lived like a kid in a candy store, wanting one of everything he saw.*

So if sin's consequences can be delayed ("Eat, drink, and be merry for tomorrow we die!"), why not live for pleasure's sake? Because it is not really living. Solomon may not have been struck down for his hedonistic lifestyle, but he was not happy, either. He was never satisfied. Pleasure never brought his life meaning. In fact, when he summed up his experience, he said it totaled less than zero: "Thus I considered all my activities which my hands had done and the labor which I exerted, and behold, all was vanity and striving after wind and there was no profit under the sun" (v. 11). It was nothing but an emotional pile-up. All that pleasure was empty of meaning, and it profited Solomon not at all.

The View from Above the Sun

If Solomon's view of life was flat and meaningless, even in the midst of every pleasure he could pursue, what consolation could one with a different perspective offer him? What might Jesus say to Solomon, or even to a modern day hedonist like Madonna?[4] Not what you might expect. Because He knows the human heart and its frailty, and its bent to sin, He cannot be shocked—even by the shock-queen herself. Madonna may have rendered David Letterman helpless on network television, but the "material girl" is no match for a loving God.

I believe He would say, first of all, "I am hurt"—hurt that individuals of great potential are wasted by misdirected desires. Hurt that others are exploited by the actions of those who are rich enough and powerful enough to scorn decency. Hurt that they have become role models for the young by the power of the media they manipulate. Hurt that they are careening down a road that will never produce satisfaction, only emptiness. I believe that the One who came from above the sun would say with tears to Madonna and others like her, "I am hurt."

> *Most pleasure seekers are trying to cover a wound. Others may not see the wound, but the one who hides it knows it is there.*

I also believe the Son of God would say, "I am sorry." Does that surprise you? Jesus was full of surprises. He surprised those who knew Him best and those who did not know Him at all. I believe He would say, "I'm sorry," because most pleasure seekers are trying to cover a wound. Others may not see the wound, but the one who hides it knows it is there. Jesus knows it too. Some pleasure seekers like Madonna have acquired a distorted view of God—that He is a celestial kill-joy whose mission is to keep anyone from having a good time. I believe Jesus would say, "I'm sorry that in your childhood you were confused about who

I am. I am sorry you can't see Me as One who wants the best for you." Many folks have said to me, "I don't believe in God." When they do, I usually say, "Tell me about the God you don't believe in." They begin to describe what they think is God's nature and His character, and I am almost always forced to say, "I don't believe in *that* God, either." Jesus would say, "I'm sorry you have such a distorted view of Me. That is simply not who I am."

Then I think Jesus would say to the hedonist, "I understand." And He does. "Therefore," stated the writer of Hebrews, "He had to be made like His brethren in all things, that He might become a merciful and faithful high priest in things pertaining to God, to make propitiation for the sins of the people. For since He Himself was tempted in that which He has suffered, He is able to come to the aid of those who are tempted" (Heb. 2:17–18). He was tempted, so He understands temptation. He suffered, so He understands suffering. He was left alone, so He understands loneliness. He understands the need to fill life's emptiness with earthly, human pleasures that do not satisfy. He does not excuse, but He understands. Perhaps Jesus would say to Madonna, "I understand that you lost your mother when you were a little girl, and that from that day on you have been hungry for understanding and unconditional love. I understand you were frightened. I understand."

> *Jesus says to every person in this world who has sold his or her soul to pleasure, "I will help."*

The last thing I believe Jesus says to every person in this world who has sold his or her soul to pleasure is "I will help." He helps like no other. "For while we were still helpless, at the right time Christ died for the ungodly. For one will hardly die for a righteous man; though perhaps for the good man someone would dare even to die. But God demonstrates His own love toward us, in that while we were yet sinners, Christ died for us" (Rom. 5:6–8). Jesus would say, "I died for your sins, as notorious as they are, because I died for the sins of the whole world. I offer unconditional love—no questions asked. And until you receive Me, you will have a hunger in your heart that cannot be filled, because I am the only One who can satisfy it." How does He help? He adopts us. The apostle Paul said it like this: "But when the fullness of the time came, God sent forth His Son, born of a woman, born under the Law, in order that He might redeem those who were under the Law, that we might receive the adoption as sons. And because you are sons, God has sent forth the Spirit of His Son into our hearts, crying, 'Abba! Father!'" (Gal. 4:4–6). God is in the adoption business. He adopted me. He wants to adopt Madonna, too.

You may have never noticed it, but the classified sections of most big city newspapers have a section called "Adoptions." It does not announce who has been adopted, but who wants to adopt. Couples who do not have children advertise to pregnant women who may be considering giving their child away. Listen to three of these entries: "California doctor-dad, at-home mom wish to adopt newborn. Will provide love, security and opportunity. Call Steve and Elaine." And another one: "Desire baby to adopt. Outdoorsman dad, stay-at-home mom, one crazy dog, wish to provide love and financial security and a great home to your newborn." Then this one: "Adoption. Joan, a Texas elementary art teacher. David, a successful professional, wish to adopt your baby and provide a wonderful life filled with love and stability. Will share photos through the years. Please call." Do they touch your heart the way they do mine?

God has an ad in His paper for Madonna and for us. It is an ad extended to all who are away from Him, pleasure seekers included—especially pleasure seekers. It goes something like this: "Behold, I stand at the door and knock; if anyone hears My voice and opens the door, I will come in to him and will dine with him, and he with Me. He who overcomes, I will grant to him to sit down with Me on My throne, as I also overcame and sat down with My Father on His throne" (Rev. 3:20–21). It promises not temporary gratification, but lasting joy. It promises a place with Jesus, in whose presence is fullness of joy, and in whose right hand are *pleasures forever.*

(Eccles. 2:1–11)

An Above-the-Sun Postscript

King Solomon, the preacher, wrote many proverbs as a young man, including the following proverb on the pursuit of pleasure:

> Can a man take fire in his bosom,
> and his clothes not be burned?
> Or can a man walk on hot coals,
> and his feet not be scorched?
> (Proverbs 6:27–28)

Sadly, Solomon failed to heed his own warning. Here's what the preacher didn't practice—and how you can apply his wisdom to your world.

Look Honestly at Your Pursuit of Pleasure

Take an honest appraisal of your temptations and their resulting pleasures and consequences. You can do this mentally, but you will discover this exercise's power if you will take out a sheet of paper and write it out. On the left-hand side of the page make a list of the pleasure *temptations* to which you succumb most frequently. Be specific. Don't just put down "escapism" or "lack of responsibility," but write down what you chase to feel better. Maybe it's drinking to excess. Or spending money carelessly. Don't just write down "lust," but specifically write down the objects of your lustful thoughts. Or maybe it's pornography. Or indulging in sexual fantasies. Instead of "lack of self-control" record that you eat too much or too often.

When you complete the list of specifics, make a new column to the right which lists the *pleasures* associated with each temptation. Then, make one more column to the right and label it *consequences*. Again, think carefully about all the consequences that attend each particular pleasure quest. Some of the consequences are small, others are enormous.

Psalm 16:4 says, "The sorrows of those will increase who run after other gods." As you take this honest look at your Temptations/Pleasures/Consequences, do you see that your sorrows increase when you chase these gods? Solomon chased other gods and, instead of finding satisfaction, his sorrows increased. Because he chased all the gods all the way, not only did his sorrows increase, but they increased to a point of despair. "So I hated life . . . my heart began to despair" (Eccles. 2:17, 20).

Our tendency is to shrug our shoulders and say, "I can't help it. The desires inside of me are simply too strong." The problem isn't that our desires are too strong, but that our desires for the right things are too weak. Yes, we have cravings for sexual pleasure and excessive escape and excessive alcohol and a host of other things. But these things do not, cannot, satisfy the deep longings of the soul. Only God can. And the real problem is that we don't desire Him enough. Even with our current desires for illicit pleasure we could not only survive but thrive if we cultivated an intense desire for God. Illicit desires would pale in comparison to a burning desire for the living God and the joy found in His presence.

Talk to God About Your Struggle

Step One: Say, "I'm sorry, God, for hurting You. I'm sorry for this, this, that, and this."

Step Two: Say, "Thank You for loving me, for caring so much and so freely about me, even when I've lived life against Your ways. I never really knew before, or maybe I never understood that You are a loving God. I had never put it together that You want what's best for me even more than I do."

Step Three: Say, "Thank You for understanding me. It's fabulous that You know what I am going through and why I've done the things I've done. So often I've felt like I'm the only one in the world who battles this temptation, and I've felt so alone. Thank You for coming here and going through life just like me."

Step Four: Cry, "Help me, Jesus! I need a fresh start. I've seen so much and done so much my heart just feels dirty. I've told myself to clean up and live right, but the temptation was just too strong. Take me, take everything about me. I need You in my life and I need Your death on the cross to get me to God. I want to be Your child. Will You have me, just as I am?"

4

A Philosopher's Solution: Think Deeper

What marks our own generation?
It is the fact that modern man thinks
there is nobody home in the universe.
                        —Francis Schaeffer

MARK TWAIN ONCE ASKED a baggage handler on a commuter train if the man thought his briefcase was strong enough to be checked and placed in the baggage compartment. The baggage handler shrugged, took Twain's case, and promptly hurled it to the pavement. "That, sir," he said, "is what she'll get in Philadelphia." Then he picked it up and struck it five or six times against the side of the train car. "And that," he continued, "is what she'll get in Chicago." Finally, he threw the case to the ground again and stomped on it vigorously until the author's books and papers spilled out, saying, "That's what she'll get in Sioux City." As Twain watched slack-jawed, the man nodded at his now mangled case and advised, "If you're going any farther than Sioux City, sir, I'd suggest you carry it on yourself."

In a sense, Twain was lucky. He saw before he boarded the train what the journey ahead would entail. The best most of us can do is observe the journey of life from the windows of our moving "train" and attempt—while the scenery whizzes by—to make some half-ordered sense of it all. Solomon was a keen observer of life. He was a contemplative king. He was a faithful recorder of reality. He saw that life was full of contrasts and ripe with paradox. But he detected an order of some kind, as well. Solomon was not content with just a clinical observation of life. He longed to understand it—to make some sense of it.

> *Solomon was not content with just a clinical observation of life. He longed to understand it—to make some sense of it.*

One of the most lyrical and often quoted passages from Solomon's book of reflections is Ecclesiastes 3:1–11. It begins, "To everything there is a season . . . ," and its fourteen couplets are familiar to many who are all but strangers to the rest of the Bible. I have heard it read at celebrations and solemn occasions alike and discovered that even atheists appreciate its poetry.

Several years ago Kodak featured an advertising campaign with the tag line, "Remember the times of your life." The ads (especially the ones for television) were of the lump-in-the-throat variety, showing all kinds of sentimental images: a mother with her newborn baby, a child learning to walk, graduations, weddings, surprise homecomings, and tearful goodbyes. I suppose the point was that Kodak helped us hang on to those moments through photographs. While a camera (and Kodak film) can capture "moments" in time, there is absolutely nothing that can capture time itself.

What is this mysterious phenomenon we call time? It is quantifiable and it is relative. Thirty minutes, 1800 seconds, is always half an hour. But those seconds are perceived differently by a student waiting for an afternoon bell and a man on death row waiting for a ruling on his execution date. An hour in the dentist chair seems longer than an hour in a fine restaurant. How long is three months? Ask a child at the end of his summer vacation and then an expectant mother who has not seen her feet in that long. How long is a year? Well, that depends. Are you a teenager waiting to get a driver's license—or a patient with terminal cancer? Times drags—and time flies.

Time is the great equalizer. Whether you are the president of the United States or you live under a bridge in Washington, D.C., you have the same twenty-four hours deposited in your "time account" each day. And it has to be spent, used up. It cannot be accumulated or saved. Is it any wonder Solomon pondered time, and the kinds of events that occur in time, as he lived out his life under the sun? This king searched the earth for meaning and came up empty-handed, but in his search he noted this: Time goes on. It does not stop for personal introspection. It does not stop for experimentation. It does not stop for pleasure or for pain. But in its passage, time accomodates every aspect of life—birth, death, joy, sorrow. Like thinkers of every age, Solomon struggled to develop a philosophy that would order and explain the intricacies of life he observed . . . but first he simply described them as they occurred, in time.

Being Born and Dying

No baby chooses the hour of birth. No man or woman predicts the hour of death. Birth and death—the bookends of this earthly life—are appointed, not selected, dates. "There is," wrote Solomon, "an appointed time for everything. And there is a time for every event under heaven—a time to give birth, and a time to die" (Eccles. 3:1–2). Parents-to-be marvel at the fact that there is a time to be born. For first-time parents especially, the hour of birth is an anxiously-awaited mystery. When will the baby come? Will it be today? Tomorrow? Next week? This much is certain: It will be at the appointed time.

No child ever born was more eagerly anticipated than the Messiah—the Son of God who would be our deliverer. Paul wrote that this child, too, was born at the appointed time: "But when the fullness of the time came, God sent forth His Son, born of a woman, born under the Law, . . . that we might receive the adoption as sons" (Gal. 4:4–5). There is a time to be born. There is also a time to die. The Creator, not the creature, determines the length of life. The psalmist understood this when he wrote,

"And in Thy book they were all written, the days that were ordained for me, when as yet there was not one of them" (Ps. 139:16). Days are ordained for us. We do not set the length of our own life. God does.

I am at the age where I no longer preside primarily over the funerals of those in my parents' generation. This past year I have buried contemporaries, and I have come to a new appreciation of the fact that each life has a number of days given to it by God. Someone I had lunch with yesterday or laughed with the day before could die today. So could I. None of that is within my understanding or my control. That is a powerful observation!

"All lives are finite. In fact, the average life lasts only 683,280 hours or 2.4 billion seconds."

Even retailers understand the impact of this idea. A recent Sharper Image catalog advertised a "Personal Life Clock"—a marble obelisk with digital numbers that flashed the number of hours, minutes, and seconds remaining in one's "statistical lifetime." "All lives are finite," the catalog glibly noted. "In fact, the average life lasts only 683,280 hours or 2.4 billion seconds. This new Timisis Personal Life Clock reminds you to live life to the fullest by displaying the . . . most profound number you will ever see." But it could be wrong by a mile. You see, those days are God-appointed and God-ordained. God's Son, too, had an appointment with death. His cry, "It is finished," from the cross was the triumphant call of the God-man whose numbered days on earth had been fulfilled. There is a time to die.

Planting and Pulling Up

Have you ever planted caladium bulbs? Caladiums are a horticultural staple in Houston, Texas, during the spring and summer months. Yard after yard in our city is accented by caladiums— white, pink, and green—and each time I see them, I think, *Someone waited.* Caladium bulbs are gnarled and ugly, and after you plant them . . . you wait. First, small, blade-like shoots appear, and then the shoots unfold into leaves. They flatten out and "show their colors," and you're on your way to Yard-of-the-Month. (Maybe.)

When caladium season is over, you can dig up your bulbs, store them in a cool, dark place, and replant them again next year. But if you miss a few bulbs, come spring you'll see caladiums inching through your ground cover in your flower beds—and the asymmetrical effect may not be what you had hoped for. Solomon observed that there is "a time to plant, and a time to uproot what is planted" (v. 2). Farmers know this, too. There is a time to plant and a time to harvest.

> *"There is . . .," Solomon observed, "a time to kill and a time to heal."*

They cannot be switched. A pattern exists, and it must be followed to achieve the desired results. What is planted must remain planted, too. The process cannot be hurried along. "Leave the bulbs alone," wrote C. S. Lewis, "and the new flowers will come up. Grub them up and hope, by fondling and sniffing, to get last year's blooms, and you will get nothing." There is a time to plant and a time to uproot.

Killing and Healing

In 1994 we marked the fiftieth anniversary of D-Day. The media did not refer to it as the "golden" anniversary, a phrase usually applied to such remembrances. There is something about that historic day that does not lend itself to the term "golden." June 6, 1944—the day the Allied forces invaded the European continent via the beaches of France—is a day that is observed in solemn, not celebratory, fashion. The cost, in terms of lives, was tremendous. Thousands of young soldiers, many of them still teenagers, were killed in the effort to drive Hitler's army from its strongholds. But heads of state and military strategists agreed that the time had come to act decisively. June 6, 1944, was a time to kill. Oddly enough, the invasion was actually planned to occur one day earlier, on June 5, but a violent storm forced the Allied leaders to delay it one day. That twenty-four-hour window gave many soldiers a little more time to jot down wills, send last letters to loved ones, and otherwise prepare for what many expected to be their final mission.

Just as there is a time for killing, there is a time for healing. The nation lost two historically significant figures in the span of a few days in May of 1994 with the deaths of former president Richard Milhous Nixon and former first lady Jaqueline Kennedy Onassis. Nixon, of course, the only U.S. president to leave office before his term expired, endured the scorn of his country in the days immediately following the Watergate scandal, but he emerged years later as something of a distinguished diplomat and statesman. In his final words to his White House staff he said, "We think that when we suffer a defeat, that all is ended. Not true. It is only a beginning, always." Nixon learned the truth of those words when he experienced, after the disaster of 1974, a time for healing. "There is . . . , " Solomon observed, "a time to kill and a time to heal" (v. 3).

Mrs. Onassis was remembered most often, in the days immediately following her death, for the role she played over three decades ago in helping an entire nation to heal after the assassination of a president. Her dignity and calm as a thirty-four-year-old widow who had witnessed the brutal murder of her husband gave strength and solace to the country that grieved with her. Her actions, both public and private, made those tragic days in November 1963, a time for healing.

Tearing Down and Building Up

I live in a city that seems to be permanently under construction. (There are freeways in Houston, Texas, that I have never seen without a sign that says—at some point—"Left lane closed ahead," or "Right lane closed ahead.") Most large cities *are* in a constant state of renewal, and building something up, especially in the inner city, usually requires tearing something else down. Old buildings are demolished because they are beyond repair or filled with asbestos, and soon gleaming new structures take their place.

The process of tearing down and building up is ongoing. Sometimes in our building up we find things worth saving, as well. A fast-food hamburger restaurant in our city is literally built around a one hundred-year-old oak, and its branches provide a beautiful setting for outdoor, on-the-deck dining. Builders of a new subway system for the city of Athens, Greece, discovered the ruins of second-century Roman baths, as well as all kinds of artifacts like sarcophagi, gold jewelry, and mosaics. The archaeological sitework delayed construction of the transit system, but planners developed a unique way to place old and new side-by-side: principal subway stations house mini-museums displaying the relics found at each site. There is a time to tear down and a time to build up.

Weeping and Laughing

Each summer I spend a week on the beach with junior and senior high school students on our annual Beach Retreat. There are lots of things that make Beach Retreat a high point for our teenagers and for me, but the sheer emotion of those few days always overwhelms me. By the time they reach their twenties, adults have usually managed to maintain a certain mid-range of emotion and never vary too much from that center, at least not publicly. But kids . . . well, that is another story. They play hard. They compete fiercely. They eat (a lot). And generally when you ask

> *There are just some things in life which can be expressed only by tears.*

them about what is really on their hearts, they tell you—straight up with no frills.

We laugh hilariously at Beach Retreat. It is just fun to be with one another and to act silly. But there is a night on Beach Retreat that we do not laugh much. We call it the Night of the Open Heart, because we open our hearts and just kind of bleed in front of one another. We confess sin. We ask for prayer. We share hurts—big ones and not-so-big ones. And every time, we cry together because there are just some things in life which can be expressed only by tears. Only in a tear do you find the three building blocks of life: albumin (protein), salt, and water. Solomon said there is "a time to weep, and a time to laugh" (v. 4). The wise person runs from neither.

Mourning and Dancing

King Solomon observed that the responses of mourning and dancing are entirely appropriate in their time. Mourning is a reasonable response to a time of grief. Dancing is a reasonable response to a time of joy. Solomon's father David knew both emotions well and exhibited, at different times, both responses. Following David's adulterous affair with Bathsheba, wife of Uriah the Hittite, the child born to them became gravely ill. David prayed for the child, fasted, and lay prostrate on the ground in his grief. Seven days went by, and then the child died. David had mourned so openly that his servants were afraid to tell their master what had happened, and they did so only after he asked them directly if his son was dead.

David's joy, however, was as public and spontaneous as his grief had been, when the occasion called for it. After successfully moving the ark of God from the house of a stranger to the holy city of Jerusalem, David danced for joy in the streets. "And David was dancing before the Lord with all his might, and David was wearing a linen ephod. So David and all the house of Israel were bringing up the ark of the LORD with shouting and the sound of the trumpet" (2 Sam. 6:14–15). When his wife Michal reprimanded him for "behavior unbecoming to a king," David told her he danced not before the people, but "before the LORD," saying "therefore I will celebrate before the LORD" (2 Sam. 6:21). There is a time for mourning and a time for dancing.

Throwing Stones . . . and Gathering Them

Solomon's statement that there is "a time to throw stones, and a time to gather stones" (v. 5) has puzzled many scholars. There are many theories about what, exactly, he was referring to, but I believe that he possibly meant that throwing stones was a defensive ploy, and gathering them was an offensive effort. The Hebrews would throw stones in an enemy's field to keep them at bay and gather stones to build their own buildings.

In 1994, the Houston Rockets made it to the finals of the National Basketball Association for only the third time in franchise history. Their victory over the New York Knicks in a grueling seven-game series gave Houston its first national title in any professional sport. There have been plenty of seasons that the Rockets survived the first round and a few forays into the second round. But typically most of our local sports teams quit playing when the regular season ends. What made the 1994 team a champion was the fact that they played ball at both ends of the floor. The team's high scorer, Hakeem Olajuwon, was also the NBA defensive player of the year. Blocked shots and steals were just as significant as three pointers and lay-ups. Knowing when to play offense and when to play defense is important in life, too. There is a time for throwing stones and for gathering them.

To Embrace and Not to Embrace

My wife, Jo Beth, and I have three sons. They are all men now, grown and going their own ways, but I still like to hug them. When they were little boys, just about any time was the right time for a hug, but as they grew older, especially in their teenage years, we learned to pick our moments. But the "golden days" for embracing come around again: Now I have four grandchildren, LeeBeth, E. J., and twin grandaughters Laurie and Landra, who are thrilled to be embraced by their old "Goosey" (granddad).

> *A hug can convey encouragement and assurance to those we love.*

With our friends, too, there is a time for embracing. A warm embrace at just the right moment can say, "You did the right thing," or "I'm with you all the way," or "I'm so happy for you." A hug can convey encouragement and assurance to those we love. There is also a time, as Solomon noted, "to shun embracing" (v. 5). Sometimes stern words, not hugs, are required. Situations arise that must be dealt with firmly, and at those times an embrace would seem inappropriate and out of place. There is a time to embrace—and a time to shun embracing.

Searching and Giving Up

Solomon's words about a time for searching bring to mind the image of a rescue worker seeking someone who is lost. Such workers labored for days after San Francisco's 1989 earthquake to locate those who were trapped in their homes and offices and in cars along the city's freeways. It is relatively easy to know when to start searching—but more difficult to know when to stop. My dad told me years ago about his attempts to revive a co-worker who had been electrocuted. He and the other men with him administered CPR for some time with no apparent success. When they felt he no longer stood a chance of being resuscitated, they stopped. Dad said he kept thinking, "We could have gone longer. Maybe we should have tried a little more. Maybe we gave up too soon." There is a time for searching, and there is a time for giving up.

Keeping and Throwing Away

Last summer, members of our church held an enormous garage sale on our church campus. Families and individuals committed the money they earned from the sale of used or unwanted items to our church's building fund. We placed small classified ads in our local papers, gathered up our "stuff," and hit the parking lot early one Saturday morning. The results were unbelievable. We had furniture, televisions, stereos, clothes, decorative items, and even a hot tub. (It sold.) There were people waiting to buy while we were still setting up—and a few items never even went on display because other sellers bought them!

Most of us have a stockpile of possessions that we will never use. The tremendous results of "The World's Biggest Garage Sale" made me wonder what might happen if we simply gave away what we do not use as a matter of routine—or sold it and gave the proceeds to God's kingdom. I suspect that we, and our churches, would be out of debt ten times over. There is a time to keep, a time to throw away, and even a time to have a garage sale . . . and give God the profit.

Tearing Apart and Sewing Together

Probably the picture Solomon had in mind when he observed that there is a time "to tear apart, and a time to sew together" (v. 7) was that of grieving. The Hebrews would tear their clothing as a demonstration of their grief and then sew the pieces together again when the time for mourning was ended. I have also seen the "tearing apart" when differences between friends, between pastors and their congregations, or even factions in denominations grow so heated and complex that separation eventually occurs. That is always a painful thing—and an occasion for grief.

While the time for "tearing apart" can come suddenly and be over just as quickly, the time for "sewing together" is often slow to commence, and its desired outcome—wholeness—may be difficult to achieve. We see evidence of this in the news each day as the emerging nations in Eastern Europe struggle to attain harmony with one another in their newly-won independence. As is true with surgery, the sutures usually require much more tedious and painstaking work than the original incision. There is a time for sewing together . . . and it is skilled, necessary work.

Keeping Silent and Speaking

Winston Churchill once said of one of his political adversaries: "He has the ability to compress the minimum amount of thought into the maximum amount of words." A wise person knows when to speak . . . and when to keep silent. I have wished many times that someone had whispered in my ear to be silent. There have been times, too, when I have been silent and should have spoken out, when I have wished someone had said, "Okay, Edwin, this is your cue. Speak up!"

"If we accept that a mother can kill even her own child, how can we tell other people not to kill each other?"

Jesus Christ illustrated the raw power of silence when He stood before His accusers, first in the home of Caiaphas and later in the court of Pilate, and said nothing. As Matthew recorded: "Now Jesus stood before the governor, and the governor questioned Him, saying, 'Are you the king of the Jews?' And Jesus said to him, 'It is as you say.' And while He was being accused by the chief priests and elders, He made no answer. Then Pilate said to Him, 'Do You not hear how many things they testify against You?' And He did not answer him with regard to even a single charge, so that the governor was quite amazed" (Matt. 27:11–14). There is nothing tougher than to stay silent when you are being unjustly accused. But Jesus knew it was a time to keep silent . . . and He did.

Those in attendance at the 1994 National Prayer Breakfast held in conjunction with the National Religious Broadcasters Convention witnessed a time for speaking when Mother Teresa took the podium and pleaded for the lives of unborn children. Barely tall enough to be seen over the lectern, this tiny nun began her address by reading a portion of Scripture, then stunned the assembled dignitaries, including the president and vice-president of the United States, by saying, "The greatest destroyer of peace today is abortion . . . [for] if we accept that a mother can kill even her own child, how can we tell other people not to kill each other?"

"Mother Teresa," wrote Charles Colson after the event, "was invariably polite and respectful. Yet she did not flinch in speaking the truth. She demonstrated civility wedded to bold conviction, confronting world leaders with a message of biblical righteousness."[1] Clearly, she viewed the breakfast as a time to speak. "Please don't kill the child," she implored her audience. "I want the child. Please give me the child." After her speech, she approached the president, pointed her finger at him, and said, "Stop killing babies." "There is," said Solomon, "a time to be silent, and a time to speak" (v. 7). May we come to know the difference.

Loving and Hating

Solomon noted in his observation of life "under the sun" that there is "a time to love, and a time to hate" (v. 8). The fact that he considered "a time to hate" a legitimate response may surprise some, but his words are quite clear. What is to be the object of our hate? Only what God hates, no more and no less—and God hates sin. "Hate evil, you who love the LORD," the psalmist wrote, and in Proverbs, Solomon listed six specific things that God hates: "haughty eyes, a lying tongue, and hands that shed innocent blood, a heart that devises wicked plans, feet that run rapidly to evil, a false witness who utters lies, and one who spreads strife among brothers" (Prov. 6:17–19).

The phrase, "hands that shed innocent blood" seems especially chilling in our present day. Newscast after newscast stuns the American public with footage of the carnage of civil war in Rwanda. Murdered bodies can be seen floating so close together in rivers that the water cannot be seen. Satellite pictures of war-torn Bosnia have all but left us numb to the senseless killing there. Millions of unborn children are legally murdered in our country each year as they rest in what should be the safest place in the world—their mothers' wombs. God hates hands that shed innocent blood, and those who are called by His name are called to hate their murderous acts as well.

There is a time to hate, but I am thankful that there is also a time to love.

Making War and Making Peace

I thought I was a pacifist at one point in my life, but I know now that I am not. There is a time to stand for what is right and what is of God, even if others oppose it. Many historians have noted that in times of war our nation has brought forward its best. Charles de Gaulle once said, "France was never her true self unless she was engaged in a great enterprise." Wisely considered and necessary warfare is an enterprise that demands the very best of a nation and of her people.

The nation of Israel faced war early in her history when God commanded the Israelites to enter the promised land of Canaan and to drive out its inhabitants. (I think some of God's chosen people may have been surprised to find out that the land *had* inhabitants!) They were commanded to fight in order to receive what God had already stated would be theirs, and they were instructed that the "clearing" of their land would not be accomplished in a single battle: "I will not drive them out before you in a single year, that the land may not become desolate, and the beasts of the field become too numerous for you. I will drive them out before you little by little, until you become fruitful and take possession of the land" (Ex. 23:29–30).

> *Peacemakers are not always heralded in the way that victorious warriors are, but they are just as significant.*

Peace, too, is a great enterprise, and Solomon noted that there was a time for it, as well. Peacemakers are not always heralded in the way that victorious warriors are, but they are just as significant. Are you a peacemaker? Do you strive for under-standing and agreement among others? Peacemakers do. They do not deal in gossip or half-truths or stir up envy or hatred. A peacemaker does not urge friends to "pray for so-and-so, be-cause he's such a rascal." Using prayer as a cloak for character assassination is not the way of a peacemaker. A peacemaker is instead quietly behind the scenes, working and praying for God's truth and His justice to prevail. There is a time for war and a time for peace . . . a time for warriors and a time for peacemak-ers.

What Does It Mean?

Solomon's under-the-sun observations are a study in contrasts, in opposites. These fourteen couplets highlight a tension that is ever present in our world. The king noted that there was a time for each of the phenomena that he observed, yet they were all at odds with one another. If this was the stuff of life, he concluded, what sense could be made of it? "What profit is there to the worker from that in which he toils?" (v. 9) he asks. From here, Solomon had the same options anyone has in explaining the apparent randomness of life. These choices could be called "philosophies of life," and they go by many names, although I will suggest three generic terms for them: chance, choice, and chosen-ness.

Chance

The philosophy that all of life is ordered by chance is one way to explain away the tensions we observe but cannot understand. Those who believe chance is life's determining cause would say, "Life is just a gamble. Sometimes you win; sometimes you lose." Or "I just happened to be in the right place at the right time. I was lucky." In the language of classical philosophy, this might be called nihilism—a viewpoint that denies any objective, moral truth and considers existence meaningless. This is the *que sera,*

sera crowd—whatever happens, happens. There is no sense to be made of life, for it is all just a matter of chance.

Elisha Shapiro, a performance artist who made a bid for the U.S. presidency on the nihilist ticket in 1988, described this view:

> There is no God, and I don't feel like replacing him with anything, and I like it that way. To me, there really isn't any significance to life, none whatsoever. No significance. And I find that's a comforting thing. You're let off the hook that way. I'm a product of . . . if I were trying to figure out what I was a product of, the best thing I could guess would be billions of years of coincidences, dumb luck.[2]

Choice

Others view life as a matter of choice. They see people as masters of their fate and the captains of their own souls. If there is a time for war and a time for peace, for love and for hate, we determine them, according to this view. We decide "what time it is" and respond accordingly. This philosophy of life has come to be known by the term "humanism," and it rejects the idea that there are supernatural forces stronger than the will of humans at work in the universe. It says that there is no other voice, no other authority, that matters.

"Of all the conceivable forms of enlightenment," wrote G. K. Chesterton, "the worst is what these people call the Inner Light. Of all horrible religions the most horrible is the worship of the god within. That Jones should worship the god within him turns out ultimately to mean that Jones shall worship Jones. Let Jones worship the sun, the moon, anything rather than the Inner Light; let Jones worship cats or crocodiles, if he can find any in his street, but not the god within."[3]

"That Jones should worship the god within him turns out ultimately to mean that Jones shall worship Jones."

Where there is no authority but each person's own, eventually chaos rules. The history of Israel records that when the nation had no king, the people "crowned" themselves: "In those days there was no king in Israel; every man did what was right in his own eyes" (Judg. 16:6). Those were Israel's darkest days.

Chosen-ness

While some see life as chance and others as choice, there is a third view widely held—that all of life is chosen or predestined. This attempt to make sense of the times of life is sometimes referred to as determinism, the philosophy that acts of our will, occurences in nature, and other social and psychological phenomena are predetermined by some cause or causes outside of ourselves. This is an ordered, not random, view of life—but in it, the order is set, and all we can do is what we have already been "determined" to do, nothing more and nothing less. Who determines these things is unimportant. The point is simply that they have already been established and are beyond our control.

A Fourth View

So what *does* it all mean? Chance, choice, or chosen-ness? I believe the truth about the times we walk through is a combination of the last two. Life is chosen—not by fate or a nebulous "higher power," but by God Himself. Yet in His chosen-ness, there is personal choice.

> *Life is chosen by God Himself. Yet in His chosen-ness, there is personal choice.*

Suppose, for example, that winter is coming. I could choose, in the middle of winter, to put on a bathing suit and jump into an outdoor pool. That would certainly be a choice. Winter is "predetermined," but I can choose how I respond to winter. Much about our lives has already been determined. Our gifts and abilities, our talents, the families we were born into—these things were chosen for us by God. But within that chosen-ness, we have been given choices. In this, we are free moral agents, or as R. C. Sproul has said, "We are free subjects who serve a sovereign king."

Solomon lived his life under the sun with little more than a casual reference to God. He believed God was there, but he related little of what he observed to God's preeminent existence. Instead, he dabbled in idolatry, hedonism, intellectualism, materialism, and philosophy. He searched for answers, and he found none. Are we not like Solomon? We live on the backside of life's tapestry, trying to make sense of the weaving with one colored strand or another of philosophy. We see the threads of life, but not its design. We see a time for this or a time for that, but we are unable to make something coherent of the whole fabric.

When do we understand? When does the tapestry take on form and meaning? Only when we see it from the upper side—from above the sun. From that view, the pattern is nothing less than pleasing and right, as King Solomon's words suggest: "He has made everything beautiful in its time. He has also set eternity in the hearts of men; yet they cannot fathom what God has done from beginning to end" (Eccles. 3:11).

(Eccles. 3:1-10)

An Above-the-Sun Postscript

Trust in the LORD with all your heart,
And do not lean on your own understanding.
In all your ways acknowledge Him,
And He will make your paths straight.
—Proverbs 3:5–6

If there are different times for every event under the sun, how are we supposed to know when to do which activity? What if we plant when it's really time to uproot? What if we scatter stones when it's really time to gather?

Suppose you are putting together a major financial package with a number of investors. Negotiations get sticky as questions of product viability surface. Should you cut your losses? Stories abound about smart businessmen who smelled a deal going sour and pulled out. Or maybe you should hang tough, using sheer determination to realize the dream. *Fortune, Money,* and the *Wall Street Journal* regularly chronicle such persistence that mushrooms into staggering success. Which should you do in your situation? Fish or cut bait? If there is a time for this, a time for that, how do you know which is which?

Or, to put it another way, how do you discover the will of God? Six practical steps will help you find God's will for your situation. The first step might sound irrelevant and impractical, but it's actually the foundation of all the other steps.

Love God

This whole enterprise called life finds fulfillment in one place—*real* relationship with God. His highest hope and grandest plan for you is a relationship with Him. He created you. He loves you, so love Him.

Examine Specific Bible Commands

Look over the Ten Commandments (Exodus 20). Do any of these relate to your family or business decisions? Check Jesus' Sermon on the Mount (Matthew 5–7). Also, look at the front pages of a Gideon Bible that show various Scriptures and place them in the normal categories of life. Ask a friend or a pastor for a Christian book that deals with the situation you are facing.

Examine General Scriptural Principles

Maybe God doesn't have a specific command like Step Two, but you might find overarching principles that apply. For example, look at your decision in light of the Golden Rule, "Do unto others as you would have done unto you." Or ask yourself, "Am I doing this for selfish gain?" (Phil. 2:3–4). Do my choices allow me to actively demonstrate unconditional love? Romans 14:23 says "whatever is not of faith is sin." Will one particular choice cause someone else to stumble (Romans 14:20)? Ask yourself, "Which alternative will bring glory to God?" And last, ask yourself, "What would Jesus do?"

Make a Pro/Con List

Honestly evaluate the pros and cons of the different choices.

Ask Godly Christians

If you are not a believer and want to try God's way with a decision, ask a Christian in your office or neighborhood. If you are a believer, sit down with a Christian friend you respect or a Bible Study teacher or a minister. Explain the entire situation and listen to their counsel.

Pray

Just flat out ask Him. Ask Him for wisdom (James 1:5) and listen for that still small voice of direction.

5

An Intellectual's Solution: Study Further

> We make men without chests and expect
> of them virtue and enterprise.
> We laugh at honour and are shocked to find
> traitors in our midst.
> We castrate and bid the geldings be fruitful.
>
> —C. S. Lewis

T HERE WERE SIX BLIND MEN from India, or so the legend goes. An elephant blocked their path, and they sought to discover by touch, what stood in front of them. One man felt the side of the animal and said, "It is a wall." Another felt the elephant's knees and said, "Oh, no, I think it must be a tree." A third touched the elephant's tail and said, "The thing is a rope." A fourth felt the ear of the elephant and said, "This is a giant fan." The fifth blind man felt the animal's tusk and said, "It is obvious. What we have is a spear." The final man touched the long trunk of the elephant and said, "All of you are wrong. It is clearly a snake."

> *An enormous question stands before each person living on this planet. It is unavoidable and all-encompassing.*

All six blind men encountered an elephant, but each had a radically different perspective on what it was. All of them were partially correct—and equally wrong. To examine only the elephant's body would lead a man to believe he faced a wall, or to touch only his trunk would make it seem like a snake. But because they examined only a portion of the animal, none of them came to the correct conclusion: The thing standing before them was an elephant!

An enormous question stands before each person living on this planet. It is unavoidable and all-encompassing. The question is this: What is the meaning of life? Three smaller questions are a part of this big question. Where did you come from? Why are you here? Where are you going? If *USA Today* or CNN polled a statistically significant sample of adults on the question, "What is the meaning of life?" I believe they would get an incredibly wide variety of answers. Most of them would be at least partially correct and most would be equally wrong. However, such a poll will probably never be taken because the meaning of life is simply too big to answer using a single tool.

King Solomon dared to ask the question. Like a traveling philosopher, he stood at life's crossroads and considered a variety of signs, each one saying, "This way to the meaning of life . . . " One pointed to pleasure; another to power. Another to religion. He earlier encountered the sign that pointed to wisdom and learning, and he followed that road as far as it could carry him. Solomon became the ultimate professor, the quintessential information-man. Gifted by God with wisdom, he pursued it as the highest good, and through education he acquired a wealth of knowledge unequaled in his day.

Most men and women today who pursue a college education do so with a specific goal in mind. Those who aspire to a career in medicine usually spend their undergraduate years studying biology. Those who seek to become attorneys may focus initially on the social sciences. Graduate school refines their studies even further, honing in on a particular specialty or niche. Solomon's educational goals were not so tightly focused. He did not pursue education as a means to an end, but as an end in itself. He majored in everything under the sun: "I, the Preacher, have been king over Israel in Jerusalem. And I set my mind to seek and explore by wisdom concerning all that has been done under heaven" (Eccles. 1:12–13a).

Solomon "set his mind to seek." He was determined, and his search was a disciplined one. He sought to thoroughly examine the wisdom of this world—and he left no stone unturned. What were the results of his exhaustive study? Listen to his preliminary report: "It is a grievous task which God has given to the sons of men to be afflicted with" (v. 13b). In other words, it is a grievous task to study, a grievous task to look intently at the scope of history. Just to live in this world as "sons of men" is a tough assignment.

"I have seen all the works which have been done under the sun," Solomon went on to say, "and behold, all is vanity and striving after wind" (v. 14). "It's meaningless," he concluded. "Been there. Done that. Now what?" Solomon determined in his exhaustive study that meaning is not found in wisdom and knowledge and that there is nothing new yet to be discovered. There is no such thing as "new" truth—but simply old truth responded to by new people. All of it was vanity in his estimation. All of it was "striving after wind."

> *There is no such thing as "new" truth—but simply old truth responded to by new people.*

Renaissance Man

What were Solomon's intellectual credentials? Was he erudite and sophisticated enough to make his pronouncement that striving after knowledge was "vanity?" He was. As he noted, "Behold, I have magnified and increased wisdom more than all who were over Jerusalem before me, and my mind has observed a wealth of wisdom and knowledge" (v. 16). That was Solomon's assessment of himself, but the details of his intellectual pursuits are recorded by others, as well. The writer of 1 Kings states that

Solomon's wisdom surpassed the wisdom of all the sons of the east and of all Egypt. He was said to be wiser than all men, and several (who must have been well-known in that day) were listed: "Ethan the Ezrahite, Heman, Calcol and Darda, the sons of Mahol; and his name was known in all the surrounding nations" (1 Kings 4:31).

But Solomon was not only "book smart," he was also creative. In fact, he could safely be called the "Renaissance man" of his day. He was a prolific writer, with three thousand proverbs to his credit—a feat that surpasses the productivity of all but a few modern authors. He was an intellectual "double threat." He possessed great insight and could articulate his understanding for the benefit and enjoyment of others. The sheer volume of his work would impress even today's best-selling giants from Robert Ludlum and Tom Clancy to Michael Crichton and John Grisham.

Not content to write only words, King Solomon penned music also. Over one thousand songs were attributed to this ancient composer—an impressive body of work in any age. He dabbled in botany and horticulture and was something of an expert on trees of all kinds. He "lectured" in the areas of zoology, ornithology, and ichthyology, too—intriguing his listeners with his extensive knowledge of animals, birds, and fish. Many scholars are considered less than captivating speakers, but Solomon must have been an exceptional one: "And men came from all peoples to hear the wisdom of Solomon, from all the kings of the earth who had heard of his wisdom" (1 Kings 4:34).

> *If Solomon lived today, he would be a "singular sensation": writer, composer, musician, scientist, statesman, teacher, and speaker.*

If Solomon lived today, he would be a "singular sensation": writer, composer, musician, scientist, statesman, teacher, and speaker. Imagine being seated next to King Solomon at a dinner party: No topic of conversation could be introduced in which he would not be well-versed. No guest within earshot would get bored. And if this man said wisdom and knowledge were vanity, he had enough of both to know what he was talking about.

Wisdom Is Not the Answer

Learned as he was, Solomon did not believe that knowledge was the answer. With all his education, he still pronounced life under the sun meaningless. Having acquired the knowledge equivalent to multiple degrees, Solomon came to three simple conclusions: "What is crooked cannot be straightened, and what is lacking cannot be counted . . . . I set my mind to know wisdom and to know madness and folly; I realized that this also is striving after wind. Because in much wisdom there is much grief, and increasing knowledge results in increasing pain" (Eccles. 1:15, 17–18). The crooked cannot be made straight through education. What is non-existent cannot be counted—even by a smart man. And more knowledge will bring more grief and more pain. Not exactly what you would expect from the world's most intelligent man.

King Solomon would contend that a thief with a Ph.D. is still a thief. An educated thief still steals; he just pulls off more complicated heists. The crooked cannot be made straight merely through schooling. We see this same truth illustrated today. Sex education has not saved our children from the consequences of immorality. We have some of the best-educated adolescents in the world, but even knowing the risks, one of every four girls and one of every three boys is sexually active by age fifteen. The typical American adult admits to having had seven sex partners since turning eighteen.[1] One Colorado high school that began distributing condoms as a part of its sex education program found that three years later the birth rate was 31 percent *higher* than the national average.[2] No amount of knowledge will make an immoral person moral. That was Solomon's first conclusion.

Next, he discovered that education does not make something of nothing. If a void exists in a person's life—education alone will not fill it. Learning will not bring an end to loneliness or estrangement. In fact, Solomon observed that more education simply brings more pain. Why? Because the more educated a person is, the more he or she understands that knowledge will

> *It is entirely possible for a professor to be granted tenure and never grasp the truth.*

never answer the question that refuses to go away: "What does this life mean?" This realization brings more grief, more agony, more sorrow. In other words, it is entirely possible for a professor to be granted tenure and never grasp the truth.

Our modern educational system does not provide the answer to our search for meaning, either. More often than not, it obscures the question—even though doing so is about as difficult as hiding an elephant. People who seek to hide from life's questions generally do so in five ways: by diversion, propaganda, indifference, the pursuit of happiness, and subjectivism.

Diversion

Diversion is quite easily achieved. Remote control in hand, we "channel surf" the airwaves for hours at a time, avoiding any question more serious than, "What else is on?" "Jay Leno isn't amusing this evening? Zap, you're gone, Jay. AMC dug a little too low in the old movie bin? Zap, take that, Cornel Wilde. Ted Koppel a bit smug tonight? Zap, try again tomorrow, Ted. You have power and autonomy. You are the king of zappers. You can cut Dick Gephardt off mid-sentence, zap."[3]

My generation has perfected diversionary tactics. We are the ones who are busy. (Have you ever had anyone over thirty admit to you they are *not* busy?) Work is totally consuming. Leisure pursuits are equally demanding. Travel plans are made months, sometimes years in advance. We are booked, so booked that we could not possibly pencil in any time for serious reflection on why we are here, much less how we got here to begin with! We have alleviated the need to examine life by racing—or zapping—through it. We have become experts at diversion, never asking the ultimate question: "When we get where we are going, where will we be?"

A man boarded a bus in New York City with every intention of traveling to Detroit, Michigan. Unknowingly, he ended up in

Kansas City, Missouri. When he got off the bus, he asked for directions: "Where is Woodward Avenue?" Nobody in Kansas City had heard of Woodward Avenue, of course, because it was in Detroit. The fellow thought people were not being very helpful or gracious, and he began to argue, saying, "I know you're putting me on. Woodward Avenue is one of the main thoroughfares here in Detroit. Tell me how to get there." "We've never heard of such a place," the bus station employees said.

Then another man spoke up. "Did you say *Detroit*?" he asked.

"That's right, Detroit."

"Sir," he said, "you're not in Detroit. You're in Kansas City."

It is easy to catch the wrong bus—and it is impossible to reach your destination that way.

> *We have alleviated the need to examine life by racing—or zapping—through it.*

Propaganda

Another means of avoiding the tough questions is through the spreading of propaganda—information meant to help or injure an institution or a cause. Television is often the primary vehicle used to serve huge portions of propaganda, frequently under the heading of "news." As television journalist Ted Koppel observed: "We now communicate with everyone . . . and say absolutely nothing. We have reconstructed the Tower of Babel and it is a television antenna. A thousand voices producing a daily parody of democracy in which everyone's opinion is afforded equal weight, regardless of substance or merit. Indeed, it can be argued that opinions of real weight tend to sink with barely a trace in television's ocean of banalities. Our society finds truth too strong a message to digest undiluted."[4] Truth is out there, somewhere. But it is buried beneath the propaganda of special interest activists whose view of life never extends beyond their own corner of creation's blanket.

Indifference

Indifference can also be used to avoid asking life's toughest questions. Some will respond that it simply does not matter what life is all about. "So what?" yawns this crowd, whose apparent lack of concern is often the symptom of "perceived invincibility." Beaches are crowded each week of spring break with half a million of them—drunken, drugged, hormone-revved men and women whose t-shirts, hats, and bumper stickers bear the slogan "Comfortably Numb." They refuse to grapple with the big questions by pretending that they do not care. But deep down, we all care—even those of us who feign indifference. We cannot help it because we are made that way.

Chuck Swindoll tells of a high school teacher continually frustrated by a class of students who would not pay attention. They wouldn't listen; they were unresponsive. One day he walked into the classroom and wrote in large letters on the blackboard, "A - P - A- T - H - Y." He underlined it twice for effect and gestured so strongly with his chalk that it broke in two. One boy on the back row woke up when he heard the noise and blinked at the word written on the board at the front of the room. "A-p-a-t-h-y. What does that mean?" he asked, punching his nearest buddy. His friend cracked one eye, shrugged his shoulders, said "Who cares," and went back to sleep. Apathy. Indifference.

The Pursuit of Happiness

Pursuing happiness can also keep us from focusing on the true meaning of life—and this pursuit of happiness is a uniquely American phenomenon. We are the only nation in the world whose constitution holds that the pursuit of happiness is every citizen's "inalienable right." A middle-aged executive whose marriage has suffered from his workaholism sees a way out in an affair with a younger, single co-worker: "Don't I have the right to a little happiness?" An unwed, pregnant woman is alarmed at the prospect of single parenthood and, feeling overwhelmed, considers aborting her child: "Don't I have the right to a little happiness?"

Happiness has become an elusive god for many in our culture. We chase it with a single-minded passion and substitute its pursuit for true purpose. Former CBS newswriter Peggy Noonan observes, ". . . We have lost the old knowledge that happiness is overrated—that, in a way, life is overrated. Our ancestors believed in two worlds, and understood this to be the solitary, poor, nasty, brutish, and short one. We are the first generations of man that actually expected to find happiness here on earth, and our search for it

> *We are the only nation in the world whose constitution holds that the pursuit of happiness is every citizen's "inalienable right."*

has caused such—unhappiness."[5] But we keep searching, because if we focus on the search, we can forget (at least temporarily) that we have found no other purpose for living.

Subjectivism

Finally, we hide from the questions of life by using the cloak of subjectivism. Never in this country's history has subjectivism been so prevalent in our educational system. We run away from absolutes with the speed and determination of an Olympic sprinter. What is life all about? What does our existence mean? The subjectivist's answer? "Whatever you want it to mean." What is truth? "Well, it's whatever is true *to you*." Our schools have adopted an "I'm okay/you're okay" stance. Anything goes as long as it is not definitive—as long as it is not an absolute. Absolutes—especially moral ones—are strictly forbidden.

When I went to school, there was a place for the teaching of absolutes. I received what I would term "character education." Teachers used words like "right" and "wrong," and they were expected to exhibit in their personal lives the kind of character they taught. Society reinforced what I was being taught in the home or at church. My parents did not have to worry about any mixed messages I might receive.

Today, parents feel the need to protect children from culture. Whereas it was once an asset to the family, culture is now a liability. Character education has been abandoned in favor of "values clarification"; the term itself certainly sounds non-offensive. Who could object to having their values "clarified"? But in values clarification programs, the teacher becomes a talk show host and the classroom becomes a bull-session. Instead of educators transmitting sound moral values to students, the students are allowed to "clarify" their own values, which are never to be criticized. The history of the word "value" is significant here: The avowed atheist Nietzsche coined the term as an alternative to an absolute right and an absolute wrong.

> *Character education has been abandoned in favor of "values clarification." Who could object to having their values "clarified"?*

A typical discussion question in this morally relativistic atmosphere might be this: "On a scale of one to seven, with one being 'never' and seven being 'always,' how frequently should you tell your parents the truth? Your peers? Strangers?" Or "What do you consider to be the best method of birth control? Is abortion a reasonable means of birth control? Is abstinence? Why or why not?" No one can be wrong, of course, because everyone is right. Actually values clarification is a misnomer. What are clarified are the individual student's wants and desires.

Former Secretary of Education and drug czar William J. Bennett is a vocal opponent of this type of educational subjectivism:

> Are we really going to do away with standards and judgments? Is anyone going to argue that a life of cheating and swindling is as worthy as a life of honest, hard work? Unless we are willing to embrace some pretty silly positions, we've got to admit the need for moral and intellectual standards. The problem is that some people tend to regard anyone who would pronounce a definitive judgment as an unsophisticated Philistine or a close-minded "elitist" trying to impose his view on everyone else.[6]

Research has shown that this kind of learning is ineffectual. Values clarification and courses in "moral reasoning" tend not to influence children's behavior—but to leave them morally adrift with no compass with which to navigate. In the best of all possible worlds, parents would be the child's primary educators, teaching their offspring moral absolutes that schools, churches, governments, institutions, and neighborhoods would reinforce. When parents do teach these absolutes but they are negated by the other institutions of society, the job of rearing responsible, morally upright citizens is harder. When parents do not teach, and society says, "Anything goes," the job is all but impossible.

Worldly Education

King Solomon pursued a worldly education. He sought wisdom and knowledge "under the sun" and concluded that all such learning was meaningless. The crooked was not made straight through intellectual pursuits, nor did vast education make something of nothing. God was excluded from the search for knowledge, and God is all but excluded in today's public education system, as well. The concept of separation of church and state, originally intended by our founding fathers to protect the personal practice of religion and prohibit the formation of a compulsory, state-sanctioned church, has been reinterpreted by the courts as a call for the complete exclusion of religious activity from public affairs.

The courts have since decided to remove voluntary student prayer, prohibit school Bible readings, remove copies of the Ten Commandments from view, remove invocations and benedictions from school activities, and remove the word "God" from school correspondence—all under the rubric of "separation of church and state."

At the same time, other philosophies deemed non-religious (and apparently not nearly so dangerous) have crept in unchecked. In 1980, The U.S. Supreme Court ruled that Kentucky schools had to remove copies of the Ten Commandments from the classrooms of that state. One year later, a text entitled "The Way to Happiness," written by the Church of Scientology founder L. Ron Hubbard was adopted for public school use and since its adoption, has been used by more than 8,300 public school teachers and administrators. One Illinois teacher deemed it "the perfect non-religious vehicle for teaching moral values"[7] to her

senior high school students. Scientology church officials estimate that 6.8 million pupils have used the text, which is distributed free and published by the church's own publishing house.

Some parents of New York City school children discovered
their schools distributing a pamphlet that included a sexual "bill
of rights" for students, including such statements as "I have the
right to decide whether to have sex and whom to have it with."
U.S. News and World Report noted that parents were "surprised
to learn that all children had the inalienable right to sleep around
and wondered who, exactly, had be-
stowed it. As it turned out, the new
'rights' sprang full-grown from the
head of someone at the City Department of Health. The pamphlets were
printed with federal money and
made their way into the schools."[8]

Decisions to remove references to
God and Judeo-Christian beliefs from
the public arena have affected not just our schools, but our
children, our families, and the moral climate of our nation. Our
first president, George Washington, warned in his farewell address that education stripped of religious principles could not
support a strong public morality: "And let us with caution
indulge the supposition that morality may be maintained without religion. Whatever may be conceded to the influence of
refined education on minds . . . reason and experience both
forbid us to expect that national morality can prevail in exclusion
of religious principle."[9]

Worldly education says credentials make someone a better
person. They will not. Worldly education says recognition or
applause will benefit a person in the long run. It will not. Worldly
education says power means something. It does not. If you do
not agree, take this little test suggested by one author: Name five
Nobel prize winners. That's right, Nobel prize winners. Just jot
their names down as they come to you. Now name five Pulitzer
prize winners. Then list the last five movies that won the "Best
Picture" designation by the Academy of Motion Picture Arts and
Sciences. Doing any better? How about the five wealthiest men
in the world? Do you know their names?

> *Worldly education
> says credentials
> make someone a
> better person.
> They will not.*

Now take another test: Name five people who really stood by you when you needed help. Name five teachers who influenced your life. Name five friends who believe in you and would shed real tears if something tragic happened in your life. How are you doing on this quiz? Better, I imagine. I did, too. That's because what counts in this world is not credentials—educational or otherwise—but concern. Values clarification and outcome-based education are poor tools for shaping lives. People—good, kind, caring, moral, upstanding individuals—make indelible marks on our lives and forge our character in the process. "Iron sharpens iron," Solomon observed, "so one man sharpens another" (Prov. 27:17). This one-on-one sharpening is frequently absent in education today, but it happens occasionally, as the following story so beautifully illlustrates.

> *People—good, kind, caring, moral, upstanding individuals— make indelible marks on our lives and forge our character in the process.*

Saved by Love

Jean Thompson was a no-nonsense elementary school teacher who gathered her students around her the first day of school for "the talk." "Boys and girls, " she began, "I love each one of you alike. You are all precious to me, and I will have no favorites in this class." That sounded good, but it was not quite the truth. Teachers are human, and they do have students they naturally like more than others. There was one student in Jean Thompson's new class that she found difficult to like at all. His name was Teddy Stoddard. Teddy never seemed to bathe. His clothes were unkempt and smelled vaguely musty all the time. When she asked him a question, Teddy would answer in monosyllables or sit with a glassy stare and not respond at all. He was not a good student. Jean admitted she took special satisfaction in marking x's on Teddy's papers with an unusual flair of her red pen. It did not hurt her in the least to place a large "F" on the top of Teddy's assignments; she did not like him.

If Jean had reviewed Teddy Stoddard's permanent record, she might have understood him better. The notes went something like this: First grade: *Teddy shows promise, but has difficulty concentrating. His home life is unstable.* Second grade: *Teddy is a good boy, but he is so serious. He has trouble getting along with the other students.* Then a small note, scribbled in the margin that year: "*Teddy's mother terminally ill.*" Third grade: *Teddy is depressed. He's falling behind the rest of the students. His mother died this year.* Fourth grade: *Teddy is hopelessly behind. He is a deeply disturbed young man who may need psychiatric help. I don't know what to do with him.*

The records were there, but Jean Thompson did not read them—and she did not understand Teddy. December came, and on the last day before the Christmas holidays, the children brought gifts to exchange with one another and gifts for their teacher. All of them were brightly wrapped except one. It was covered in brown paper and scotch tape, and it was marked "from Teddy for Mrs. Thompson." She was surprised that Teddy brought a gift at all. When she opened it, however, the class began to laugh. It contained a rhinestone bracelet with several stones missing and a half-used bottle of perfume. But something in Jean told her to make a fuss, and she put the bracelet on, holding up her wrist for all to see, as she dabbed it with perfume. "Isn't it beautiful," she asked, and the children nodded in agreement.

That afternoon, when the children scrambled out of the room at the final bell, Teddy approached Mrs. Thompson's desk. He had never come forward to speak to her before. "Mrs. Thompson," he said, "you smell like my mother used to smell— and her bracelet looks good on you, too. Thank you for liking my presents."

When he walked out, Jean Thompson sank to her knees and prayed, "God, I sought to be a teacher of facts and not a lover of children. Forgive me for misunderstanding Teddy." And the next morning she arrived in class a changed teacher. She began to take an avid interest in every child in her class and especially in Teddy. She tutored him so that he was able to catch up to the other students. She looked for things that she might praise him for, no matter how small they might seem. Teddy had never encountered that kind of love before, and he blossomed in the light of her encouragement. It was a good year for Teddy.

The next year brought another class of children to Mrs. Thompson's class, and Teddy moved on. Many years went by before she received this note: "Dear Mrs. Thompson: I graduated from high school today, second in my class. I thought you might want to know. Love, Teddy Stoddard." Four more years passed, and she received another note: "Dear Mrs. Thompson: I graduated valedictorian. The university was tough, with working and studying and all—but I liked it. Love, Teddy Stoddard." A few more years went by, and Mrs. Thompson thought of Teddy now and then and wondered how he was getting along. She was thrilled when she received this brief letter from her former pupil: "Dear Mrs. Thompson: You can now call me Theodore J. Stoddard, M.D. Would you ever have believed it? By the way, I'm getting married on July 26th, and I would love for you to come and sit where my mother would have sat. You're all the family I have. My dad died this year. Hope to see you soon. Love, Teddy."

Jean Thompson went to Teddy's wedding, and she sat in the place of honor that would have been his mother's. She sat there because she deserved that distinction. She had recognized promise in this motherless child and poured her heart into his education for those few months many years before. Her interest gave him confidence. Her tutoring grounded him in the basics. Her kindness became an island of security for him in a very shaky world. He succeeded not because the system saved him; it did not. Teddy needed more than the system could deliver. He needed uncompromising, unapologetic love. He needed a role model after which he could pattern his life.

> *No amount of education will make something out of nothing. Only love can do that.*

Will education help us find meaning in life? No, it cannot. The system is inherently flawed, when, as William Bennett said, "There are greater, more certain, and more immediate penalties in this country for serving up a single rotten hamburger than for

furnishing a thousand school children with a rotten education."[10] No amount of learning, Solomon said, will make the
crooked straight. No amount of education will make something
out of nothing. Only love can do that. And only love answers the
big questions.

What is life all about? It is about this: God loved man so much
that He sent His only Son from above the sun to live and die
under the sun for all humanity. That lesson can stand our full
weight. That truth can stand our closest scrutiny. That story
never gets old, no matter how many times it is told, whether you
are a struggling student, or a Ph.D., like Solomon. Without love,
worldly learning is empty. Without God, human knowledge is
meaningless. True wisdom begins when we acknowledge our
Maker and believe in Him. "The fear of the LORD is the beginning
of wisdom, and the knowledge of the Holy One is understanding" (Prov. 9:10). Anything less is simply "busy work" in
this classroom we call life.

(Eccles. 1:12–18)

An Above-the-Sun Postscript

The fear of the LORD is the beginning of
wisdom,
And the knowledge of the Holy One is
understanding.
—Proverbs 9:10

Solomon engaged in the most fervent quest for wisdom in world history and he still came up empty. What are we to learn from Solomon's quest and conclusions? What practical insights do we get from him so that we can answer the big questions? Three steps will give you far more joy than Solomon discovered.

Admit the Inadequacy of Worldly Wisdom

Just admit it. Humbly acknowledge to yourself and to God that acquiring knowledge "ain't gonna do the trick." What's the worst case scenario if you pursue knowledge as the "end all, be all" of human existence? The worst case scenario is knowing more will increase your pain. You will discover pain you never knew existed. You will learn about more philosophies and world views and cultures, and realize that none of them adequately explain why you are here and where you are going.

What's the best case scenario? Knowing more simply won't satisfy. Take one lonely person, add the best education the world can offer and what do you get? A well-educated lonely person. Possessing worldly knowledge and degrees never soothes the gnawing pain and loneliness of the heart. Advanced degrees, thousands of books read, and clever up-to-date things to say at parties only ease the gnawing for a brief time.

Seek God

If you are a skeptic, wondering whether Christianity is true, examine the evidence. Does God exist? Is the Bible the Word of God? Is Jesus the Son of God? Can you have a dynamic relationship with Him? What do you need to do to have that relationship? Look at history, science, archeology. Use reason and seek the evidence, weigh it honestly, and live by the truths you discover. (See the appendix "An Appeal to the Open-Minded Skeptic" at the end of this book.)

If you are a believer, Jeremiah 29:13–14 was written for you. God says, "Seek Me and find Me when you seek Me with all of your heart." Spend time with God. Read His word. Pray. God says you will find Him, the Creator and Sustainer. He wants to have a great relationship with you. All you have to do is seek and He promises to be found.

Fear God

In other words, obey Him in all that you do. The compartmentalization of life is a modern malady. When you think, speak, or act, do so truthfully and clearly, understanding that all of life is an act of worship.

6

A Materialist's Solution: Acquire More

> The most terrible thing about materialism,
> even more terrible than its proneness to
> violence, is its boredom.
> —Malcolm Muggeridge

THE PLACE WAS CHICAGO, ILLINOIS; the year was 1923. Nine of the world's wealthiest and most successful men gathered for a meeting at the city's Edgewater Beach Hotel. Almost anyone in that day would have exchanged places with any of these well-known executives. They were powerful and rich. The world was their oyster. But only twenty-five years later, their days at Edgewater were a dim memory and all but two were dead. None had lived the easy life their tremendous resources seemed to promise.

Charles Schwab, the president of the nation's largest independent steel company, lived on borrowed money the last five years of his life and died bankrupt. Samuel Insul, the president of a giant utility company, died a penniless fugitive from justice in a foreign country. Gas company executive Howard Hopson suffered from insanity. Wheat speculator Arthur Cotton died destitute. Richard Whitney, president of the New York Stock Exchange, was released from Sing Sing prison. Albert Fall, a member of the president's cabinet, was pardoned from prison so that he could die at home. Wall Street's greatest bear, Jesse Livermore, committed suicide as did Ivan Krueger, the head of a great monopoly. Bank president Leon Fraser also took his own life.

The most dangerous love affair any man or woman will ever experience in this life is a love affair with money. Money is a deceitful object of desire, because it can never deliver what it promises. Solomon, probably the richest man in the world, then or now, concluded that money was a fickle lover, and its accumulation not a worthy life-goal. "He who loves money," he wrote, "will not be satisfied with money, nor he who loves abundance with its income. This too is vanity" (Eccles. 5:10). Money is a means of exchange, but it is so much more than that. Money is, and always has been, equated with power. That is why it is frequently pursued with such passion.

> *The most dangerous love affair in this life is a love affair with money.*

It is no sin to be rich. But money is not neutral and the individual who thinks so is only being foolish. Jesus once used the Aramaic term "mammon" to refer to wealth, and in doing so, He assigned it a personal and spiritual aspect. Saying, "You cannot serve God and mammon," He personified mammon as a rival god—and a force that sought to dominate man. Mammon—wealth or riches—vies with God for man's attention, and its pull can be incredibly strong. G. K. Chesterton once wryly observed that to be clever enough to *get* a great deal of money, one must be stupid enough to *want* it—but the history books are full of such "clever and stupid" men, and Solomon heads the list.

How could King Solomon know for certain that money did not satisfy? Because he had plenty—and he was miserable. His reputation as a wealthy ruler extended far and wide; in fact, one of his "press releases" must have intrigued the Queen of Sheba herself, for she traveled from Ethiopia to Israel to meet him. I imagine she was fairly sure the man would be no match for his press clippings, but her expectations were far surpassed by what she saw:

> When the Queen of Sheba perceived all the wisdom of Solomon, the house that he built, the food of his table, the seating of his servants, the attendance of his waiters and their attire, his cupbearers, and the stairway by which he went up to the house of the LORD, there was no more spirit in her. [We would say he "blew her away."] Then she said to the king, "It was a true report which I heard in my own land, about your words and your wisdom. Nevertheless, I did not believe the reports until I came and my eyes have seen it. And behold, the half was not told me. You exceed in wisdom and prosperity the report which I heard. How blessed are your men! How blessed are these your servants who stand before you continually and hear your wisdom. Blessed be the LORD your God who delighted in you to set you on the throne of Israel because the LORD loved Israel forever. Therefore, He made you king to do justice and righteousness." (1 Kings 10:4–9)

There is more. In response to what she saw, she gave Solomon a gift of 120 talents of gold—roughly $3.5 million—and a generous cache of spices and precious stones. She responded to his wealth and power in the only way she knew how: by giving him even more. (Who says the rich do not get richer?) Solomon's annual income in gold alone was the equivalent of $25 million, yet the queen said the half of his riches had not been told! In other words, there was more to this man's fortune than met the eye, and Solomon himself told "the rest of the story."

Power Corrupts

First, he observed that money is power and power corrupts. And as Lord Acton accurately concluded, "absolute power corrupts absolutely." Look at Solomon's words: "If you see oppression of the poor and denial of justice and righteousness in the province, do not be shocked at the sight, for one official watches over another official, and there are higher officials over them" (Eccles. 5:8). What a contemporary picture of bureaucratic government! It is the picture of a monarch appointing one official over another, until all accountability is lost. The president says the problem is with Congress; the Senate says it is the House; the House says it is the Senate or the special interest lobbies or the cabinet. And the finger pointing continues, but nothing changes.

When a drunk driver who is worth millions of dollars injures someone in an automobile accident, does he get the same treatment as the man whose net worth is zero? Usually not. Because whom we know and what we have can give us an advantage in due process in our corruptible society. It was as true in Solomon's day as it is today.

> *Power corrupts and absolute power corrupts absolutely.*

Power corrupts and absolute power corrupts absolutely. Solomon was the monarch of Israel, and there was no higher court in the land than his royal chamber. The buck, so to speak, stopped there. The men and women of his nation could only hope the power of the office had not corrupted their sovereign as well.

Make no mistake. Power corrupts. It was said of Charles Colson, that he was so loyal to former President Richard Nixon that he would have run over his own grandmother to achieve Nixon's re-election. Colson and his associates were willing to do whatever it took to keep their man in power. C. S. Lewis wrote that the "magician's bargain" lures us to give up our souls to get power in return. But when we do give up our souls, the power we get does not belong to us. Instead, we belong to it, as "slaves and puppets of that to which we have given our souls." The nature of "mammon"—of worldly wealth and power—will never change. That is why it is critical that we elect and promote people of true character to positions of leadership.

Make Room for the Wanna-Be's

He who loves money will not be satisfied with it or its income because, "When good things increase, those who consume them increase" (v. 11). In other words, if you have a love affair with money, it will become increasingly difficult to know who your true friends are. Consider, for example, the entourage that typically follows a world-class athlete. There is the manager, the agent, the publicist, the attorney, and the bodyguard(s). Are they friends or are they employees? When Joe Louis was the heavy-weight boxing champion of the world, he helped many who were less fortunate than he. There were literally hundreds of folks he "looked after" who loved him—idolized him. But when Louis lost his heavyweight title, his wealth, and his health, he found himself a lonely man. "Where are my friends?" he must have wondered. Perhaps a better question would have been, "Who are my friends?" The powerful man who retains his power may never know. Christina Onassis, daughter of Greek shipping tycoon Aristotle Onassis, was said to have paid companions thousands of dollars each month just to spend time with her. Although she was unbelievably wealthy, she never found happiness and spent millions of dollars trying to be accepted and loved. Who were her true friends? Sadly, she never knew. Those with wealth and fame can never be entirely sure who is a "wanna-be" and who is the real thing.

A Good Night's Sleep

Those who aspire to riches can expect to forfeit a portion of their peace of mind, as well. "The sleep of a working man is pleasant," noted Solomon, "whether he eats little or much, but the full stomach of the rich man does not allow him to sleep" (v. 12). My dad was a working man. He worked for twenty-five years for the Mississippi Light Company, and his days usually began at 3:30 or 4:00 A.M. During World War II, he held two full-time jobs and routinely put in ten to twelve hours a day, six days a week—and they were hard days. He climbed poles; he wired attics; he lifted and pushed and pulled until his muscles ached.

When Dad returned home in the evenings, however, he still had enough energy to play with me. We shot basketball, tossed the football, wrestled, and ran. Every evening, we sat down to dinner together—my brother, my mother, my dad and I. There were always plenty of vegetables from the garden: peas, toma-toes, turnip greens, okra and beans—and lots of homemade cornbread, pies and cakes. Dad would eat a hearty meal, drink four or five cups of strong black coffee, get up from the table, yawn about three times . . . and fall sound asleep. Just like that!

Working people like my dad seldom suffer from insomnia. They sleep soundly at night. Rich men—kings and princes—wander sleepless through the dark like Shakespeare's King Henry V on the eve of the battle of Agincourt, full of wonder (and perhaps a touch envious) of the peaceful slumber of so many "common men." Legend has it that the Russian novelist Leo Tolstoy would feed any man who came begging to his doorway, so long as he had calloused hands. Most of us today would go hungry at Tolstoy's castle. We work, yes, but our hands are smooth, and our sleep is sometimes fitful. "Where did the market close today?" we wonder, or "What new product is my competitor developing?" "Are my investments performing well?" "Have I covered every angle in this merger?"

With worldly success comes worldly responsibility, and Solomon wanted his listeners to know that riches have a price. He is not under pressure from a senate sub-committee to reveal his diaries—he's telling it all because he *wants* to reveal the half that has not yet been told about wealth or materialism in a life lived strictly under the sun.

"It Was Nothing but Agony"

Joey Coyle could echo Solomon's revelations about the dark side of wealth. Just weeks before he was to be immortalized in a Hollywood movie, this forty-year-old electrician hanged himself with an electrical cord in his hometown of Philadelphia. *Money for Nothing* was the ironic title of the film that told the story of his recovery of $1.2 million that spilled from the back of an armored truck and his subsequent spending spree. Coyle became something of a folk hero to those who dreamed of finding millions of dollars and getting away with it. Director Ramon Menendez said he wanted the movie to show "what it means for a kid like that to find money. He thinks he has choices, but the money makes him paranoid."[1]

With worldly success comes worldly responsibility.

Coyle and two friends were driving behind an armored truck on February 26, 1981, when its back doors swung open and sacks of money fell out. Coyle retrieved the unmarked bills and started spending them freely, handing out $100 bills all over his neighborhood. The ensuing FBI investigation of the missing money caused Coyle to panic, and authorities picked him up a few days later at JFK International trying to board a flight to Mexico. His boots were stuffed with $105,000 cash. A jury found him innocent of theft by reason of temporary insanity in February of 1992, although he was later convicted of drug possession and of delivering a controlled substance.

> *Solomon revealed that hoarding money will break a man's heart.*

What was it like for the then-unemployed longshoreman to be unbelievably rich for a few days? "I wouldn't put nobody in my situation," Coyle said. "Everybody's thinking: 'That must have been great.' Little do they know it was nothing but agony and despair. I musta [sic] aged in those six days twenty years. You have no idea what money does to you—especially that kind of money."[2]

A Heart Breaker

Finally, Solomon revealed that hoarding money will break a man's heart: "There is a grievous evil which I have seen under the sun: riches being hoarded by their owner to his hurt" (v. 13). "It's about money," said Fast Eddie, the pool-playing hustler played by actor Paul Newman in *The Color of Money.* "The best is the guy with the most." In Solomon's day, and in ours, plenty of people concur—and spend their lives grasping and grabbing for more and more. The stakes are incredibly high. Steve Ross, CEO of Time-Warner (and reportedly the highest paid executive in the United States) earned $78 million in 1990. That same year, six hundred other Time-Warner employees were laid off. The average annual compensation of CEOs rose to $1.9 million in 1990, even though corporate profits were down 7 percent.[3]

Jimmy Johnson, former head coach of the Super Bowl champion Dallas Cowboys, earned over $1 million a year for his efforts and was known for his habit of carrying (and handing out) $100 bills like they were "ones." Johnson achieved recognition for his accomplishments, but his focus on money—and winning—cost him something. When he took over the Cowboys in 1989, Johnson divorced his wife of twenty-six years, explaining that he needed to focus completely on his job. His $50,000 speaking fee dissuades any who would desire his presence at a social function, and his drive to be the best almost completely alienated him from other meaningful relationships. "I don't want to make him sound shallow," said son Brent, "but Dad has his work and then his private life. He doesn't have a whole lot of interests. He's got football, my brother Chad and me, and his girlfriend, Rhonda. He's got a few friends—very few—and he's got his fish. I like the fish, but not as much as he does. I guess, when you think about it, the fish are easy. They're not demanding—not like a dog, say, that might need his time or that might want to be petted every now and then."[4] Today, Johnson does not have the Cowboys, either.

One of the world's wealthiest men, Ted Turner, has amassed a personal fortune estimated to exceed $3 billion. In 1980, Turner confided to his business advisor that he had four great ambitions for his life: to turn station WTCG into a national network, to go into the movie business, to be the country's wealthiest man, and to be president of the United States.

Eighteen-year-old Turner enrolled in Brown University in the 1950s and majored in the classics, to his businessman father's disgust. While he did well academically, he was eventually expelled and went to work for his father's business, Turner Advertising in Charleston, South Carolina. He married for the first time in 1960 and divorced his wife while she was pregnant with their first child. Two years later he married again. By this time, his parents had separated and, in 1963, his father (a millionare himself by age fifty) committed suicide and left the family business to his son.

Strategically building his empire one block at a time, Turner never looked back—or so it seemed. But in 1982, in front of thousands of Georgetown University students, the man who appeared bullet-proof exposed a deep, deep heartbreak: "In the middle of a rip-roaring speech about entrepreneurship, Ted pulled out a well-worn copy of Success magazine, the journal his father used to read to him in the car on those long trips to inspect their billboards. His own face was on the cover. His booming voice trickled to a whisper, and he stared up into the rafters: 'Is this enough?' he asked in a hoarse voice. 'Is this enough for you, Dad?'"[5]

If you have a love affair with money you will never discover true riches because you will never have them. If you have a love affair with money, you will not enjoy your meals as much or sleep as well as the man who does not share your mistress of mammon. If you have a love affair with money and horde it, you will do so at your own peril. And finally, as Turner's father proved, if you have a love affair with money you will not have anything *but* money to leave your family—and you can be sure of one thing: it is as likely to hurt them as it is to help.

> *There is no inherent virtue in being poor, and there is no inherent sin in being rich.*

Wealth does not last. That's right. It doesn't last. "As he had come naked from his mother's womb," said Solomon, "so he will return as he came. He will take nothing from the fruit of his labor that he can carry in his hand. And this also is a grievous evil—exactly as a man is born, thus will he die. So, what is the advantage to him who toils for the wind?" (vv. 15–16). Remember comedian Jack Benny? Benny was known as a stingy tightwad who hoarded his money. Folks used to say, "If Jack can't take it with him, Jack won't go." But Jack is gone. And his money is still here.

Solomon does not gloss over anything in his report on materialism. Does he have anything positive to say, you might ask? He does. "Here is what I have seen to be good and fitting: to eat, to drink and enjoy oneself in all one's labor in which he toils under the sun during the few years of his life which God has given him; for this is his reward. Furthermore, as for every man to whom God has given riches and wealth, He has also empowered him to eat from them and to receive his reward and rejoice in his labor; this is the gift of God" (vv. 18–19).

There is no inherent virtue in being poor, and there is no inherent sin in being rich. The secret, Solomon seems to say, is in realizing that however God has blessed us, we cannot carry any of it with us. It must be enjoyed here and not held too tightly. When we do that, we will not even worry about growing old; we are just filled with gladness and occupied with whatever our hands find to do: "For he will not often consider the years of his life, because God keeps him occupied with the gladness of his heart" (v. 20).

The cynic might wonder how it is possible to focus more on living than on money when "big money" is at stake. A news story involving a well-known athlete proves that it is possible. Ryne Sandberg, ten-time All-Star second baseman for the Chicago Cubs, stunned the baseball world by announcing his retirement on June 13, 1994. "Millions of dollars can't buy job satisfaction for Cubs' favorite son,"[6] the headlines read, as Sandberg walked away from a minimum of $16.1 million remaining on his contract. "Pride and performance come first over salary and getting paid," said the thirty-four-year old. "I am not the kind of person who would have the Cubs pay my salary when I am unhappy with my performance."[7]

Those who know him say Sandberg's decision is consistent with his character. "This is a good example that shows money can't make you happy," said Baltimore Orioles manager Johnny Oates, a Cubs coach from 1984–87. "It takes a strong man to do what he has done." White Sox shortstop Ozzie Guillen agreed. "I know Ryne has to be 100 percent sure of what he wants. What's amazing about it is he walked away from the money. I tip my hat to the man."

Ryne Sandberg loved the game of baseball more than the money, but he loved life most of all. His announcement made at a hastily-called press conference was emotional, but upbeat: "This is a special day for me; it's as special as Opening Day in 1982."[8] Sandberg expressed his desire to spend more time with his wife Cindy, and his children, Lindsey and Justin. Noting Michael Jordan's foray into baseball following his retirement from pro basketball, Sandberg laughingly said he harbored no other sports aspirations, ruling out basketball, football, and hockey. Baseball was a living, but it wasn't a life. The money was good, but it wasn't all that mattered. Ryne Sandberg did not allow himself to be defined by what he did.

Chairmen of the Bored

Sandberg quit while he still loved the game. But if the money is good, most players are willing to hang in and "take the check" even when they're bored with the whole routine. Why? Solomon observed three reasons: competitiveness, laziness, and workaholism. Solomon described the competitive man this way: "And I have seen that every labor and every skill which is done is the result of rivalry between a man and his neighbor. This too is vanity and striving after wind" (Eccles. 4:4). The competitive man is out to win. He wants to outdistance the field, and make a lot of money in the process. Often he does.

The Competitive Person

Houston, Texas, restauranteur Ghulam Bombaywala came to the United States as an immigrant. He applied for a job as a dishwasher at a well-known eating establishment, where he was told his English was not good enough for him to qualify. "Give me a chance," he pleaded with the owner. "I want to work my way through school." But the owner refused. When he was turned down, his competitive spirit kicked in. "One day," he told the owner, "I'm going to buy you out and own this restaurant you think I'm not good enough to work in." The restaurant owner smiled condescendingly, and the immigrant went up the street and got another dishwashing job.

Six years went by before Bombaywala returned to the first restaurant, and offered the same owner a price for his business. A deal was struck, and he owns the restaurant to this day. As they closed the transaction, the now-successful immigrant looked at the man who had refused him a job years before and said, "You don't remember me, do you? I'm the guy you said wasn't good enough to be your dishwasher. I want you to know I said I'd buy you out one day, and now I have."

The Lazy Person

That same competitive spirit motivates a lot of folks today. They want to be the one with the most toys, because "the one with the most toys, wins." But there is also a man who finds no

There is dignity in work—even menial work—but the lazy man will never know.

joy at all in work, and that is the lazy man: "The fool folds his hands and consumes his own flesh" (v. 5). It sounds suspiciously like the welfare state, does it not? I believe one of the saddest things taking place in our country today is the enabling of well-bodied persons to "fold their hands" and do nothing with federal assistance. As long as there is an unmanned mop or broom, an unattended counter, or an unfilled position, we are doing those on welfare a grave disservice by paying them. When Solomon says the man with folded hands "consumes his own flesh," he means that he destroys his own dignity.

There is dignity in work—even menial work—but the lazy man will never know. Inactivity is by no means limited to the welfare system, either. It is entirely possible to be lazy and gainfully employed. This man or woman warms a seat and collects a paycheck, but does little else. Nothing about his work inspires him or fires his imagination. Nothing short of dynamite will stir him from his lethargy. He's simply there doing time, hands folded, and watching the clock. His job doesn't feed his self-esteem, it feeds on it—and he gets no sense of satisfaction in having done something well. He's simply and literally killing time.

The Workaholic

Then there is the workaholic, to whom work *is* life. "There was a certain man without a dependent, having neither a son nor a brother, yet there was no end to all his labor. Indeed, his eyes were not satisfied with riches and he never asked, 'And for whom am I laboring and depriving myself of pleasure?' This too is vanity and it is a grievous task" (v. 8). The workaholic is at the job morning, noon, and night. While the lazy man derives no satisfaction or esteem from work, the workaholic gets *all* of his enjoyment from work. Why is he working? He does not know; he just is. Who is he working for? He does not know; he just is. What is he working for? Because he does not know anything else to do.

Within each man—the competitive man, the lazy man, and the workaholic—there is a built-in boredom that remains unchallenged, either by activity or the lack of it. None of them are satisfied. A reporter at Michael Jordan's retirement press conference raised his hand and almost apologetically asked what was probably the most profound question voiced that day. "Are you going to get a job?" he queried. Jordan, and the others in the room, laughed. The superstar said, no, he was not planning to, since he had more money than he could spend in ten lifetimes. He had every advantage the material world could give, but maybe, just maybe, the reporter knew that there is something in work that goes beyond money. Maybe he sensed that Jordan was bored and still searching for something meaningful in his life. Maybe the man who seemed to have everything sensed that something was still missing.

The great tragedy of materialism is that money can buy what *seems* to be happiness and what *seems* to be peace. To those who search for meaning in this realm, I would say, "Don't let success blind you." What money buys is pseudo-happiness, and pseudo-peace, but it is not the real thing. Ask a super-salesman who just closed the biggest deal of his life how long the thrill lasted. Ask a lottery winner how soon the "high" wore off. The pay-off is never what we think it will be. Real satisfaction is found more in the living, the doing, than in the amassing of wealth or the building of empires. "Why should we be in such desperate haste to succeed, and in such desperate enterprises?" asked Henry David Thoreau. "If a man does not keep pace with his companions, perhaps it is because he hears a different drummer. Let him step to the music he hears, however distant or far away."

> *What money buys is pseudo-happiness, and pseudo-peace, but it is not the real thing.*

A psychologist spent four and a half years surveying over four thousand executives who would be termed very successful by the world's standards. Six out of ten said their lives were empty and had no personal meaning. Six out of ten! To the super-achievers, I would say, "Invest in what lasts." Souls last. God's kingdom lasts. Nothing else will. Investing time, talent, and resources in these will reap benefits not only now, but in eternity.

Best-selling business author Tom Peters has said that being a "real success" in the business world is costly. According to Peters, a star in that arena will miss a lot of little league games and birthday parties. He or she will go on vacations with a portable phone, a modem, and a fax. Quiet nights with family or friends will be distant memories. In all probability, the business superstar will go through a marriage or two on the way to the top because few spouses will be able to sympathize with or endure the kinds of sacrifices required to succeed. When Peters was asked if a man or woman could somehow do it all, he answered with one word: No.

Everything Is a Gift

To the Michael Jordans, the Jimmy Johnsons and the Ted Turners of our culture, a warning is in order: Do not think you are responsible for all you have. When we are in trouble, many of us are quick to fall to our knees and say, "Oh, God, help me!" But how slow we are when we are fresh with success to say, "Oh, God, thank you!" The triumphs of life are gifts, not merit badges. Sometimes people get what they deserve for their hard work and effort, but just as often they do not. The Bible says that every good thing in life is a gift from the Father above who is the source of life itself (see James 1:17).

A newspaper reporter went to interview a successful entrepreneur . "How did you do it?" he asked. "How did you make all this money?"

"I'm glad you asked," he replied. "Actually, it's a rather wonderful story. You see, when my wife and I married, we started out with a roof over our heads, some food in our pantry, and five cents between us. I took that nickel, went down to the grocery store, bought an apple, and shined it up. Then I sold it for ten cents."

"What did you do then?" the reporter asked.

"Well," he said, "then I bought two more apples, shined them up, and sold them for twenty cents." The reporter was beginning to catch on and thought this would be a great human interest story.

"Then what? Then what?" he asked excitedly.

"Then my father-in-law died and left us $20 million," the businessman said. He had fooled himself into thinking he had done something, forgetting that he had received something. Don't forget all that you have been given, and remember to spend time with the Giver.

Existentialist philosopher Camus wrote a story of a diamond merchant who lived in a small village and married a beautiful girl. He often went on trips to buy and sell stones, but his wife stayed home, never leaving the village. Finally, he convinced her to accompany him on a trip into the city. He had several appointments one afternoon, but he gave his wife plenty of spending money and told her to enjoy herself while he was away. After her husband left, the wife remembered a lustful dream she had had since she was a young girl. Now she had the opportunity to fulfill her sensual dream, but she feared what her husband would do if he discovered her unfaithfulness. So instead of acting on her impulse, she wandered the streets in ambivalence until he returned. They had a lovely dinner together. They walked around a bit. Then they went up to their room and got into bed. The husband fell asleep quickly, but his wife could not. She tossed and turned, remembering her dream. Finally, Camus said, she rose from bed, dressed, walked out into the night, and indulged her fantasy. Early the next morning she returned quietly, showered, undressed, and got back into bed with her unknowing husband. Then she began to sob, crying so loudly that she woke her mate. "What is the matter?" he asked. "Nothing," she replied. And that was the end of the story.

Don't forget all that you have been given, and remember to spend time with the Giver.

That is the way under-the-sun stories told by existentialists end. But there is an above-the-sun footnote to be added: The loneliest day in our lives is when we experience our wildest dreams and come away empty. Success cannot fill us. Money cannot satisfy. The wealthy person's chief advantage over those who are not is that he or she has already discovered that money does not bring happiness. True success is being right in the middle of God's plan—a place where your great love and the world's deep hunger meet.

(Eccles. 5:8–20)

An-Above-the-Sun Postscript

> Two things I asked of Thee,
> Do not refuse me before I die:
> Keep deception and lies far from me,
> Give me neither poverty nor riches;
> Feed me with the food that is my portion,
> Lest I be full and deny Thee and say, "Who is
> the LORD?"
> Or lest I be in want and steal,
> And profane the name of my God."
> —Proverbs 30:7–9

If the acquisition of things doesn't satisfy our deep longings, but rather feeds the hunger, what are we to do? The burning question is, how can we be in the world without letting the world get into us? Richard Foster in his book, *Celebration of Discipline*, details two parts of the life of simplicity.

Cultivate an Inward Simplicity

Otherwise, we will only pump up a phony simplicity for others to see. If simplicity reigns in our hearts, it will flow naturally into simple lifestyle. Seek first the Kingdom of God. Don't seek first to give more money to the church or spend less on your own lifestyle, but actively seek first the Kingdom of God.

I can just hear someone saying, "Oh, come on! What's that supposed to mean? That sounds so vague and so irrelevant. Try again."

The truth is, if you don't establish the inward reality of simplicity, you will only play at outward simplicity for a short while. Eventually you will tire of the effort (that you don't really believe in) and return to the rat race. Seeking the Kingdom isn't vague, it's spending time with God. Reading His word. Mulling around in your mind truths learned from reading. Praying those back to God, asking Him to remake you into a Christ-like person.

Practice an Outward Simplicity

First, "buy things for their value rather than their status." Evaluate purchases of cars, clothes, houses, etc. in this light. Foster writes, "Stop trying to impress people with your clothes and impress them with you life."

Second, "develop a habit of giving things away." If you find that you are becoming attached to some possession, consider giving it to someone who needs it.

7

A Religionist's Solution: Do Church

> Although there seemed to be,
> and indeed were, a thousand roads
> by which a man could walk through the world,
> there was not a single one which did not
> lead sooner or later either to the
> Beatific or Miserific Vision.
>
> —C. S. Lewis

I F A MAN ARRIVED FROM another country, presented himself to you, and said, "Show me what America is like," where would you begin your cultural field trip? A shopping mall? The ball park? A busy downtown street corner? I think I might be tempted to start at the nearest cafeteria. You see capitalism at work in the cafeteria. A product—food—is offered for a competitive price. You see all kinds of interesting social interplay: Businessmen and women catch a quick bite between appointments; couples talk quietly (or not at all) through their meals; mothers with small children try to eat with one hand and feed their little ones with the other. Around noon or six o'clock in the evening, the cafeteria is a regular people-watcher's paradise.

But the real key to a cafeteria can be summed up in one word: choice. Most people go to the cafeteria, not because it is the cheapest place to eat or the most exclusive. Not because the food achieves gourmet status, although it is usually consistent or because the presentation is lovely. They go because there they can *choose* a meal suited to their own particular tastes. Meat-and-potato people eat at the cafeteria; so do vegetarians and salad lovers. Someone who is yearning for a big chicken-fried steak can dine happily with a companion who is thinking more along the lines of enchiladas or caesar salad. There are no hard-and-fast rules, either. If you like jello (and your mom will let you) you can have jello in every flavor, and nothing else!

> Americans are big on choice. We like options; we dislike absolutes.

Americans, you see, are big on choice. We like options; we dislike absolutes. We are shoppers, and we shop for everything from meals to meaning. *Time* magazine's cover story in its April 1993 issue, "The Generation Who Forgot God," reported that many of those who "forgot" God in early adulthood are now shopping for Him—or at least for spiritual satisfaction—through new "designer churches" or more traditional forms of worship. Syndicated columnist Cal Thomas observed in his book *The Things That Matter Most* that religion is making something of a comeback as "sixties flower children have found permission to explore their inner selves without having to acknowledge the existence of a personal God who might require something from them and want to do something for them . . . ."[1]

Researcher George Barna concurs with these observations, saying:

> For most Americans, the search for meaning in life continues. Despite our technological sophistication and political savvy, millions of adults are desperately seeking the keys that will unlock the secrets to achieve significance in life and bring them greater fulfillment. As a nation, we are exploring many avenues. Comparatively few have arrived at what is deemed to be a reasonable or satisfying conclusion. [2]

But we are looking—and the spiritual realm is an important arena of our search. Consider that a recent book based on "a self-study program of spiritual psychotherapy" sold over half-a-million copies within a month of its first printing in 1993 and remained on the *New York Times* bestseller list for over nine months. This book by New Age preacher/teacher Marianne Williamson, entitled *A Return to Love*, captured the attention of ordinary folks and well-known celebrities with its grab-bag of pseudo-religious "choices." It used traditional Christian terminology, incorporated tenets of eastern mysticism and pop psychology, and preached a soft, benign gospel of love as the answer to the world's ills.

It was a "cafeteria" book in the truest sense of the word. Few were offended; many were intrigued. Its author, a former bookstore owner and cabaret singer, says she discovered meaning through her study of *A Course in Miracles* and based her book upon its teaching. "The Course . . . claims no monopoly on God. It is a statement of universal spiritual themes. There's only one truth, spoken different ways, and The Course is just one path to it out of many," she stated.[3]

If book sales are any indication, Americans today are ravenously hungry for religious enlightenment.

Williamson's own book, she says, "is written as a guide to the miraculous application of love as a balm on every wound. Whether our psychic pain is in the area of relationships, health, career, or elsewhere, love is a potent force, the cure, the Answer."[4] So much for target marketing. Like your local cafeteria, there is no one this book was not for—and it sold like hotcakes.

If book sales are any indication, Americans today are ravenously hungry for religious enlightenment. *A Return to Love* is only one example. Recently high on nearly every fiction bestseller list was *The Celestine Prophecy*, with author James Redfield's "nine key insights into life itself." While some of Redfield's suppositions are rather bizarre (for example, the idea that as our "spiritual energy" increases we humans can actually become invisible), readers like school psychologist Gael Smith feel the book rings true and "offers hope that life is more than a series of random things that can't be controlled."[5]

Solomon's Spiritual Search

Solomon hoped so, too. Remember his search? He had exhausted every avenue in his pursuit of meaning and purpose in life. He tried pleasure and materialism to satisfy his senses, philosophy and education to satisfy his mind. His motto was "Been there. Done that," and as long as he was young, "Now what?" He experienced all that he could, for as long as he could, paying little attention to God in the process. When he had experienced everything under the sun, nothing satisfied. Humans, he began to realize, are an inseparable union of body, mind, and *spirit*, and although he had enjoyed something of a mental and physical feast, he had experienced a spiritual famine. Like so many today, when his choices did not yield what he was looking for, he turned his attention back to God: "He [God] has made everything appropriate [or beautiful] in its time. He has also set eternity in their hearts, so that man will not find out the work which God has done from the beginning to the end" (Eccles. 3:11).

This world was never designed to fill our deepest hunger.

He found the wide world he had explored to be smaller than the "world without end" in his heart. When we look within we see eternity, because eternity is what God has placed within us. Solomon tried to fill an above-the-sun hunger with under-the-sun living, and it didn't work—not because he didn't try hard enough, but because it was never meant to! This world was never designed to fill our deepest hunger.

There are God-planned answers to every desire in this world, save one. If we are hungry, there is food that will satisfy our hunger. If we are thirsty, there is water to quench our thirst. If we desire human companionship, there are those who will be our friends. If we desire mystery, the earth is ripe with it. If we desire beauty, it is everywhere.

But for the man or woman who recognizes a deep need within to *connect* with the eternal—this world has no answer. Augustine said that there is a God-shaped vacuum in our hearts that cannot be filled by any created thing, but only by the Creator Himself.

We long for the eternal, because God has planted that longing in our hearts, but we live in the temporal. We are a little like the chick in the children's story who becomes separated from the mother hen and asks every animal it subsequently encounters, "Are you my mommy?" We instinctively know that something essential is missing—and that we're not finding it here.

Furthermore, our dilemma is unique in all of creation. I don't believe a fish is dissatisfied swimming around in the water. Fish don't dream of the day they will walk out of the water and onto dry land. They were made for water; they are satisfied with it. The fish doesn't say, "There's got to be something more than this." But God has put eternity inside of us, and we *strongly suspect* there is more to life than we can see.

When Solomon looked within, he saw eternity. When he looked without, he saw the gifts of God: "I know that there is nothing better for them than to rejoice and to do good in all one's lifetime; moreover, that every man who eats and drinks sees good in all his labor—it is the gift of God" (vv. 12–13). It is a gift to celebrate. I have never known anyone who could genuinely and deeply rejoice who did not have a relationship with God. Those who do not know God can certainly have a good time— they can laugh, travel, spend money, give gifts, and enjoy life, but only those who know God in Jesus Christ can truly *rejoice*. To rejoice is a gift from God.

It is also a gift from God "to do good." The ability to positively impact others and our world is a privilege from God. We are not here just to breathe the world's air and eat its food—to take up space. The Bible says that God has "ordained" good works for us beforehand that we might walk in them. That is our privilege, our gift. The fact that we have an appetite is a gift; everyone in this world does not. In the last years of his life, John D. Rockefeller could eat very little. Just one or two bites of food and a sip of water might be all he consumed in a day. I am told he once walked down a New York City street and, seeing a beggar eating a hotdog, said, "I'd give a million dollars to be able to eat that hotdog." He had lost his appetite.

Finally, Solomon observed, it is a gift to be able to work. We spend our early adult years gaining the skills to work, and then occupy our best years preparing for retirement—but it is a gift simply to do the work itself.

Then Solomon looked up. "I know that everything God does will remain forever," he said (v. 14). In other words, "What God has done is permanent, and perfect." What God has done is rightly done. " . . . There is nothing to add to it, and there is nothing to take from it, for God has so worked that men should fear Him" (v. 14b). We are to fear God, he concluded. Quite a switch from today's New Age idea that we *are* God! That does not mean that we are to be cowed in His presence or that we are to run from Him as we would a roaring lion. But after we look within and look without, we must look up— and see our holy God for who He is. Our society has all but lost this sense of awe.

> *God will not be reduced to a manageable size.*

Our "Too Small" Deity

When my granddaughter LeeBeth was six, my wife Jo Beth and I took her to Disney World. We had been warned ahead of time that she would finally become so tired we would have to carry her—but that never happened. (Her grandparents wouldn't have minded being carried at several points, however.) One especially interesting Magic Kingdom exhibit was called, "Honey, I Shrunk the Kids," after the movie by the same name. I am over six feet tall, but in this area, I felt like an ant. The grass was about twenty feet high. Giant sprinklers showered water over us. We felt as if we had been pushed down until we were just a few inches tall. "Honey, I Shrunk the Kids" made me think of how we have "pushed God down" until He seems to be nothing but a board game token of Himself.

Why do we do it? He is infinite, and we are finite; we cannot comprehend His nature or His ways. Since we do not particularly want to fear, reverence, serve, or obey Him, we seek instead to make Him smaller than He is. But God will not be reduced to a manageable size. Writing of the Christ-figure Aslan in his *Chronicles of Narnia*, C. S. Lewis said, "Aslan is not a tame lion." And God is not a tame-able God.

Babylonian literature tells the story of a man who wanted to believe in God but did not. He went to a Jewish teacher, saying, "If you'll show me God, I'll believe. Just show Him to me." The teacher said, "I will show you God—but first, go outside and gaze up at the sun for five minutes." The man went outside, but he could not look at the sun for even a minute. He told the teacher that he failed, that the sun was too bright to gaze upon. The Jewish teacher nodded in agreement, and said, "You could not look upon a minor creation of God for a minute—and yet you want to see Him who put the brilliance in the stars. You cannot. He is too big." He is too big, and the distance between us is too great. For me to try to understand all about God would be about as reasonable as expecting my dog Sonny to understand all about calculus—and Sonny's a smart dog.

What Kind of God Would You Like?

Solomon knew God as well as anyone in his day, but his extended pleasure cruise through hedonism, materialism, philosophy, and education carried him further and further away from God's presence. Once he knew a "nearby God," but he drifted from Him like a swimmer at high tide drifts from fixed landmarks on the beach. No one cataclysmic event took place that severed their relationship; Solomon simply slipped away. Inattention to God's commands was partly to blame, but so were rebelliousness and pride. Solomon wanted a far-away God, and God simply honored his desire.

I came to know God through His Son Jesus Christ as a twelve-year-old boy in Laurel, Mississippi. He was real to me through my growing up years, but when I went away to the University of Alabama as a freshman engineering student, I gradually began to drift away from God. I never intended to. I never made a conscious decision to stop reading my Bible or praying or attending church. But eventually I did.

One weekend I went home for a visit, and I stopped by to see Aunt Gladys and Uncle Howard. They did not have any children, but Aunt Gladys and Uncle Howard had always treated my brother and me as if we were their own. They were always there with a listening ear, a kind word, or a challenge. Theirs was one of the warmest, most loving homes I have ever known. That weekend as usual, there was music in the house, and they were singing a little chorus that went like this: "Get the new look from the Old Book; Get the new look from the Bible. Get the new look from the Old Book; Get the new look from God's Word. The inward look, the outward look, the upward look from the Old, Old, Book; Get the new look from the Old Book; Get the new look from the Bible."

I was not particularly interested in music at that time in my life, let alone music about God or the Bible. But they made me learn that song, and it has remained in my memory for nearly forty years. I understand that there are those who do not believe in God and who dismiss the God of the Bible saying, "Those people wanted a God, so they invented one for themselves." The Bible, they would argue, is simply man's way of working out the kind of God he would like. I don't buy that for a second. If I wanted to work out my own God, it would not be the God of the Bible. Oh no, my God would be a good-time God. I would invent the kind of God who winked at sin, encouraged me to do better, but never held me accountable. My kind of God would say, "Oh, Edwin, you really ought to do better, but I understand—just keep on trying because that's what counts." When I reached the end of my life he would "cover" me if I came up short in the righteousness department, and never say a word about it. My kind of God would extend credit and never expect payment. What kind of God would you like?

Religion, Cafeteria-Style

Today it seems as though we can *have* whatever kind of God we want. All we have to do is invent him. Our society is so poisoned against absolutes of any kind that no one would tell another his god was "false," no matter who or what it was. Russ Chandler, religion writer and award winning journalist for the *Los Angeles Times*, says that where religion is concerned, anything goes today:

> The Institute of Metaphysics in Los Angeles can advertise itself as a New Age Center and at the same time hold a fund-raising jamboree with "the rousing music of oldtime Gospel" . . . the four-times married former Mrs. California Terry Cole-Whitaker, who was ordained by the Los Angeles Church of Religious Science, can bid farewell to her supersize San Diego congregation, dump "the Reverend" from

her title, and proclaim a health and wealth individualism through her Adventures in Enlightenment Foundation—and never miss a beat nor lose her following."[6]

While a 1984 Gallup Poll indicated that an amazing 82 percent of Americans said "growing into a deeper relationship with God" was important to them, and 60 percent said they were more interested in "spiritual things" than they had been five years earlier, 60 percent also rejected the idea that a person should be limited to a single faith.[7] "In my opinion," writes Chandler, "the insidious danger of the New Age—insofar as one can corral this moving, many-sided, cultural transformation—is its view of reality. It admits to no absolutes. This all seems so tolerant. Everyone is so right. It doesn't matter if you're praying to your inner light, to Sophia, to the Trinity, to whomever. If it works for you, it's fine. After all, there are no standards."[8]

"Open minds, like open mouths, were meant to close down on something."

You see, if God is not interested in us, if He is not all-powerful, omniscient, or all-knowing, if God is impotent in our affairs and is only a dottering, senile grandfather on heaven's front porch—then it *doesn't* matter what we believe. But if He is who He says that He is, it matters a great deal. In fact, nothing matters more. Our culture bears a striking resemblance to that of the end of the Roman Empire, when unreason was rampant. Belief in the occult grew then as it has today, and the subjectiveness of a person's own conscience was the prevailing yardstick of truth. Then, like now, people who no longer believed in the good or evil or God's truth could be led to believe in almost anything. In fact, belief in almost anything was a sign of being open-minded, a state modern man regards highly, although G.K. Chesterton said that open minds, like open mouths, were meant to close down on something.

This delight with open-mindedness disappears, however, when absolutes are professed—particularly Biblical absolutes, as Peter Kreeft reveals: "If you confess at a fashionable cocktail party that you personally love to play with porcupines, or plan to sell CIA secrets to the communists, or that you are considering becoming a Palestinian terrorist, you will find a buzzing, fascinated crowd around you, eager to listen. But if you confess that you believe that Jesus is God, that He died to save us from sin, or that there really are a Heaven and a Hell, you will very soon be talking to empty air, with a distinct chill in it."[9]

The King's Confessional

King Solomon searched for a spiritual answer to the meaning of life by doing what millions are doing today: attending church. The church he attended would have been considered a "mainstream" congregation in his time. It was the Jewish temple of Jerusalem—and Solomon not only attended—he built it! In fact, Solomon was known as "Qoheleth," or "the preacher" in the Hebrew language. This king was a preacher/teacher who spoke to assembled crowds but failed to practice what he preached. He supervised the construction of the beautiful temple whose very design trumpeted the glory of God—but he failed to worship that God "in spirit and in truth."

Solomon attended all the services. He participated in all of the feasts. He probably knew all the priests by their first names. He was externally faithful in every way as far as the religious community was concerned. He was an insider. But in his autobiography, he confesses that his private devotion was never equal to his public worship. Today, Solomon would be called a hypocrite, and his religion would be considered a sham. His worship was insincere—just another element of a vain and meaningless existence. His words, however, reveal that he understood what true worship required: "Guard your steps as you go in to the house of God . . . ." (Eccles. 5:1a).

"When you go into the House of God," he said, "go in on tip-toe." Approach God with care, in other words. When Moses saw God's presence in a burning bush, he took off his shoes. He was on holy ground, and he knew it. So many of us "do church" and worship in a casual, unprepared manner. We don't anticipate God's presence or His voice. We're apathetic, unconcerned. My Mississippi kinfolks used to say, "You don't go to church flat-footed." But many of us frequently do.

Then Solomon says, "Draw near to listen," and avoid offering what he calls "the sacrifice of fools." What is the sacrifice of fools? It is the kind of worship that never shows itself in our daily lives. A fool gives God the sacrifice of singing and praying and giving and sharing, and then goes out and lives as he pleases. The fool's worship never changes him. When we go through the motions of church and worship and Christianity, and our hearts remain the same, we have offered the sacrifice of fools.

> *A fool gives God the sacrifice of singing and praying and giving and sharing, and then goes out and lives as he pleases.*

Once I spent a wonderful morning of private worship in my study at home. I spent time in prayer and praise, and it was so refreshing. God came down in a wonderful way and gave me fresh new insight in my study time and a renewed energy for the day. I felt "good all under" like the old Hanes underwear ads used to say. After I had showered and dressed, I kissed Jo Beth at the door and said, "Have a great day!" All was still well at that point. Then my wife said, "Would you mind taking out the trash?" Who *does not* mind taking out the trash? Is there anyone on this earth that actually enjoys taking out the trash? So I got mad, and she could tell.

To begin with, the trash was overflowing. And I couldn't find the little twistie thing you tie the bag with. We have an able-bodied son who had walked by the same can four or five times already that morning—and he did not even make up his bed. *Here I am, the spiritual leader of this home, the head of this household, elbow-deep in garbage,* I said to myself. I was mad about it. Then it hit me: How can it be that the man who was so pure and prayed-up and carefree five minutes ago is now "fit to be tied" (no pun intended)? How can this be the same guy? All that praying, all that listening, all that studying and crying and cleansing and confessing—how can it be? Nothing that I got in the quiet of my study had transferred to the chaos of my kitchen—not one thing.

You see, we exist in a transitional period called life. We live on earth, midway between heaven and hell. Hell is ugly and profane and filthy. It is filled with horrors and God is absent. But heaven is the very opposite. Heaven is beautiful and marvelous. It is filled with praise and pleasure and uninterrupted worship. Best of all, God is there. We worship on earth, but we do evil here, too. Midway between a hideous hell and a beautiful heaven, we sometimes fail to translate our worship to our world. Instead we offer the sacrifice of fools.

Did Solomon have any other advice about worship? You bet he did. He warned us against making foolish promises to God. "When you make a vow to God, do not be late in paying it, for He takes no delight in fools. Pay what you vow! It is better that you should not vow than that you should vow and not pay. Do not let your speech cause you to sin and do not say in the presence of the messenger of God that it was a mistake. Why should God be angry on account of your voice and destroy the work of your hands?" (vv. 4–6).

> *A promise made to God becomes a covenant with Him, and God does not take such vows lightly.*

I wonder how many times God has heard prayers like these? "Oh, God, if you'll get me out of this tight place, I'm yours from now on," or "Lord, if you'll just help me do this thing, I'm going to start being a better father or being a better husband or going to church or telling the truth." The trouble with these "emergency" prayers with promises attached is that God takes our promises to Him very seriously. A promise made to God becomes a covenant with Him, and God does not take such vows lightly.

Why did Solomon offer this particular piece of advice? Because he made a lot of promises to God he didn't keep. God forbade his ever-increasing collection of concubines, but he continued to keep them and even increased their number. God forbade Solomon to stockpile materials for war, but he amassed horsemen and chariots by the thousands and stored them in neighboring cities. These acts of disobedience rendered his worship invalid, and he warns others against imitating them. But tacked on to the end of his warnings about worship, he reveals the secret of real worship when he says, "For in many dreams and in many words there is emptiness. Rather, fear God" (v. 7).

Real worship begins with the fear of God—not a frightened fear, but a reverent fear. Anyone who has lost the fear of God has lost the ability to worship, because worship requires awe and wonder for who God is and for what He has done. Worship requires respect for that which cannot be explained. I sometimes envy children their capacity for wonder. My grandson E. J. and I were out for a walk one day when a big, rattle-trap dump truck lumbered up the street. There were shovels in the back and bits of mud flying off the tires, and E. J. was thrilled. "Oh boy, oh boy!" he said, over and over. It was just an old truck, but it inspired wonder in him.

Now LeeBeth, our granddaughter, is not impressed with dump trucks, not in the least. LeeBeth has been around a little longer and seen a little more. Even our trip to Disney World, wonderful as it was, did not leave her speechless—until the lake parade. We came in from a long day at the park and LeeBeth, Jo Beth, and I settled into our room. It was about 9:55 P.M., and I noticed on a card by the phone that at 10:00 P.M., right outside our window, there would be a parade on the lake with lighted boats and fireworks. And it would all begin in just a few minutes.

"LeeBeth," I said, "I am sorry that we had to come in. I wish we were still out there."

"I do too," she said.

"You're not really tired, are you?" I asked her.

"No," she said, "I'm not tired."

"Me neither," I replied. "You know what we need, LeeBeth? We need just one more parade, don't you think?"

"Oh, Goosey," she said, "we need one more parade. We sure do."

"Tell you what," I said. "I think I'm just going to order a special parade for you and me, just outside our window. What do you say?"

"You're teasing!" she said. But those Disney people know how to make an old grandad look good.

"No, I'm not," I said, pulling the drapes open. It was dark. No lights on the water. Yet.

"Let's just watch," I told her. Then I started counting—and before I could say "three," there were lights and rockets and the sounds of a parade. Her face filled with wonder. She was in awe of it all! I felt like a king. (Thank you, Disney.)

LeeBeth at sixteen would not have been filled with awe at the lake parade. She would not have been willing to believe that I had arranged a parade on a moment's notice for the two of us. But at six she was. Some scientists say that one day we will be able to explain everything about the world we live in. If that sad day ever comes, I hope I'm not around to see it—but I'm not convinced that it will come. Because we live in a universe that is filled with awe and wonder, "crammed with heaven," as Elizabeth Browning said, but "only he who sees takes off his shoes" in reverent fear.

If wonder does not move us to gratitude, something is deeply wrong with our hearts. I agree wholeheartedly with the man who said he pitied the atheist because he had no one to thank for the good things he had received. Worship begins with wonder, awe, and mystery; it carries us to gratitude, thanksgiving, and love for God and life. The Westminster Shorter Catechism says that our "chief end" is "to glorify God and enjoy Him forever." That is the finest definition of worship I know.

Three Imperatives for True Worship

"Cafeteria-style" worship has no requirements. "Do church" any way you choose. Believe what you like. Worship whatever god appeals to you. Disregard any requirements that are made of you and just select the aspects of religion that suit your own special circumstances and your sense of style. But there are requirements for real worship. The Bible gives three absolutes, three great "musts" for worship.

New Birth

Jesus states the first requirement for true worship in John 3:7, when He tells His friend Nicodemus, "You must be born again." The first necessity of worship is new birth. Until we are "born again," we are unequipped to approach a holy God in genuine worship. This notion makes many uncomfortable. They would prefer a come-as-you-are God, who would allow anyone fellowship with Him, with no questions asked. But God is holy and righteous, and we need a complete change of heart to stand in His presence. This new birth is available to anyone who will confess his failures (that's the s-word: sin), turn from them, and accept Jesus Christ's death and resurrection as his only hope for righteousness. The man or woman who does this is new-born: "Therefore if any man is in Christ, he is a new creature; the old things passed away; behold, new things have come" (2 Cor. 5:17). A new, clean heart is required before true worship can take place.

> *God is holy and righteous, and we need a complete change of heart to stand in His presence.*

Jesus Christ

The second requirement for worship is found in John 3:14: "the Son of Man must be lifted up." Jesus Christ is the Son of Man. He was "lifted up" on Calvary's cross, where He died sinless on our behalf. Without His act of atonement, there is no relationship between God and us, and worship is not possible. Jesus Christ is to be at the center of our worship as "the way, the truth and the life." Worship that does not acknowledge Him as Savior and Lord and "lift Him up" is not authentic worship.

Worship becomes real when Jesus Christ is the center of it all. All the way through the Old Testament, patterns and symbols point to Christ as He is revealed in the New Testament. That is why the Old Testament is seen as the New Testament concealed, and the New Testament as the Old Testament revealed. The tabernacle built by Moses in the Sinai wilderness was a little woodshed covered with the hides of animals, but that tabernacle was a picture of how we come to God.

When a person walked into the tabernacle, he saw the brazen altar—a "preview" of the sacrifice of Jesus Christ for our sins. Then he saw the laver—a basin for washing the hands—and it was a foreshadowing of the blood of Jesus that must cleanse us from sin before we can come before God. The table of the show bread was a picture of Jesus Christ, the Bread of Life who nourishes us. And the incense was a reminder of the intercession of Christ, who sits at the right hand of God, pleading on our behalf. Just beyond the veil was the Holy of Holies. When Jesus died on the cross, that veil was ripped from top to bottom—from God to humanity—to give us access to His very throne! There, above the mercy seat, the glory of God dwelt. And in the presence of that shekinah glory, true worship was possible.

Worship in Spirit and Truth

Finally, those who would worship God must worship Him in the way He prescribes: "in spirit and truth." Jesus told the Samaritan woman He encountered at the well, "You worship that which you do not know; we worship that which we know, for salvation is from the Jews. But an hour is coming, and now is, when the true worshipers shall worship the Father in spirit and truth; for such people the Father seeks to be His worshipers" (John 4:22–23). The first "must" of worship is new birth. The second "must" is the cross of Christ. The third "must" is genuine, vibrant worship in spirit and truth. Worship in spirit is an affair of the heart. Worship in truth is a matter of the mind. Our spirit is the part of us that is most like God. When we worship in spirit, our immortal, invisible nature meets the immortal, invisible nature of God.

> *When we worship in spirit, our immortal, invisible nature meets the immortal, invisible nature of God.*

Worship in spirit is an expression of joy, not the fulfillment of a duty. My wife and I recently celebrated our thirty-fifth wedding anniversary. If I gave Jo Beth a dozen red roses for our anniversary, she would hug me and say "Oh, thank you, Edwin! I love you, too. You're so sweet to remember our day this way. This is marvelous!" But if I shrugged, and said something like, "Don't mention it. It's my duty as a husband," her whole countenance would change. (And I would be making a big mistake.) If instead I said, "Joby, it's a joy and my privilege because I love you," that would give her pleasure. Do you see the difference?

Each moment that my spirit meets God's spirit in worship is a moment of joy, not duty.

True worshipers will also worship God "in truth." Many people today have the idea that it's not necessary to worship in truth as long as we worship sincerely. Remember—it is possible to be sincere—and sincerely wrong. But to worship in truth we must follow the One who says He is the Truth, Jesus—the Son of God.

Solomon looked back on his life, on how he had "done church," and he realized his worship was false. It had the *form* of godliness, but none of the *power*. Solomon was the preacher/teacher of the people, but he did not practice what he preached. The moments, the hours, that he spent in the temple were empty hours, but more than that, he understood that every hour of his life could have been an hour of worship—no matter where he was! Solomon was made in God's very image, and so are we. When God looks at us, He longs to see that image—not a clouded mirror that reflects the sacrifice of fools. He wants our devotion and our love, not our excuses or our foolish sacrifices.

The great Russian writer Dostoyevsky said that we need worship more than God does, a fact Solomon discovered late and many others have never known at all: "The one essential condition of human existence is that man should always be able to bow down before something infinitely great. If men are deprived of the infinitely great, they will not go on living and will die of despair. The Infinite and the Eternal are as essential for man as the little planet on which he dwells." Of all the choices available to us, none holds more promise than the choice to worship the Living God, in spirit and in truth. Solomon would say, "Choose well."

(Eccles. 3:11–15; 5:1–7)

An Above-the-Sun Postscript

The name of the LORD is a strong tower;
The righteous runs into it and is safe.
—Proverbs 18:10

If you want to stop playing church, how do you go about it? What steps should you take to authentically worship God?

God says, "without faith it is impossible to please Him," (Heb. 11:6), so one simply cannot worship Him without being a believer, having a personal relationship with Him.

Worship takes two forms, public and private. Ideally, the public worship we give to Christ on Sunday morning represents the culmination of a week of private worship, so let's begin with the private forms and move to the public.

Private Worship

The heart of worship is submission and exaltation.

Be Still

Just be quiet. In prayer give to God all the items of your "stress list": work, household responsibilities, financial burdens, relationship problems. God can handle all these things so much better than we can anyway, so give them all to Him—at least for a time of worship.

Confess Your Sins

Ask the Holy Spirit to bring to mind all the sins you have committed. Then confess them, one by one. When we confess our sins, God is faithful to not only forgive our sins, but to keep on cleansing us of all impurity (1 John 1:9). Spend some time in prayer, allowing the Healer and Forgiver to love, heal, and restore you.

Adore Him

Remember, the heart of worship is our submission and His exaltation. Read passages of Scripture and follow the verses with prayed whispers of agreement. Revelation 4:11 cries, "You are worthy, our Lord and God, to receive glory and honor and power, for You created all things and by Your will they were created and have their being." Tell God why you love Him, His mercy, His holiness, and His might. Tell God that He is the best thing that ever happened to you, and express how much you love and appreciate Him.

Adoring God occurs when you read passages of Scripture to Him, out loud or silently. He is adored when you pray words of praise and thanksgiving. And He is adored when you sing to Him. Buy a hymnal or a songbook and sing in the privacy of your room or your car or your office or some secluded spot. Another great way to worship the Lord by singing is to use a worship tape or CD. There are literally hundreds available so shop around until you find one that you like.

Practice the Presence of God

Worship God as you go. God designed us to worship Him not just for a few moments, but moment by moment as we offer our entire lives to Him (Rom. 12:1). As you work, talk on the phone, drive, eat, play golf, or jog, practice the presence of God. Thank Him for the little blessings along your way, and praise Him for who He is in your life as you live each day.

Public Worship

A week spent worshiping God privately finds delightful fulfillment in the gathering of other believers. We feel a certain expectancy, an excitement, as we experience God with dozens, hundreds, or even thousands of worshipers.

Prepare for Public Worship

The night before church go to bed a little earlier. Eat and drink healthy food so that your mind and body feel fresh and nourished the next morning. Plan ahead to avoid the last-minute scramble gathering children and belongings.

Preparation continues when you arrive at church. You would never enter an important meeting cold, with your thoughts all out of order; how much more one needs to enter God's presence prepared. Be early, so that you can enter the sanctuary and be still. As in private worship, be still and confess your sins. Finally, as the service begins, give yourself wholeheartedly to worshiping your King. You will experience a joy and an ecstasy as you join with others in shared adoration of the Lord.

Part III

Now What?
Above-the-Sun
Meaning

8

Get Perspective

I had always believed that the world involved magic
now I thought perhaps it involved a magician . . .
This world of ours has some purpose;
and if there is a purpose, there is a person.
I had always felt life first as a story:
and if there is a story there is a storyteller.
—G. K. Chesterton

LIFE'S DEFINING MOMENT came for Roy Riegel when he picked up a fumble during the 1929 Rose Bowl and ran as fast as he could . . . toward the other team's goal. His mistake set up the winning touchdown for the opposition. Ralph Branca may not be a household name, but many will never forget the pitch he threw in the last game of the 1951 National League playoffs. It was a defining moment. Bobby Thompson eyed the pitch and pelted "the shot heard 'round the world"—a home run that won his team the pennant and probably the most famous home run in baseball history.

Chris Webber's defining moment came when the young basketball star called time out during the 1993 NCAA finals, only to discover his team had no time outs remaining. Speed skater

Dan Jansen's life changed forever when he took the mark in his favorite race in the 1988 Calgary Winter Olympics, determined to win a gold medal for his sister Jane, who had died of leukemia just hours before. Rounding the last turn, the blade on Jansen's skate caught the ice and sent him skidding into the wall. He fell again in his next race; he also finished out of medal contention in two races in Albertville in 1992. Defining moments.

What happened to Roy Riegel? I don't know. Perhaps he finally forgot his blunder or went on to somehow use it to his, or someone else's, advantage. But Ralph Branca turned his "defining moment" into a turning point. With the memory of a pitch he would like to take back fresh in his mind, he changed out of his uniform, closed his locker, and went on with his life. He married, raised a family, and had a successful business career. Today he is a major force in an organization called BAT, dedicated to assisting old ballplayers "who have suffered tragedies more permanent than dealing the wrong pitch at the wrong moment." [1]

Life is ripe with moments that can make us or break us, depending on our perspective.

Chris Webber established Time Out Inc., a non-profit agency "to help kids who need a time out to get going again."[2] He was able not only to laugh about his famous blunder but to use it as a springboard to help others. And Dan Jansen? He wears a gold medal from the 1994 Winter Olympics in Lillehammer, Norway, which he won in world-record time in a 1,000 meter race no one expected him to take. Millions of television viewers watched as he skated to the side of the rink, embraced his tearful wife, and took his infant daughter in his arms to begin a long-awaited Olympic victory lap. His baby daughter's name? Jane, after the aunt in whose memory Jansen raced—and lost—six years before.

Life is ripe with moments like these—moments that can make us or break us, depending on our perspective. I believe the defining moment came for Solomon when he reached the end of his extended, existential safari and discovered that there was nothing under the sun that could give his life meaning or purpose. He had seen it all, tried it all, had it all, done it all. There was no satisfaction to be found in any avenue of flatland living he pursued—none. "I've been there," he must have said. "I've done that. Now what?"

A Flatland De-Briefing: Four Unsatisfying Conclusions

Solomon reported his observations of life in the flatlands like an astronaut returning from space or a pilot from a wartime reconnaissance mission. His de-briefing is recorded in Ecclesiastes, chapter 6, and it includes four unsatisfying conclusions and four unanswerable questions. His first conclusion is that it is possible to have the best this world can offer without having satisfaction. "There is an evil which I have seen under the sun and it is prevalent among men—a man to whom God has given riches and wealth and honor so that his soul lacks nothing of all that he desires, but God has not empowered him to eat from them . . . ." (Eccles. 6:1–2). Wealthy, revered, powerful people are not rarely but *frequently* unsatisfied when they attain the things they desire. True satisfaction, Solomon seems to say, comes not from the things God gives, but from the Giver Himself.

Even the blessings of many children and a long, long life are nothing without a satisfied soul: "If a man fathers a hundred children and lives many years, however many they be, but his soul is not satisfied with good things. . . . " (Eccles. 6:3a). The word Solomon used for soul was *nephish*, and it represented the spiritual, eternal part of a person. The gnawing appetite of his *nephish* was not sated by the things he hoped might fill him—and they were good things! There was no sense of joy, no sense of contentment, no sense of satisfaction.

Second, Solomon said, it is possible for a person's death to be unattended by grief. Solomon suspected that when he died, no one would truly grieve over him. Imagine that! He was the richest, the wisest, the best-educated, most erudite, accomplished man of his day. But he knew that his achievements were vain trophies that had never filled the longing in his soul—and he did not believe they would be enough to win him a lasting place in the hearts of those who knew him, either. The idea that someone might actually love him for himself was apparently foreign to him.

"If a man . . . does not even have a proper burial," he said, "better the miscarriage than he, for it comes in futility and goes into obscurity; and its name is covered in obscurity" (vv. 3b–4). If no one grieves when we die, Solomon reasoned, we would be better off never having been born. If they attend our burial only as a necessary prerequisite to the reading of the will, then our life wasn't worth as much as a miscarriage. When a child was stillborn in Solomon's day, he would not be given a name, because it was believed this would help the parent overcome their loss more quickly. They would call the child "it," allowing it to pass into obscurity.

According to Solomon's third conclusion, someone who lives and dies without being deeply mourned is to be pitied more than the miscarried "it" who never had a name or a life at all. "It never sees the sun and it never knows anything; it is better off than he. Even if the other man lives a thousand years twice and does not enjoy good things—do not all go to one place?" (vv. 5–6). The Bible records the story of another man, Job, who in a time of great grief and personal loss, cursed the day that he was born. Job suffered the loss of his health, his wealth, his family, and his friends. Sick, poor, and utterly abandoned, he believed it would have been better if he had never been born. Solomon had everything that Job lost, and still he arrived at the same conclusion!

Solomon's report from the flatlands could almost be called "Straight Talk from a Pessimist," could it not? Better to never breathe one breath of this world's air, he argued, than to live a long life that never satisfies self or touches others. Better a wake for a nameless child than a state funeral for a famous man where no one cries. As a pastor, part of my job is to officiate at the religious ceremonies of life: weddings, baptisms, and funerals. I have officiated at funeral services for the rich and famous, tremendously powerful elite before just a handful of people—and not seen a tear in the house. And I have buried some folks whose names would not be recognized, but whose services were virtually "standing room only" and whose losses were deeply mourned. It is not unusual in these circumstances for a member of the family to tell me later "I had no idea he (or she) touched this many lives." Perhaps they were teachers or good, patient listeners or generous givers or faithful friends. One thing is certain: Solomon would have envied them.

Finally, the king concluded, it is possible for a person to experience labor without reward and to attain wisdom without advantage. "All a man's labor is for his mouth and yet the appetite is not satisfied. For what advantage does the wise man have over the fool? What advantage does the poor man have, knowing how to walk before the living? What the eyes see is better than what the soul desires. This too is futility and a striving after wind" (vv.

Wise people will not necessarily enjoy great advantage because of their wisdom, either.

7–9). The primary reason we work is to put food on our tables. Only after our basic needs for food and shelter are met, do we begin to worry about whether we *like* our jobs, or whether our egos are satisfied by them. Work was never meant to be our salvation. It is not a big enough reason to get up every morning, in and of itself. I know people who have worked hard all their lives and never had much to show for it—men and women whose labor was not rewarded with anything more than a place to live and food to eat. And I know others whose hard work has brought them great *financial* reward, but who are not satisfied by simply making more money. Financial success does not bring satisfaction.

Wise people will not necessarily enjoy great advantage because of their wisdom, either. In fact, men and women of wisdom are frequently overlooked in favor of those whose gifts are more readily visible. Solomon could definitely speak as an authority on the futility of wisdom, because there was no man in his day wiser than he. There is, he discovered, simply no advantage that under-the-sun living can provide to satisfy man's soul, his *nephish*. Wealth won't do it, and neither will longevity, education, hard work, or a house full of children. Solomon could not get any soul satisfaction from these, no matter how hard he tried.

Solomon at the end of his earthly search suffered from what I like to call the "Mick Jagger Syndrome." Jagger is the celebrity front man for the rock and roll band, the Rolling Stones. This fifty-something multi-millionaire grandfather has embarked on yet another world tour with his thirty-year-old band, but in the sixties he was an unknown performer/musician until a song called *Satisfaction* propelled the Stones to stardom. The song became the cry for a generation of young adults that experimented with everything from methamphetamines and marijuana to the Maharishi Mahesh Yoga in their search for meaning—but it could just as easily be the theme for the burned-out super-achievers of the nineties: "I can't get no. . . satisfaction." Perhaps one of the thousand or more songs Solomon penned contained similar lyrics!

Further De-Briefing: Four Unanswerable Questions

As is often the case, Solomon's search led him not to answers, but to more questions. His first question is implied: "Whatever exists has already been named, and it is known what man is . . ." (v. 10a). Do we really have choices? he wondered. Is all of life predestined? Are we preprogrammed with inclinations and impulses that will determine who we are? Solomon rightly noted that everything that existed had already been named, and in the Hebrew culture, once a thing was named, it was *defined.* (For this reason, the Jew would not speak the name of God. God called Himself "I Am that I Am," and their rendering of that name was "Yahweh," but to utter it presumed that they had Him defined, and they did not.)

> *Do we really have choices? Is all of life predestined?*

It was God who said light would be named light, and darkness would be called darkness. He named the ball of fire in the daytime sky the sun and the changing disc in the nightime sky the moon. What are we to do, Solomon wondered, in a universe in which everything is named? Especially when we, too, have been named, "and it is known what man is." We were created out of the dust of the ground and would return to it. Dirt to dirt —that was Solomon's destiny under the sun. And under the sun, it is our destiny as well. Do we have choices? he wanted to know. Nothing he had observed provided him with an answer.

Second, Solomon wanted to know if we had recourse. If everything was named—if God made the choices—could we argue? Was there a system of appeals at work in the universe? We "cannot dispute with him who is stronger than he is," Solomon wrote (v. 10b). Was God in that category? Could He be disputed?

A Broadway show was called *"Arms Too Short to Box with God."* Solomon couldn't be sure, but he suspected that God was in a different weight category. Can a man argue with God? Or is God some kind of celestial Evander Holyfield in comparison to our fly-weight status as human beings? Can we appeal to under-the-sun reason and have His words overruled? Or *does* His word rule supremely? Solomon had no answer.

If, as Solomon suspected, our choices were limited and our recourse with God questionable, could we at least determine for ourselves what was good and what was not? Did we have a measuring stick for defining goodness? "For who knows," he asked, "what is good for a man during his lifetime, during the few years of his futile life? He will spend them like a shadow" (v. 12a).

Judith Viorst has written a wonderful book for children (and their parents) called *Alexander and the Terrible, Horrible, No-Good, Very-Bad Day.* Alexander has to eat food he doesn't like. He has to wear his railroad train pajamas to bed, and he hates his railroad train pajamas. The dog wants to sleep with his brother, not with him. To Alexander's way of thinking, not much about his day was good. Solomon's question is about as negative as Alexander's very bad day. "Who knows what is good?" he asks—and the subtext is, "Could anything *be* good at all?"

Two women lived together for several years and neither had ever married. Suddenly, one woman disappeared. Her roommate had no word from her and did not know what had happened to her friend. After a year, the missing woman called.

"I got married," she said.

"Oh, that's good!" her old roommate replied.

"Well—not all good," she said. "I married someone twice my age."

"Oh, that's bad."

"Well, not all bad," said the first woman. "He was a rich man."

"A rich man? That's certainly good," her roommate said.

"Actually, it's not all good because he left all his money to his children by his first wife."

"Oh, that's bad."

"Well, not all bad," the first woman corrected. "He did build me a beautiful home."

"That's good," her friend replied.

"Well, not all good," the first woman said. "The home burned down."

"Oh, that's bad!"

"Not all bad," she said with a laugh. "The old tightwad was in the house when it burned."

That's how it is with us. We can't tell what's good from what's bad in this life. If standards for "goodness" existed under the sun, Solomon did not find them. He was asking if anyone else had! What is good for a man during his lifetime? The king did not know. His under-the-sun search yielded no clues.

Solomon's final question was, "Who knows about the future?" "For who can tell a man what will be after him under the sun?" (v. 12b). Solomon, in all of his learning and all of his traveling, found no one with the ability to accurately predict the future. He himself could not. Today we can predict within varying degrees of probability anything from tomorrow's weather to fluctuations in the bond market. But no one can say with any certainty what will be in this world after he is gone.

The King's Conclusion

Solomon had precious little to show for the longest, most extensive, most thoroughly-complete, and well-funded search for meaning ever recorded in history. He had seen and done everything under the sun, but he came away with more questions than answers. What is the meaning of life? What is our purpose? He was clueless. Riches? No satisfaction. Labor? No satisfaction. Education? No satisfaction. Religion? No satisfaction. Hedonism? No satisfaction.

Perhaps that is why Voltaire said if there is no God, it would be necessary for us to invent him. We need there to be more to life than we can know and experience under the sun. Solomon's eventual question, "Now what?" was his most important one. What happens when life deals a crushing blow? What happens when the paths we thought would lead to answers turn out to be dead ends instead? What happens when everything we depend on is lost? These are the defining moments of life. To meet them successfully, a change of perspective is in order. Meet Job—a man on the verge of an enormous paradigm shift—and fasten your seat belt for an encounter with above-the-sun reality.

> *We need there to be more to life than we can know and experience under the sun.*

Job Asks Why

Nearly five hundred years before the rule of Solomon in Israel, a man named Job lived in the land of Uz, southeast of the Dead Sea. Job had it all. He was respected, brilliant, rich, and righteous. "He was the greatest," the Bible says, "of all the men of the East." But then something happened to Job. Overnight, he saw the things that he valued stripped from him. He lost his health, his wealth, his family, and his good name. A band of mercenaries stole his oxen and donkeys and murdered his servants. Fire fell from heaven and consumed his sheep and their shepherds. Another band of soldiers raided his flock of camels and killed the servants who looked after them. While his sons and daughters were eating and drinking in the home of the eldest brother, a whirlwind struck the house and it fell on them, killing them all. Then, as if that weren't enough tragedy for one man to endure, Job's body was covered with horrible sores from the crown of his head to the bottom of his feet.

When life deals you a tough blow, you find out who your friends are. Job's friends were named Eliphaz, Bildad, and Zophar, but they weren't much help. Without question, the kindest thing they did was mourn with him in complete silence for seven days. Their helpfulness decreased as their conversation increased. They assumed (and told Job so) that he must be suffering because of some unknown sin he had committed. Accusations flew. Emotionalism escalated. Questions were asked by Job and by his friends. They asked God all kinds of questions—most of them having to do with *why* Job was experiencing such pain. God never answered a single question. Then when Eliphaz, Bildad, Zophar and Job *shut up*, God *spoke up*.

Solomon had four unanswerable questions about life. Job and his friends must have asked God a hundred questions about His mysterious ways. Do you suppose that when God finally spoke, He went down a list of their questions and answered them in turn? He did not. His response to Job is the longest recorded monologue of God anywhere in the Bible, and in it, He answers not a single one of Job's questions—but instead He asks Job sixty-four of His own!

> *God is always the subject—never the object. He is always the One who asks—not the One who answers.*

Where were you, Job, when the sun was set in the sky? Where were you when the foundation of the world was put into place? Big questions. Small questions. "Have you ever in your life commanded the morning and caused the dawn to know its place?" God asked His earth-bound interrogator? "Can you lift up your voice to the clouds, so that an abundance of water may cover you? Can you send forth lightnings that they may go and say to you, 'Here we are'?" (Job 38:12, 34–35). What is the point? Don't miss it. We are not the questioner—God is. We are not the teacher—God is. We are not the center of the universe. We are not the ones who hold all things together—God is!

God is always the subject—never the object. He is always the One who asks—not the One who answers. Where is the meaning in our under-the-sun existence, whether it is happy or sad, fortunate or unfortunate? It is found only in an above-the-sun God! This life will never have meaning for us until we come face-to-face with our Creator.

What did Job do when God put *him* to the test? He listened in silence to every one of God's questions—and with each one, he began to see his place, his purpose in the universe more clearly. "Behold, I am insignificant; what can I reply to Thee? I lay my hand on my mouth. Once I have spoken, and I will not answer;

even twice, and I will add no more" (Job 40:4–5). Job said that he repented "in dust and ashes" and acknowledged that he had failed to understand Who it was he had been questioning. "I have heard of Thee by the hearing of the ear; but now my eye sees Thee . . . ." (Job 42:5).

Every person who encounters the living, holy God comes away from that meeting with the same testimony. The Almighty cannot be captured with words. His awesome power and majesty is literally inexpressible. God did not answer Job's questions; He answered *Job*. And Job was unable to adequately express what he had seen and heard. God revealed Himself to Job, and Job offered the only appropriate response: He worshiped Him.

Solomon unraveled a multi-colored skein of worldly wisdom and followed it to the very end, until finally, he looked up. All that is under the sun is meaningless without the view from above the sun. Only God can provide that perspective. A man can bail out, fog out, burn out, or blow out—but he will never understand what it means to truly *live* apart from a relationship with the Living God. He is the Person behind the purpose. He is the Storyteller behind the story of life. He is the Magician behind any magic we might meet in this under-the-sun existence. Every door of human satisfaction closed on Job. Every door closed on Solomon. Every door will eventually close on us, too. When the doors of life close, what is left is simply faith in God. He asks; we answer—with submission, confidence, faith, and worship.

Do You Really Love God?

St. Augustine proposed an imaginary story in his sermon entitled *The Pure Love of God*. Do you really love God? Augustine asked. Do you love Him with all your heart, soul, mind, and strength, which is the first and greatest commandment? Then he proposed a way to discover the answer. Suppose God came to a person and said, "The world and all that is in it can be yours. I will give you perfect health. Whatever your heart desires, you may have. I will even do away with sin and enable you to live forever." It sounds good, doesn't it? The whole world at your disposal—no sin, eternal life. It sounds too good, perhaps.

"There is only one thing you will not have," God would say in this imaginary tale. "You will never see My face. The choice is yours. I will respect your wish."

Augustine said if there was a quiver in a person's heart at the words, "You will never see My face," it is quite possible that he really might love God. If a man decided to turn away from all that the world could offer for the joy of seeing God's face, his love might be true. It sounds to me like a pretty good test of whether a man loved God with all that he had or hoped to be.

The only real satisfaction to be found in this life is found in the love of God. We can choose Him through His Son Jesus Christ and know Him as we are known. Only then does satisfaction come—but then it comes from everywhere in little things and big things. Because when the soul is satisfied, the other things may be enjoyed for what they are: gifts from a God who is unchanging and good.

My mother is in heaven. I have not seen her in several years, but I like to remember her as I saw her so many afternoons of my childhood. I would round the corner of the little alley behind our house, walking along the fence where the garbage cans stood, and pass through our little gate. Then I would begin to sniff the air, to see if Mother was making a pound cake. In those days, she baked two or three a week—and if she were in the kitchen cooking one of those cakes, I could smell it a hundred yards away. If Mother were in the kitchen making a cake, she would almost always be singing a little chorus that went something like this:

> In the morning, I see His face;
> In the evening, His form I trace.
> In the darkness, His voice I know;
> I see Jesus everywhere I go.

I do not know how many times I heard that song as a child. She must have sung it a thousand times. (And I must have eaten a thousand slices of pound cake.) But I do know this: My mother knew real satisfaction in her life under the sun because she knew God through Jesus Christ. She saw Him everywhere. He made her life rich and full of meaning and purpose. He has made mine rich and full as well. And today my mother sings in the presence of the source of her satisfaction, whose name is Jesus. Apart from

Him, nothing makes sense. All is vanity. With Him, with His perspective, life under the sun is only a sweet prelude to a symphony that is yet to come. Do you see Him? Do you love Him? Will you say yes to His plan and His purpose for your life? If you will, that yes will be your defining moment and the way to true and lasting satisfaction, now and forevermore.

(Eccles. 6:1–12)

An Above-the-Sun Postscript

He who walks in integrity walks securely,
But he who perverts his ways will be found out.
—Proverbs 10:9

If you are not a Christian or if you are and are feeling hopelessly caught up in the rat race, how do you experience one of these defining moments? How do you get this perspective?

Unfortunately, most defining moments are not only unplanned but also painful. Too often God cannot get our attention apart from a tragedy. We forget the lessons of history, toss aside the hard-won lessons of friends and family, seemingly only willing to learn from personal experience. However, if you are ready to be wise, to learn from Solomon, and to ask yourself some hard questions, you can still bring that defining moment into perspective. Honestly answer the following questions:

1. How much money will it take for me to be fulfilled?

2. How much higher up the corporate ladder do I have to rise to be fulfilled? Is it possible to be "up there" and still be dissatisfied? What more will it take then?

3. How many more high-tech comforts do I need? If I can just own one vacation home will that take care of the deep longings? Do I know people with these things who aren't fulfilled?

4. How many more sexual conquests will it take for me to be satisfied? Will I ever reach the satiation point? Do I know anyone who has had their hunger met in this area and is now content?

The problem with all these things is that they are just things. What more will it take for you to realize that things cannot love you? How many things do you have to cram into that God-shaped vacuum before you realize that nothing fits?

On the other hand, One who is not a thing but the Maker of things *does* love you and He loves you without a single condition. But He won't share your heart's adoration with any of the things He has made. You either keep cramming these things into the vacuum and forsake Him or you forsake them and find deep pleasure and everlasting satisfaction.

Honest questions answered honestly can bring you the right perspective. God alone is worthy of your life, love, energy, and trust. What will it take for you to give all you are to Him?

Try this exercise. Write your obituary. What do you want said of you? What did you really accomplish? As you write your obituary, did you invest your life or waste it? Are you leaving a legacy in the lives of others? Writing the ideal obituary requires that we seriously reflect on what really matters in life, what we will give our lives for. Once you have the ideal life written out, what steps do you need to take to make it happen? Remember—"one life to live—soon will be past—only what's done for God will last."

9

Know What Is Good and What Is Better

Morality means choice. Choice means priorities.
Priorities mean a hierarchy. A hierarchy
means something at the top, a standard.
That is the greatest good. If you have no
greatest good, you have no hierarchy of goods.
If you have no hierarchy, you have no priorities.
If you have no priorities, you cannot make
intelligent choices. If you cannot make
intelligent moral choices, you have no morality.
—Peter Kreeft

A WOMAN ENTERED AN AIRPORT gift shop with an hour or so to spare before her flight. She purchased a newspaper and a small package of cookies and then settled into a chair near the appropriate gate to wait. She opened her paper and began to read. A gentleman sat down opposite her, resting his briefcase and a cup of coffee on the small table between them. He opened his paper, too. As she read, she reached for a cookie from the bag in the center of the table, and popped one into her mouth. A few minutes went by, and she reached for another cookie—but they had been moved. The package, now half-empty, was sitting on top of the briefcase belonging to the man beside her.

"How unbelievably rude!" she thought, moving the cookies back to her side of the table and taking another one. Then she heard the rustle of cellophane and watched him remove the last cookie from the package. This was too much. She put down her paper and glared at the seemingly non-plussed cookie thief, who shrugged his shoulders, broke the remaining cookie in two, and offered her half! Angrily gathering her things, she gave him one final, withering stare and moved to the other side of the waiting area.

Her fury did not subside until half an hour into her flight, when she reached into her bag for a pen and pulled out . . . her unopened package of cookies!

Perspective is critical, is it not? Every decision we make is based on a world view that reflects our understanding of reality. "Well, you could have fooled me," someone might say, "I didn't know I had a world view." We all do. Having a consistent world view is almost like having a pair of eye glasses with lenses cut and ground just for us. It enables us to see life more clearly and to perceive with greater accuracy the things around us.

What kinds of things comprise our world view? First, our perception of God. Is there a God? If there is, is He knowable? Is He interested? Is He all-knowing, all-powerful, and all-seeing? The second step in developing world view involves ultimate reality. What is real in this universe? What underlying truths or principles have been at work, are at work, and will be at work in our world? What relationships exist between these principles? The third component of a world view is our perspective of knowledge. What is its true nature? What limits exist in its understanding? How is its validity determined? Fourth, is ethics. Are some things morally right and others morally wrong? Is "rightness" or "wrongness" absolute or situational? Is our conscience invio-

> *Every decision we make is based on a world view that reflects our understanding of reality.*

late? Finally, what *are* we—the apex of creation or a higher form of animal life? What is our relationship to God and to our world? Where do we "fit" into the grand scheme of things?

A world view is much more practical than it sounds and is fundamental to every aspect of our lives. If our view is consistent with what we believe about God, ultimate reality, knowledge, ethics, and mankind, our world will be in focus. Every thought, every relationship, every decision will be perceived through its lenses—and the more consistent and coherent our world view is, the clearer each image we see will appear.

Solomon's search for meaning in life was a search for his own world view. When none of the under-the-sun avenues provided satisfactory answers, he began to understand that a change of perspective was in order. The seventh chapter of Ecclesiastes, his written testimonial, provides an unedited look at the formation of a world view. Solomon realized that the answers he was looking for would not come from under the sun—but from above it. His perspective was changing—and a series of value judgments between what is "good" and what is "better" served to bring his world view into sharper focus.

Four "Good/Better" Proverbs

We have all heard our share of proverbs. A proverb is a collection of words wrapped around a kernel of truth. "A stitch in time saves nine" and "Early to bed, early to rise, makes a man healthy, wealthy, and wise," are familiar proverbs. One of my favorite proverbs is, "It has to get dark before you see the stars." A funny-sounding one that I have heard a lot is "You can't make a silk purse out of a sow's ear," but I am told a scientist recently did exactly that, just to prove that it could be done. So much for *that* kernel of truth.

A Good Name

Solomon used four proverbs to establish a hierarchy of good, contrasting that which is good with that which is better. "A good name," he says, "is better than a good ointment, and the day of one's death is better than the day of one's birth" (Eccles. 7:1).

That is strange wisdom when taken in pieces, but profound truth when viewed as a whole. It was common practice in Solomon's day for people to cover themselves in sweet-smelling perfumes or ointments to create a favorable impression. But a good name, he reasoned, goes further than a cosmetic cover-up. Ointment is good—but a good name is better. Then he joined that thought with another: The day of one's death is better than the day of one's birth. Why? Because between birth and death, we make a name for ourselves.

A name *can* carry good or bad connotations. Depending on the "Marys" you have known, you may think someone named Mary is either wonderful, or wretched. At birth you can only speculate—but chances are, on the day of a person's death, you will *know*. The day of death is better than the day of birth, Solomon said, because on the day of death, all the returns will be in. The person will be known for who he or she was. In other words, the truth beats a smokescreen every time! If there is a choice between sham and reality—reality is the better of the two.

The Reality of Death

The second and third proverbs have to do with learning. "It is better to go to a house of mourning than to go to a house of feasting, because that is the end of every man, and the living takes it to heart" (v. 2). Death is the inevitable end of everyone, and death can be a valuable teacher. In fact, life's blessings cannot be truly understood or enjoyed apart from the reality of death. It forces us to ask the big questions and to prioritize. Death slows us down and sobers us up. It has been said, accurately I believe, that a man is not ready to live until he is ready to die.

I read from the Bible often in public. It is part of my job as a pastor. Most of the time, especially if I am reading a familiar passage, I am convinced people are only half-listening. If their minds are wandering, they probably hear something like this: "In My Father's house. . . (Look at Ron over there—I think he's dozing.) if it were not so. . . (It's almost noon—I wonder if he's finished?) I go to prepare a place. . . ." Even at weddings, I'm not sure that the bride and groom hear much except, "I now pronounce you husband and wife."

But funerals are different. At funerals, I can read, "In my Father's house are many dwelling places; if it were not so, I would have told you; for I go to prepare a place for you," and I am sure that all there who loved their father or mother or husband or wife or friend are riveted on each and every word. Why? Because heaven takes on incredible significance when someone we love lives

Life's blessings cannot be truly understood or enjoyed apart from the reality of death.

there. Death makes everything about life seem more real. We are sensitive to God's teaching in times of pain and sadness as we are at no other time.

The Lessons of Sorrow

"Sorrow is better than laughter," Solomon also wrote, "for when a face is sad a heart may be happy. The mind of the wise is in the house of mourning, while the mind of fools is in the house of pleasure" (v. 3–4).

Two holiday letters enclosed in Christmas cards illustrate this beautifully. Recipients of the first letter read:

Dear Friends:

What a great year! Jim was named president of the bank. We celebrated by buying a Mercedes and flying to the Orient. In addition to Boy Scout work, Jim was the co-chairman of the United Fund. He continues on the board of Grace Hospital and is treasurer of the local Kiwanis chapter. His first love is still conservation and he's heading the committee to fight Dutch Elm disease.

After completing my term as Junior League president, I swore I'd take life easy, but I'm more involved than ever. I accepted the vice presidency of the garden club, and am active in the DAR. I ran the bake sale for the Eastern Star and we made $680. I also squeezed in a flower arranging class offered by a Japanese exchange student. All of this with my leg in a cast! Dumb me fell off a ladder while hanging curtains at the USO.

Jim Jr. was elected class president and won his letters in football and basketball. He's on the all-state debate team and placed second in the National Oratory Contest. We were surprised to read in the paper that he'd won a $100 prize in the American Legion essay contest—we never even knew he entered! Junior has been accepted by Harvard and Yale, and can't make up his mind. Linda was elected vice president of her class, homecoming queen, and the sweetheart of the Phi Delts, and she was a finalist in the regional swim meet.

Look forward to hearing from you.

Love, Alice.

The second writer's year was not so terrific, by contrast:

Dear Friends:

We've had a rotten year. Bill was passed over for a promotion again, so he quit. He hasn't lined anything up yet but he's listed with the employment agencies and looks in the want ads every day. In the meantime, he's drinking like a fish.

Bill Jr. was defeated for homeroom monitor. He flunked French and will have to go to summer school to graduate. College is out. Bob hasn't had a haircut since August and had to hock his Honda to pay for its repairs. Thank God he didn't lose his leg. We were pretty worried.

Mary is protesting something and shaved her head two weeks ago. My mother-in-law's May visit lasted until August and now I'm back in therapy. As I write this the whole family is down with the flu and I'm exhausted. We hope next year is better. It couldn't be much worse.

Love, Jane.

Alice's friends may have enjoyed her letter more than those who received Jane's—but I believe the second family probably learned more during their difficult year. Laughter is good, but where real learning is concerned, sorrow is often better.

Foolish Flattery

Finally, Solomon said, flattery seems good, but honest feedback is better: "It is better to listen to the rebuke of a wise man than for one to listen to the song of fools. For as the crackling of thorn bushes under a pot, so is the laughter of the fool, and this too is futility" (v. 6). It is better, according to Solomon, to be corrected by a friend who knows and loves us than to receive the foolish flattery of a member of the less-than-wise crowd. Praise from the lips of a fool has the same result as thorny branches used for kindling: lots of sparks, but no real heat. The effect may be pleasant—but it is not at all useful.

Solomon's understanding of what was good and what was better was shaped slowly over time, but it is possible for our priorities to be overhauled in an illuminating instant. Inspirational writer Og Mandino told the story of such a person in his book, *The Choice*. Mark Christopher was an insurance salesman whose career had taken off like a rocket. He was his company's youngest vice president, and his nickname was "Mr. Success." When he wasn't selling, speaking, or teaching as an adjunct professor at a nearby university, he focused his winning passion on golf.

Then came the morning Christopher would never forget. He was up at 6:30 A.M. on a Sunday, waiting for his buddies to pick him up on the way to the country club, when his two sons surprised him with a shout: "Happy Father's Day, Dad!" They attacked him with hugs and kisses, and then presented him with homemade cards, each bearing the greeting "to the greatest father in the world." He thanked them both, and they enjoyed a few minutes of small talk. Then Christopher really began to look at his boys, seeing them as if for the first time.

> *It is possible for our priorities to be overhauled in an illuminating instant.*

Perhaps it was no more than an illusion created by the early morning mist seeping through the screen door, but Glenn, my twelve year old, seemed to be aging before my eyes. Or maybe it was just the first time I had taken a good look at him since I couldn't remember when. He was handsome and, luckily for him, was getting to look more and more like his mother. Gosh, he had grown up. There was even a hint of fuzz above his upper lip; his hands seemed immense, and his voice had a break in it. Between my long hours at the office and university plus my weekends on the golf course, I hadn't noticed his gradual transition from the infant I once bathed every night to the young man who now sat before me. The horrible thought suddenly hit me that he would be off to college in five years and more or less out of my life in ten. I turned my attention to Todd who was struggling to read aloud from the back of his giant cereal box. He was already in the first grade. It was only yesterday, wasn't it, that I had paced outside the delivery room until I heard his first cry? Where did those six years go?[1]

When the horn honked and his buddies called for him, Christopher made his apologies and stayed home instead. The next morning he dictated his letter of resignation to his boss. What was better had been distinguished once and for all from what was merely good.

Four Wise Warnings

Following these four proverbs that draw the line between good and better, Solomon offered four warnings meant to further refine a man's world view.

Dishonesty and Deception

"Oppression makes a wise man mad," he said, "and a bribe corrupts the heart" (v. 7). There are forces at work in the world that will harm the wise man and the good man, the king seemed to say. He warned those who would listen to "play it straight" and avoid dishonesty and deceit in all their dealings.

A young brother and sister negotiated a trade. The brother agreed to trade all of his marbles for all of his sister's candy. The sister was unsure and needed time to think it over. She went in her room and returned after a few minutes. "Okay," she said, "I'll do it." The boy went to collect his marbles and began to have second thoughts. There were four or five cat's eyes that were his favorites, and he didn't want to part with them. So he pulled them out at the last minute and hid them under his pillow. The rest he offered to his sister. "Here are all my marbles," he said. "And here is all my candy," she replied.

That night the little girl slept soundly, but her brother lay awake all night tossing and turning, wondering if she really had given him all of her candy. Dishonesty and deception are oppressive. They "press down" the man or woman who employs them. Beware of them, Solomon warned. They can be crippling.

Impatience and Pride

Then Solomon spoke a warning about impatience and pride: "The end of a matter is better than its beginning; patience of spirit is better than haughtiness of spirit" (v. 8). Many people today congratulate themselves on their impatience, considering it some kind of back-handed virtue. But impatience is a mark of pride, not power. We are in such a hurry to get things done, but Solomon said that the end of a thing—that which we must wait for—is actually better than its beginning—that which we can do right away. A great beginning is important, but many who have made great beginnings have experienced terrible endings.

> *No one has ever embarked on a sinful undertaking that wasn't initially appealing.*

Satan promises great beginnings. No one has ever embarked on a sinful undertaking that wasn't initially appealing. Sin always looks good at the outset. But the end of sin has a payday someday. The eventual result is tragedy, whether it manifests itself in disease, disaster, or death. It is possible to overcome a bad beginning, but you cannot change a bad ending. Beginning well is good—but ending well is critical.

Anger

Solomon warned against anger, too. "Do not be eager in your heart to be angry," he said, "for anger resides in the bosom of fools" (v. 9). How many times has someone said, "I've got a short temper, that's all"? It is no badge of honor to be short-tempered and quick to anger. The person who allows anger to establish residence in his or her heart is a fool, the king said.

I once asked an acquaintance who was quite familiar with the PGA tour which professional golfer was particularly unpopular to play with. He told me that years ago there was a fellow by the name of Bobby Cole that fit the bill. No one wanted to play with Bob Cole because he was angry all the time. He made cutting remarks. He was bitter. He made the other golfers around him mad, too.

Bobby Cole's partner at the Masters in Augusta one year was Sam Snead. Everybody loved Sam Snead. He was gracious and kind and, in general, just wonderful to be around. He coached and encouraged others and rarely had a negative word to say to anyone. But after ten or twelve holes with obnoxious Bob Cole, even Sam Snead's patience was wearing a bit thin.

They approached the next hole, a lay up with a dog leg to the right, near some tall pine trees. Snead took out a three iron and laid up right down the middle. Then he turned to Cole as he was preparing to lay up with his iron and said, "Son, when I was your age and playing this hole, I would take my driver and fade my shot right around the corner, over those pine trees. It would save me about 100 yards—but that might be a little tough for you."

Cole's anger flashed and he immediately said to Sam Snead, "I can do anything you've ever done. Get out of my way." He put up his iron and took out his driver and then hit a fabulous drive with a slight fade on it. It hit the tops of the pine trees Snead had pointed to and fell down into the deep rough. As both golfers began walking toward their shots, Snead looked back at Bobby Cole and said, "Nice try, son, but I forgot to mention that when I was your age those pine trees were only shoulder-high."

> *Someone who lives in the past has no immediate opportunities*

Solomon wrote in Proverbs that a hot tempered person stirs up strife, but one who is slow to anger can head off contention. An anger that constantly churns just under the surface can do great damage. The wise person is never in a hurry to give in to anger.

The Good Old Days

Finally, Solomon warned about the dangers of living in the past. "Do not say, 'Why is it that the former days were better than these?' For it is not from wisdom that you say this" (v. 10). I have discovered that those who talk incessantly of the good old days don't always recall them very clearly. Generally speaking, the good old days were not quite as good as we remember them to be. But even if they were—they are still gone. Someone who lives in the past has no immediate opportunities because the present is the only thing we have the power to participate in fully. "The great thing," said C. S. Lewis, "is to be found at one's post as a child of God, living each day as though it were our last, but planning as though our world might last a hundred years."[2] Beware of the kind of nostalgia that continually says, "If only. . ." and "What if. . ." Memories that please are tremendous; memories that plague are destructive. It is essential to know the difference.

Two Wise Conclusions

Can you see how Solomon's world view began to take shape as he made judgments between what is good and what is better? He added two wise conclusions to his previous proverbs and warnings: Value wisdom and consider God.

Value Wisdom

"Wisdom along with an inheritance is good," the king said. No argument there. "And an advantage to those who see the sun. For wisdom is protection just as money is protection. But the advantage of knowledge is that wisdom preserves the lives of its possessors" (vv. 11–12).

Solomon possessed wisdom as no other person. His wisdom was God-given and super-abundant. But as he reflected on his life and the paths he had taken, the king realized he had not used what he had been given. He took short cuts. He followed dead ends. He tried in vain to satisfy his appetites and to fill his soul. Finally, the man who had been everywhere and done everything testified to the value of his original gift—wisdom. It not only protects a man, he said, but it preserves him from the vanity of endless searching.

Our times— all of them— are in the hand of God.

Consider God

What did Solomon's wisdom reveal? That he should consider God. Instead of exhausting himself in under-the-sun pursuits, the king could have sought the one thing that would have

157

yielded true satisfaction: a relationship with the living God. "Consider the work of God," Solomon said. "For who is able to straighten what He has bent? In the day of prosperity be happy, but in the day of adversity consider—God has made the one as well as the other so that man may not discover anything that will be after him" (vv. 13–14).

Remember, God is intimately involved in our affairs. Solomon's father, King David, said it this way: "But as for me, I trust in Thee, O LORD, I say 'Thou art my God.' My times are in Thy hand . . . . " (Ps. 31:14–15a).

When I die, what I am will all be gone.

Our times—all of them—are in the hand of God. In times of happiness, Solomon advised, consider God and rejoice! Celebrate good news and happy occasions in the days of prosperity. And when times of sorrow come, consider God and take heart—for He has made them as well.

I believe God gives us enough blessings in our hands to counter-balance the burdens on our backs. Between our blessings and our burdens, we can manage to walk upright if only we will consider God. Death loomed before Solomon as it looms before us, and we do not know what will be in this world after we depart. The bigger question is this: What will become of *us*? The answer is that in the hand God, we lose *what* we are, but *who* we are remains. When I die, what I am—my possessions, my status, my profession—will all be gone. But who I am will remain. Who we are depends on the choices or judgments we have made about the two things that are eternal: God and our souls.

Life's Three Key Relationships

There are three key relationships in life: our relationship to ourselves, our relationship to others, and our relationship to God. Solomon's beliefs about these relationships also expressed his emerging world view.

Our Relationship to Ourselves

What did the king say about our relationship to ourselves? "I tested all this with wisdom, and I said 'I will be wise,' but it was far from me. What has been is remote and exceedingly mysterious. Who can discover it?" (v. 23). The epitaph of every philosopher who has ever lived is the same: "I'm not as wise as I thought. In fact, I'm not even sure I understand myself." Brilliant, gifted Solomon learned so much in his lifetime, but he confessed that his wisdom was inadequate—especially when it came to understanding himself!

Solomon confessed that his wisdom was inadequate—especially when it came to understanding himself!

Socrates said, "Know thyself." The truth is, no one ever truly knows himself. Our own soul can seem as remote and untouchable as the sun. We can send powerful instruments into space that allow us to learn more about the stars than we will ever comprehend about ourselves! When King David asked God to search his heart and to know him, he expressed the broken cry of someone who tried and failed to plumb his own soul's depth. I've heard words come out of my own mouth that surprised me. "Why did I say that?" I sometimes wonder. "Why did I respond in such an inappropriate way?" I do not know myself as thoroughly as I might imagine. No one does.

Our Relationship to Others

Just as we cannot ever completely know ourselves, we cannot ever totally understand another person. Solomon's scrutiny of others was as intense as his examination of himself. His conclusion was that relationships with others can be disappointing and even dangerous. "And I discovered more bitter than death the woman whose heart is snares and nets, whose hands are chains. One who is pleasing to God will escape from her, but the sinner will be captured by her. 'Behold I have discovered this,' says the Preacher, 'adding one thing to another to find an explanation, which I am still seeking but have not found. I have found one man among a thousand, but I have not found a woman among all these'" (vv. 26–28).

This king systematically tested or investigated his relationships with others and observed one particularly dangerous kind of relationship: the liaison between a man and a manipulative woman. I believe early in Solomon's life he experienced an affair with a woman like the one he described and found himself trapped as a result. He learned that it is impossible to be married, indulge in an affair, and keep life in focus. An unfaithful husband confided to me once that he never knew genuine fear until he started having an affair. Then he began carrying a gun because he believed that if his lover's husband found out about them, the man would attempt to kill him. If his own wife found out, he said, she would leave him. If his children knew, he would be disgraced, and his relationship with them ruined. The lure of another woman became a trap, not a way to freedom.

Solomon reported sadly that only one man in the thousand that he knew was upright and trustworthy. Only one. And of the women he knew (his wives and concubines alone numbered one thousand), not one did he find to be upright or wise. What was he really saying? Simply this: It is the rare, rare person under the sun who has life together. That is why we are so often disappointed or disillusioned when we look to other men or women for a sense of our own purpose. They frequently are as lost as we are! Earthly relationships and human wisdom will not satisfy.

Our Relationship to God

What did Solomon discover about our relationship with God? "Behold, I have found only this, that God made men upright, but they have sought out many devices" (v. 29). God's first man and woman, Adam and Eve, were beautiful, upright people. They looked to Him for everything, and He was in fellowship with them constantly—until they sought their own devices at the urging of Satan and believed the lies he spoke about God. From that day until now, we have continued to seek our own schemes, our own devices—and have reaped the consequences of our actions.

There is a church in northern California that has portraits of famous people hanging in its vestibule. There is a portrait of Socrates and another of Eleanor Roosevelt. There is a portrait of Abraham Lincoln and Ghandi and Jesus. These words are written in beautiful gold letters over the assembled portraits: "And we are all children of God. . . ." I am sure people pass by those portraits every day and marvel at the universal brotherhood of man. There is only one problem: The universal brotherhood of man (and the universal fatherhood of God) is an inclusive, benevolent, politically correct, loving lie. The quote in gold letters is even a quote from the Bible—but it is incomplete. "We are all children of God," the Scripture says, "through faith in our Lord Jesus Christ" (Gal. 3:26).

There is no universal brotherhood apart from Him. But through Him, we are "adopted" into the family of God, and we become joint heirs with Christ to the very Kingdom of God. The heresies of this world aren't hatched whole from the minds of brilliant lunatics; they are spun from half-truths left unexamined and incomplete. We are like sheep, Jesus said, who have wandered away and followed after our own schemes and desires. But we were created for something different—something more.

> *The universal brotherhood of man is an inclusive, benevolent, politically correct, loving lie.*

The truth about our relationship to God is that we matter to Him. Regardless of what we have done or not done, we matter to Him. God loves unconditionally, and the boundaries He has placed around our lives are not to keep us from joy, but from harm. The aim of Christianity, G. K. Chesterton said, is to allow good things to run wild.[3] God knows, that left to our own devices we will stray and will bring ourselves grief, but within His boundaries our lives can truly count for something. Within His boundaries there is meaning and purpose.

The greatest lie perpetrated today is that God's way does not work. The second greatest lie is that man's way does. The truth is there are no values that are working in this world today but God's. No other set of values—no other world view but His—is operating successfully. The apostle Paul said, "I know whom I have believed and I am convinced that He is able to guard what I have entrusted to Him . . . ." (2 Tim. 1:12). We cannot fully know ourselves. We cannot fully know or rely on other men. But we can be absolutely certain that God can keep whatever is committed to Him. When He is recognized as the highest good, everything else makes sense. Everything else works.

> *The greatest lie perpetrated today is that God's way does not work. The second greatest lie is that man's way does.*

Suppose a man loses his briefcase on a cross-country trip. When he arrives at the airport terminal, he sees the ticket manager and says, "I've lost my bag." The ticket manager will ask for a description. The man might say, "It's a brown, leather case about this long and this high. It has a handle—no strap. Oh, and a little sticker with my name and address." The ticket manager's next question will certainly be, "Did you check your bag with us, sir, or carry it on yourself?"

If the passenger failed to check his case but set it down to get a cup of coffee in the lobby and returned to find it gone, the manager might offer to announce it over the public address system, but he would feel no further obligation. After all, the bag was not checked to the airline. The bag was never in its possession—and never its responsibility.

Oh, but if the bag was checked, it would be a different story. The man would show his claim check. A search would ensue. Telephone calls would be made. Airlines take responsibility for bags that are checked onto their planes. I know, I've had lost bags returned to my home at all kinds of odd hours, and if a bag could not be found, its value has been awarded instead.

The first step to a world view that works is a right relationship with God. When we make that commitment of our lives to Him—God commits Himself to us, totally and permanently. Then we are turned "right-side up." "To the modern man the heavens are actually below the earth. The explanation is simple;

he is standing on his head; which is a very weak pedestal to stand on. But when he has found his feet again he knows it. Christianity satisfies suddenly and perfectly man's ancestral instinct for being the right way up. Joy is the gigantic secret of the Christian."[4] Then, even in the midst of a culture that is following its own schemes and devices, we can be certain that our world will remain in focus and that we will see life for the adventure of faith that it is and always has been.

(Eccles. 7:1–14)

An Above-the-Sun Postscript

There is a way which seems right to a man,
But its end is the way of death.
—Proverbs 14:12

Everyone possesses a world view. Do you have the right world view? Isn't every world view just how each person perceives reality? And if so, who's to say one world view is right and another wrong?

A world view should first correspond to facts and reject demonstrably false notions. Internal consistency provides the second test of a world view. The presence of contraditions logically renders any world view invalid. Third, an integrated or unified theory that envelops facts, theories, and principles will provide a coherent explanation of the world around us. Fourth, a good world view maintains a balance between simplicity and complexity. Fifth, multiple disciplines and arenas of life supply the evidence for the veracity of the world view. Sixth, a good world view can not only withstand the charges of competing visions, but can also refute them.

So, does your world view correspond with reality, with facts plainly evident? Is your world view consistent, or rife with contradictions? Can it explain origin, destiny, and condition? Is it relevant to life? [5] Two practical tests can both illuminate and transform your perspective.

First, the Checkbook-Calendar-Thoughts Test. Take a moment to scan your check register and see where your money went. Track one month's expenditures and you will discover the priorities of your life.

Next, look at your calendar covering the last month. Where did your time go? Whatever you invest your precious minutes in the most, you value the most. Lastly, consciously examine your thoughts for a week as you drift off to sleep and as you wake up. Generally, whatever your mind is contemplating at rest clues you in to your priorities.

The second practical test for transforming your perspective is the Existential Shock Test. You don't have to leave home to see what's really important in life. Jolts to our world view can come by way of visiting shut-ins and nursing home residents, visiting prisoners, tutoring inner city youth regularly, and comforting at AIDS hospices.

10

Accept Life's Mysteries

I shall know why when time is over
And I have ceased to wonder why.
Christ shall explain each separate anguish
In the fair schoolroom of the sky.
                              —Emily Dickinson

C HICAGO CARDINAL JOSEPH BERNARDIN had been a priest for more than forty years and a bishop for nearly thirty when he was accused of sexual misconduct by Steven Cook in the spring of 1994 and sued for $10 million in civil damages. Cook alleged that Bernardin molested him nearly twenty years ago when he was a young Catholic considering a career in the priesthood. He initially accused another priest and then sometime later claimed to remember that Bernardin, too, had seduced him. These memories were said to have surfaced when Cook was hypnotized by a Philadelphia therapist whose services he sought for help in dealing with the stress of his AIDS infection.

When it became clear that Cook's therapist had neither the training nor credentials to substantiate his claims in court, Cook was sent to a clinical psychologist specializing in hypnotism for a second opinion. As a result, he was persuaded to drop the case and later recanted his story, but Bernardin had already suffered tremendous public humiliation as a result of Cook's false accusations. "My life," the Cardinal told *Newsweek* magazine, "will never be the same."[1]

Bernardin was unjustly accused, and although he was publicly exonerated, he understood that he would never be completely free from the accusations. His ordeal is proof (as if it were needed) that we live in a world where bad things happen to good people. Justice is delayed and at times even denied to good men, and evil men are too frequently able to escape it. Solomon observed the ambiguity of life under the sun this way: "I have seen everything during my lifetime of futility; there is a righteous man who perishes in his righteousness, and there is a wicked man who prolongs his life in wickedness" (Eccles. 7:15).

> *We live in a world where bad things happen to good people.*

He had seen the good die young and the wicked live to a ripe old age. He had seen things in his life under the sun that defied his idea of fairness. These injustices astounded King Solomon, and they astound us, too. A few years ago, a book called *When Bad Things Happen to Good People*, written by a prominent rabbi, became a national bestseller. Why do they happen?

Why would a vivacious, inquisitive elementary school teacher with a husband and young children perish before her family's eyes in an ill-fated space shuttle launch? Why would an innocent child be led away from his mother in a London shopping mall and brutally beaten to death by two other boys too young to be tried for their crime as adults? Why?

Wolfgang Mozart, perhaps the most brilliant musical genius to have lived on this earth, died a pauper at thirty-five. Not a single person attended his burial. What other symphonies could he have written—with what more could he have thrilled future generations—if he had lived even another decade? Oswald Chambers, a beloved devotional writer and trainer of young pastors, died in relative obscurity somewhere in Egypt at the age of forty-three. His classic devotional *My Utmost for His Highest*, first published in 1935, has been printed over sixty times and its latest edition was recently ranked third among non-fiction Christian bestselling titles.

Peter Marshall, a brilliant Scottish immigrant preacher and former chaplain of the United States Senate, died at forty-seven. Marshall's charismatic prayers in the Senate chambers touched thousands of hearts and lives. German theologian Dietrich Bonhoeffer died at the age of thirty-nine at the hands of his Nazi captors. He was jailed for his unbending stand for the church at a time when speaking for God was considered foolhardy.

Jim Elliot was twenty-nine when he and four fellow missionaries were murdered by Auca Indians in the Ecuadorian jungle in 1957. Elliot's journals, and his widow Elisabeth's writings, have inspired countless men and women to live with abandon for the cause of Jesus Christ. These and others whose names will never be known lived lives we would call "too short" and were gone too soon. How can their untimely losses be explained? And how can it be that the very Son of God lived only thirty-three years on this earth before He was betrayed by His own and executed on false charges?

"I've seen it all," Solomon said, "and I can make sense of none of it." Not only do good men perish—wicked men prosper. Solomon himself was succeeded by some of the vilest rulers in the history of Israel. Manasseh, son of King Hezekiah, ascended the throne when he was twelve and ruled for fifty-five years. He murdered members of his own family, slaughtered thousands, and filled the Jewish temple with pagan idols. The Bible says the sins of Manasseh were reflected on generation after generation after generation—but this godless, profane, vicious tyrant remained in power for fifty-five years and was the picture of health until the day he died! Why?

Joseph Stalin murdered millions of his own people—and once explained his strategy as a despot by plucking all the feathers from a live chicken and noting that afterward, it stayed near him for warmth. How can mean, murdering, vindictive men live so long and so well, while those who are good, upright, and kind come to tragic ends? Does it bother you? It bothers me. And it bothered Solomon, too.

Who Determines What Is Fair?

If we cry out at injustice, it must be because we carry within us an innate sense of fairness—a sense that is shaped by values we may or may not be able to express. Smith College religion instructor Philip Zaleski illustrates this to his students periodically by administering what he calls "a peculiar little test." The test is simple. He offers a list of fifteen varying items and asks his students to rank them using whatever scale they deem most appropriate. They review the list—"mouse, boy, sun, angel, ant, crab, Norwegian pine, corn, amoeba, hamburger, potato, Moby Dick, Taj Mahal, Rolls Royce, the idea of good"[2]—and plunge in. The results, he says, are always fascinating.

It's not news when good things happen to good people or when bad people receive their due. Only when the opposite occurs.

If a student ranks "crab" over "corn," his choice says something about what he believes a crab or corn to *be*. And while the cumulative effect of the exercise may be "all over the board," no one student could have completed it without a clearly defined, individual sense of hierarchy. Is it fair to boil a crab and unfair to boil a mouse? What is a mouse that a crab is not? Who decides what "fairness" is based upon?

Perhaps Solomon perceived this dilemma only too well and understood that while great injustice or delayed justice challenged his understanding, more often than not, a normative justice quietly prevailed. The exceptions were simply more notable, as they are today. It's not news when good things happen to good people or when bad people receive their due. Only when the opposite occurs. Generally speaking, good things do happen to good people and bad things do happen to bad people, but when they do not, we become reflective.

The Beauty of Balance

At these times, "Do not be excessively righteous," Solomon cautioned, "and do not be overly wise. Why should you ruin yourself? Do not be excessively wicked, and do not be a fool.

Why should you die before your time? It is good that you grasp one thing, and also not let go of the other; for the one who fears God comes forth with both of them" (vv. 16–18). What is he saying? Strive for a trusting balance that allows for some things to be unexplained. Don't run for the shelters of self-righteousness or wisdom or fling yourself into a lifestyle of wickedness as a response to the "randomness" of life. Neither defense mechanism is reliable.

The super-righteous are not only just as vulnerable as the wicked, they're offensive to almost everyone. You've probably seen them in action. They are the sanctimonious "saints" who speak down to "lesser mortals," attemping to impart their exclusive knowledge of the Almighty to anyone who will listen and to some who will not! The Bible speaks of them as immature, but they would never view themselves that way. Oh no, their quiet times are always anointed, and their understanding of Scripture is bullet-proof. Just ask them (if you have to). The only trouble is that their piousness doesn't guarantee them justice or protect them from life's dilemmas.

Wisdom is no shelter from injustice either, Solomon warned. He was certainly most qualified to say so. Even the super-intellectual receives no guarantees against grief or trouble. The brilliant Christian apologist and author C. S. Lewis found his tremendous intellect of little comfort when he lost his wife to cancer just three short years after they were wed: "I thought I could describe a state; make a map of sorrow. Sorrow, however, turns out to be not a state, but a process. It needs not a map but a history, and if I don't stop writing that history at some quite arbitrary point, there's no reason why I should ever stop. There is something new to be chronicled every day."[3] Lewis never "made sense" of his wife's untimely death, in spite of his thorough and articulate examination of its aftermath.

> *If righteousness and wisdom provide no hedge against the ambiguities of life, why not just revel in wickedness?*

If righteousness and wisdom provide no hedge against the ambiguities of life, why not just revel in wickedness? Because it will hasten your death, said Solomon. I believe the majority of adults who die prematurely do so not because of some wicked twist of fate, but as a result of their own lifestyle choices. Drug and alcohol abuse, sexual promiscuity, poor health habits, and a haphazard approach to safety are just a few examples. Someone who seeks to live his life out purely on the basis of his appetites may in fact shorten it.

The answer is not found in the extremes of super-righteousness or wickedness but in allowing ourselves to be held somewhere between the two by the fear of God. Far from being simply an argument for moderation in everything, Solomon's solution is actually quite daring. It requires nothing less than faith: ". . . not a pathetic sentiment, but robust, vigorous confidence built on the fact that God is holy love. Faith is the heroic effort of your life [whereby] you fling yourself in reckless confidence on God."[4]

Our lives are held in balance when we fear God. Our reverent awe of the Almighty keeps us from becoming too self-righteous and judgmental or too wicked and immoral. Balance comes when we focus, not on the mysterious ambiguities of life, but on the character and nature of God. Only when we see Him for who He is can we understand our own impoverished state, as Solomon noted: "Indeed, there is not a righteous man on earth who continually does good and who never sins" (v. 20).

No One Is Righteous

It is relatively easy for us to recognize sin in one another. It is much more difficult to recognize it in ourselves. Worship—fear of God—enables us to see clearly our own sin. Years ago the *London Times* ran an article asking the question, "What is wrong with the world?" It encouraged readers to respond. I am sure the editor must have read the following reply more than once before its profound truth sunk in:

Dear Sir:

In response to your question, "What is wrong with the world?"
—I am.

Yours truly,

G. K. Chesterton

We are what is wrong with the world. God's standard is absolute righteousness, and when we see His holiness, we understand our own impossible limitations. No matter how skilled we may be at dodging our sins, we cannot make them disappear. We cannot deliver ourselves or one another from the capriciousness of this topsy-turvy world, because not one of us is righteous. Sadly, when we see the corruption in our hearts, we are more likely to call for help from others who are in the same boat than we are to reach out to God.

> *We need to cry out to God. He alone is able to save us. His opinion of us is the only one that matters.*

This was true in Moses' day, too. Because intimacy with God can be a risky business, the children of Israel preferred God to speak to them through Moses. "In this way," Richard Foster says, "they could maintain religious respectability without the attendant risks. . . but it was a step away from the sense of immediacy, the sense of the cloud by day and the pillar of fire by night." By enlisting a mediator between ourselves and God, we believe we are saved from His piercing scrutiny, and protected from any compelling need to change our ways.

Caught in our inadequacy, we cry out to others who are just as phony as we are when it comes to righteousness. Instead, we need to cry out to God. He alone is able to save us. His opinion of us —His assessment of the condition of our hearts—is the only one that matters. The flattery or criticism of the world is meaningless, as Solomon noted: "Also, do not take seriously all words which are spoken, lest you hear your servant cursing you. For you also have realized that you likewise have many times cursed others" (vv. 21–22).

We Are God's

It is always a mistake to let the world tell us who we are. The person who allows the world's assessment of his abilities to define him denies the sovereign power of God. I know far too many people who will never teach a Bible class, never sing a solo, never serve God in a ministry, or speak out on His behalf in a meaningful way because they've been wounded by criticism.

Knowing that we belong to God can allow us to "ride out" the injustices and mysteries of life.

John Calvin said that we are not our own, but God's—and that we would be wise to forget both ourselves and the things that are ours, living and dying to Him, and allowing His wisdom and will to preside over our every action. God's sovereignty is more powerful than our present circumstances, the whims of fate, or the unfullfilled prophecies of others. The best response to criticism is to ask God, "Is it true?" If there is an element of truth to it, it is a call to repentence—and we must repent, change, and move on.

Knowing that we belong to God can allow us to "ride out" the injustices and mysteries of life believing that while *we* may not be in control, *He* is. He knows what He is doing. Our assignment is to learn to yield to the divine wisdom of God, saying, "Lord, I don't understand . . . and it doesn't seem fair . . . but I believe in You, and I surrender my will to Yours. Show me Your way so that I might walk in it." Acknowledge God *as* God. We dethrone Him in our hearts, writer Elisabeth Elliot said, when we demand that He act in ways that satisfy *our* idea of justice. His ways, though often mysterious, are always best.

His Mysterious Ways

The Bible is rich with stories of unlikely heroes, victorious underdogs, and surprise endings. Solomon's own father, David, could attest to that. It was certainly not *fair* that David became king. He was the youngest son of his father Jesse and selected over seven strapping, able brothers—each of whom was recommended for the job. But Samuel was listening to God—and God had another plan. He wanted David—shepherd-boy, lion-killer, and sensitive poet/singer—to succeed King Saul. But first. . . He wanted him to wait.

For fourteen years, David stayed in hiding—anointed king but yet uncrowned—he ran constantly from Saul and his army, with a bounty on his head. Why couldn't *Samuel* have waited? Why give the title and withold the office? Why spend years sitting around campfires and hiding in caves? Why couldn't David have been doing something more productive? Because God was preparing David for godly leadership, that's why! Around those fires, in those forced marches, God was building into David the "stuff" he would need to rule the nation of Israel. He was equipping him for the future. God knew what He was doing. He was building within David a heart for Him.

Moses, the mediator, had to learn to wait, too. The voice of God in a burning bush spoke to a burned-out, former prince who had all but given up on leading anyone anywhere. The "right" time for Moses to become a deliverer would have been at the height of his popularity, not the height of his obscurity—right? Well, yes, except God had a better plan. Moses took off his shoes. He worshiped. And God sent him back to Egypt—the scene of the crime—with a tall order: to bring the children of Israel (a million-plus of them) out of bondage, conquer a new land, and establish a nation in Canaan.

There was only one problem. Moses didn't feel like a leader; he was not sure of himself anymore. Who would want an insecure national leader? God, of course. Because Moses didn't need to be sure of Moses—he only needed to be sure of God.

"How will they know I have any authority?" Moses asked God.

"Here, Moses," God replied, "I'll show you some miraculous things to do. Take this staff, for example. Throw it down. It will become a snake. Pick it back up, and it will be your staff again. Or try this: put your hand inside your cloak and draw it out slowly. It will be leprous—as white as snow. Then do it again, and your hand will be restored."

Moses must have still looked unconvinced because God kept going.

"If this doesn't reassure them, Moses, take some water from the Nile River and pour it on the ground. As you do, it will become blood."

Moses was warming to the special effects. He didn't really want to mention it, but in case the Almighty had overlooked it, he felt he must bring one last thing to His attention. "These are great," he hedged, "but there's still one problem. I'm pretty slow of tongue, Lord, and I don't speak very well. Perhaps someone who didn't stutter would be better for what you have in mind. There seems to be a lot to say."

I think this was where Moses might have expected God to offer to heal his affected speech. That would have been *fair*, would it not? But that is not what happened. Instead, God told Moses he would use his brother Aaron as a stand-in. Does that strike you as strange? Why didn't God say, "Moses, I'm going to heal you right now of your slow and stammering speech, so that you'll be able to speak with the eloquence of Charlton Heston, who will play your role centuries later"? Couldn't He have done that? Of course He could—but He didn't. God knew what He was doing.

The greatest evangelist in the history of the church, the apostle Paul, was handicapped—physically challenged. He suffered mightily from an unknown affliction of the flesh, although he prayed repeatedly for it to be removed. I am sure his reasons were virtually unselfish. He was an itinerant preacher—he traveled from church to church, country to country—and probably could have covered more territory had he been well. No man labored harder for the kingdom of God than Paul—didn't he deserve to be made physically whole?

God knew what He was doing. He had a better plan. He gave Paul great revelations to inspire him and great pain to humble him. Paul called his ailment his "thorn" and confessed that it kept him from exalting himself! God did not remove it—but He did give Paul the grace to bear it: "And He has said to me, 'My grace is sufficient for you, for power is perfected in weakness.' Most gladly, therefore, I will rather boast about my weaknesses, that the power of Christ may dwell in me. Therefore I am well content with weaknesses, with insults, with distresses, with persecutions, with difficulties, for Christ's sake; for when I am weak, then I am strong" (2 Cor. 12:9–10).

Paul carried his true treasure—Jesus—in the "earthen vessel" of his broken body to the glory of God. He had no interest in imparting the glory of Paul, but he was passionate about imparting to others the glory of God. His life illustrates a principle that Solomon emphasized: We are clay pots—most of us "cracked," but we can exalt God in our broken places. Every life has "if onlies": If only I had known my father . . . If only I had married someone else . . . If only I had gotten that job . . . If only, if only, if only. Our lives may be full of injustices that are beyond our control, but it *is* up to us to see that they are *not* full of bitterness or regret. "On the contrary," Paul wrote, "who are you, O man, who answers back to God? The thing molded will not say to the molder, 'Why did you make me like this,' will it? Or does not the potter have a right over the clay, to make from the same lump one vessel for honorable use, and another for common use?" (Rom. 9:20–21). God certainly could have healed Paul . . . but He didn't. And He knew what He was doing.

Joseph suffered repeated injustices. Although he was his father Jacob's favorite, no one else seemed too keen on Joseph. His brothers considered murdering him, left him to die, then decided on impulse to sell him to traders on their way to Egypt. He became a slave, rose to a position of trust in a rich man's household, was sexually harrassed by that man's wife, and then went to jail when she falsely accused him of rape. He showed kindness to his fellow prisoners and was then forgotten. Joseph spent nearly all of his adult life separated from his father, his family, and his homeland. He had every excuse to become bitter. God had given him great dreams as a young man, but many years went by with no sign that they would ever be fulfilled.

> *What happened to Joseph was not fair, but he believed that God knew what He was doing and that He had a better plan.*

When circumstances brought him face to face with his brothers decades later, he had no thoughts of revenge. Instead, he gently revealed his true identity to them and spoke these wise (but amazing) words: "And now do not be grieved or angry with yourselves, because you sold me here; for God sent me before you to preserve life. . . .it was not you who sent me here, but God . . . ." (Gen. 45:5, 8a). Joseph's life looked like a series of repeated tragedies and what happened to him was not *fair*, but he believed that God knew what He was doing and that He had a better plan.

Daniel was a young Israelite deported to the land of Babylon at the age of sixteen and hand-picked for government service. He was handsome, wise, and quick-witted—just the kind of "recruit" the Babylonians were interested in assimilating into their pagan culture. Once in King Nebuchadnezzar's court, an attempt began to re-program Daniel and his companions, changing their names and their diets so that they would lose their Jewish identification. But his friends were young men of great character, and they refused to worship Babylonian gods, even though the king commanded it. Instead, they prayed to their God when the call to worship was sounded.

Charges of treason were brought against three men—Shadrach, Meshach, and Abed-nego—for their refusal to worship Nebuchadnezzar's golden images, and they were brought before the king. He gave them an opportunity to reconsider or be cast into a blazing furnace; they said no to his second offer as well: "If it be so, our God whom we serve is able to deliver us from the furnace of blazing fire; and He will deliver us out of your hand, O king. But even if he does not, let it be known to you, O king, that we are not going to serve your gods or worship the golden image that you have set up" (Dan. 3:17–18).

God could save these men out of the fire—or He could choose not to. They acknowledged His sovereignty. They might live or they might die but either way, they were determined to be faithful to God. Nebuchadnezzar was furious. He ordered the fire to be stoked seven times hotter than normal, and the three men were bound and thrown in. The furnace was so hot the men who carried them up were consumed, but Shadrach, Meshach, and Abed-nego fell inside.

When Nebuchadnezzer peered inside, he saw not three bound men, but four—loosed and walking around in the middle of the fire unharmed. The fourth man, the king said, was like "a son of the gods." Nebuchadnezzar called them out of the furnace and they walked out unharmed—no singed hair, no burned clothing. In fact, they didn't even smell like smoke! When he saw this, the king responded: "Blessed be the God of Shadrach, Meshach and Abed-nego, who has sent His angel and delivered His servants who put their trust in Him, violating the king's command, and yielded up their bodies so as not to serve or worship any god except their own God" (v. 8). Nebuchadnezzar worshiped their God, too, and passed a decree that made speaking against Him an offense punishable by death because "there is no other god who is able to deliver in this way" (v. 29).

A Just God in an Unjust World

Justice does not always rule in our world. History illustrates it. Headlines confirm it. Solomon observed and recorded many injustices that puzzled him. He saw bad men die and receive the respect due saints. He saw justice delayed and give evil ample opportunity to flourish.

> *Justice does not always rule in our world. History illustrates it; headlines confirm it.*

It never made sense to him. "All this I have seen and applied my mind to every deed that has been done under the sun wherein a man has exercised authority over another man to his hurt. So then, I have seen the wicked buried, those who used to go in and out from the holy place, and they are soon forgotten in the city where they did thus. This too is futility" (Eccles. 8:9–10). But while we see delayed justice as an outrage, in truth it is only an interlude for repentence provided by a just—and merciful—God.

When someone else has sinned, I am all for swift and timely justice. Our human courts cannot guarantee justice, however. Although I am convinced that our country's legal system is the best in the world, it cannot (and does not) provide justice for every plaintiff. David Frost has said that a jury is twelve individuals who vote on who has the best lawyer. Tragically, many times that is true. But a day will come when every man and woman who has ever lived will receive justice from the Judge whose pronouncements are never wrong. His name is Almighty God.

Between now and then—in the seeming injustice of our fallen world—we have time for repentence. We have time to get it right. Instead of wringing our hands at the inequities and mysteries of this life, we should be thankful for a sovereign God

179

whose kindness allows the time and space to repent. Solomon said that he saw every work of God, and his conclusion was that "man cannot discover the work which has been done under the sun. Even though man should seek laboriously, he will not discover; and though the wise man should say, 'I know,' he cannot discover" (v. 17). God is at work, although we cannot always understand.

We will never have all the answers in this life. We will be confused at times. We will see things that defy our ideas of justice. We will witness troubling events. But our God is so powerful, so true, so just, that He can "hit straight licks with crooked sticks." His will ultimately will be done. In every mystery of life, God's sovereign grace and love will sustain us. He makes that which is crooked, straight. He makes that which is dark, light. He weaves the threads of our lives into something beautiful and good when we submit to Him in love and worship. "It will be well," Solomon said, "for those who fear God" (v. 12). Fear Him. It *will* be well.

(Eccles. 8:10–17)

An Above-the-Sun Postscript

Anxiety in the heart of a man weighs it down,
But a good word makes it glad
—Proverbs 12:25

In a world of injustice, how should we respond? When we face trials and suffering, how should we think? How should we act?

Be Honest with God

Remember, Christianity is all about a personal relationship with the Lord. We are children of our Heavenly Father and Jesus says we can call Him "Friend." With this Father/Friend relationship we can be honest because He already knows all that we feel before we articulate it and because He loves us without any conditions.

God never said He would love you unless you were angry or disappointed. He loves you in spite of your anger and disappointment, so be honest with your emotions and questions. God can handle any emotion. He wants to handle it.

Also, be honest with trustworthy friends. Find some friends in whom you can pour out your heart and tell them you need to talk, and you need them only to listen. You are not looking for advice, counsel, or correction, merely the listening ear of a friend who understands and will walk through the fire with you.

Focus on Him

This can be excruciatingly difficult when you feel pounded on by life's sledgehammer. Pain may make you believe that it's impossible to look at anything but the blows, but you must try.

Physical and emotional pain certainly hinder our ability to focus, but ultimately we will choose to sink or choose to walk—like Peter in the Gospel of Matthew. But sinking or walking is only the result! What determines the result is a prior choice—will you focus on the storms of life or on the prize of life?

Dwell on His Attributes.

Who do you know the Lord to be? What has He shown you about Himself recently? Remember when you first came to know Him? How sweet was His love? How challenging was His holiness? How exhilirating His grace?

Think back to blessings and victories. Remember a specific answer to prayer, when He helped you through another difficult time. Consider the battles that only the Lord could conquer in your life and He won. The point of dwelling on His attributes and remembering blessings and victories is this: *never deny in the darkness what God reveals to you in the light.* God proved Himself a God of Love, Holiness, and Grace in the light; focus on Him as a God of Love, Holiness, and Grace in the darkness. God hasn't changed, only your circumstances have.

Examine Yourself.

Please hear me when I say suffering and injustice are not always consequences of sin in your life, but sometimes they are. Job suffered and God Himself said Job was blameless, so rest assured that suffering doesn't prove sin. If you are committing sins actively or passively, know that you are now reaping or will soon reap what you sow. Perhaps an honest and meticulous examination of yourself will yield areas of impurity. If so, confess to God your sins. Repent of them. Repentance means to turn 180 degrees. Ask God to cleanse you, to forgive you, to shower mercy upon you.

Fight Tenaciously.

Adversity can destroy your life, but it can also make you stronger. No one experiencing suffering likes to hear this, and I know it rings hollow to those immersed in pain. Still, to quit or surrender to bitterness or hopelessness merely prolonge your misery.

Question, Rage, Grieve, Talk.

After a season of giving free reign to your natural emotions you will come to a fork. Will you continue to walk in despair and bitterness, or will you surrender your will to the mysteries and character of God. God will not, as He showed with Job, answer your questions. Ultimately, at that fork in the road, you will decide to live alone in bitter anger or walk hand in hand with the Lord. "The alternative to disappointment with God seems to be disappointment without God."[5]

The Lord doesn't require you to understand the why's of His ways or the why's of your circumstances. He doesn't expect you to like or appreciate the circumstances themselves. He definitely doesn't ask you to trust your circumstances. He does ask you to trust Him, love Him, and worship Him. "Though He slay me," says Job, "Yet I will trust Him" (Job 13:15).

Remember not only is He your Creator and Sustainer, but also your Savior. He redeemed you for a price that caused Him immeasurable pain. *Emmanuel* means "God With Us." He understands our pain. He became flesh two thousand years ago not only to die on the cross, but also to walk through our human experience. God knows and cares. You ask, "Where is He when I suffer?" He is Emmanuel, God With Us. He is here.

11

Seize the Day

Mr. Meant-to has a comrade
And his name is Didn't-do,
Have you ever chanced to meet them?
Did they ever call on you?
These two fellows live together
In the house of Never-win
And I'm told that it is haunted
By the ghost of might-have-been.
—Samuel Johnson

T HE FOLLOWING ADVERTISEMENT appeared in London newspapers in 1900: "MEN WANTED FOR HAZARDOUS JOURNEY. Small wages, bitter cold, long months of complete darkness, constant danger, safe return doubtful. Honor and recognition in case of success. Ernest Shackleton."[1] Sir Ernest Shackleton had placed this ad to recruit men for the National Antarctic Expedition and was overwhelmed by the tremendous response that it generated. "It seemed," he later said, "as though all the men in Great Britain were determined to accompany me . . . ."[2] Although the expedition subsequently failed to reach the South Pole, it was not for lack of able-bodied, ambitious volunteers.

Life *is* a hazardous journey. King Solomon examined it from beginning to end—its randomness, its mystery, its futility, its pain, and its promise—and shared his findings freely in a rambling, stream-of-consciousness memoir called Ecclesiastes. When every avenue under the sun had been exhausted in his search for meaning in life, Solomon re-considered the God of his youth. Pleasure was ultimately fleeting; philosophy, empty; materialism and education, unsatisfying. Even worldly religion failed to fill the vacuum in his life. Flatland living had yielded no answers. Although he had everything the world could give, it could not satisfy him.

Solomon eventually did what we should do when we discover we are lost. He went back to the place where his journey began. He traded his under-the-sun world view for God's above-the-sun perspective and began to reason from that vantage point. He made value judgments based on the belief that "this world is not conclusion—another lies beyond . . . . "[3] He came to a peaceful co-existence with the ambiguities and injustices of life by embracing the sovereignty of God. Then King Solomon offered some utterly practical, "Been there. Done that" advice to fellow travelers on the hazardous journey.

Choose Life

Solomon minced no words with his audience. Even though God is sovereign, he told them, life is uncertain, and death is certain. "For I have taken all this to my heart and explain it that righteous men, wise men, and their deeds are in the hand of God. Man does not know whether it will be love or hatred; anything awaits him. It is the same for all. There is one fate for the righteous and for the wicked; for the good, for the clean, and for the unclean; for the man who offers a sacrifice and for the one who does not sacrifice. As the good man is, so is the sinner; as the swearer is, so is the one who is afraid to swear" (Eccles. 9:1–2).

> *Whether good or evil, we all will die. What is more, life is as uncertain as death is certain.*

Death, in other words, is "politically correct"—painfully so. Whether good or evil, we all will die. What is more, life is as uncertain as death is certain. Love or hatred can lie ahead, and there is no way for us to know which of the two we will encounter on any given day. The recent award-winning film *Schindler's List* chillingly captured this truth. The Nazi concentration camps were filled with terror. The prisoners knew death was inevitable; they witnessed someone's every day. But would their own come today—or tomorrow? Next week—or next month? No one knew.

Many of us are like Woody Allen—we are not afraid to die, but we just don't want to be there when it happens.

No technology developed since Solomon lived has made it any more possible to predict the future. Ours is a capricious world. Love might await or hatred might lurk. Anything can happen. Jane Elder has been a member of the Second Baptist Church of Houston, Texas for over fifty years. Now approaching ninety "years young," Jane still serves faithfully on our staff, directing various missions efforts, teaching, and leading others to Christ. She has never married, but who knows? One day soon Jane might fall in love and have a big church wedding! Love might come along—and Jane assures me she's open to that!

Anything can happen. Simply glance at the newspaper headlines. Murder is a routine occurrence in hundreds of cities across our nation. News that an innocent victim has been found dead hardly raises an eyebrow anymore. The uncertainty of life was underscored in a startling way by the death of a young Houston Police Department rookie whose funeral was conducted at our church. He was shot and killed in his own patrol car by a handcuffed prisoner who had been searched three times for a weapon! Hatred might be ahead. It is impossible to know when hatred will touch or change or even end a life.

If someone had said just a little over a decade ago that a former movie actor who was old enough to receive Social Security would be elected president of the United States, who would have believed it? Who, in the mid-1908s, would have predicted that communism would slowly die from within, like an undiagnosed cancer?

Life is uncertain. But death is certain. We are all going to die. Many of us are like Woody Allen—we are not afraid to die, but we just don't want to be there when it happens. Death is a fact of life that must be addressed. It is like an elephant in the living room: we can decorate around it, but it's impossible to ignore. Death is also absolute. The book of Hebrews says everyone has an appointment with death—and it is an appointment we cannot cancel. Robert Bolt writes in *A Man for All Seasons*, "Death comes for us all; even at our birth—even at our birth death does but stand aside a little. And every day he looks toward us and muses somewhat to himself whether that day or the next he will draw nigh. It is the law of nature, and the will of God."[4]

Between life and death, Solomon says, there is evil and insanity: "This is an evil in all that is done under the sun, that there is one fate for all men. Furthermore, the hearts of the sons of men are full of evil, and insanity is in their hearts throughout their lives. Afterwards, they go to the dead" (v. 3). Two brothers are tried for the murder of their parents and claim self-defense. A wife mutilates her husband and charges him with abuse. A former football star buries his wife, is charged with her murder, writes a suicide note then leads police on a surreal, nationally-televised "chase" back to his home, where he allows himself to be arrested. Does anyone doubt that the hearts of men are full of evil and insanity?

> *Life is uncertain, and death is certain—but Solomon's unstinting advice is: "Choose life."*

What does Solomon say in light of all this? Choose life! "For whoever is joined with all the living, there is hope; surely a live dog is better than a dead lion. For the living know they will die; but the dead do not know anything, nor have they any longer a reward, for their memory is forgotten. Indeed their love, their hate, and their zeal have already perished, and they will no longer have a share in all that is done under the sun" (vv. 4–6).

Life is uncertain, and death is certain—but Solomon's unstinting advice is: "Choose life." There is a difference between submitting to existence and choosing to live. Life is not what happens to us while we are waiting to die. Truly living is a choice.

A company in Las Vegas called "Thrillseekers Unlimited" specializes in what it calls an "adrenalin vacation." Owner Rick Hopkins enthusiastically promotes a week of skydiving, bungee jumping, firewalking, paragliding, and rock climbing for the not-so-faint-of-heart. While some might argue that this "full immersion" approach to choosing life is actually more like cheating death, the *thought* is certainly exhilarating! I like the spirit of men like S. L. Potter, a La Mesa, California, resident who bungee jumped for the first time at age one hundred! Potter's children, ages sixty-eight to seventy-four, were vehemently opposed to the leap, but Potter climbed a 210-foot tower and successfully executed his jump. His first words when he got off the cord? "Give me back my teeth!"

> *As long as there is life, there is hope for meaning and for change.*

The motto of the State of South Carolina where I lived and worked for many years is *Dum Spiro Spero*, literally, "While I breathe, I hope." Solomon, in spite of all he had seen of this world, was thoroughly pro-life. A live dog, he pointed out, is better than a dead lion. A dog in Solomon's day was a scavenger; there were no pampered housepets like we have today. Dogs were filthy, vicious, and often carried disease. The lion, however, was the revered patriarch of the animal kingdom. "There are three things which are stately in their march," the king proclaimed, "even four which are stately when they walk: the lion which is mighty among beasts and does not retreat before any, the strutting cock, the male goat also, and a king when his army is with him" (Prov. 30:30–31). But the lowest of the animals alive, he reasoned, is better than the highest, dead.

As long as there is life, there is hope for meaning and for change. As long as there is life, it is possible for us to contribute to our world. But when we die, our memory is eventually forgotten, regardless of what we have done, or how many monuments have been erected in our honor. Even with his above-the-sun perspective, Solomon saw great value in this life lived under the sun. "Choose life," he said, and his words echoed those of another mighty leader of Israel named Moses, when he challenged the people to follow God and inhabit the promised land: "I call heaven and earth to witness against you today, that I have set before you life and death, the blessing and the curse. So *choose life* in order that you may live, you and your descendants, by loving the LORD your God, by obeying His voice, and by holding fast to Him; for this is your life and the length of your days . . . ." (Deut. 30:19–20a).

Live It to the Hilt

Life is to be chosen, Solomon challenged, then fully lived. "Wherever you are," missionary Jim Elliot once wrote, "be all there. Live to the hilt every situation you believe to be the will of God." Jesus intended His followers to live abundant lives, not mediocre ones. "The thief comes only to steal, and kill and destroy; I came that they might have life, and might have it abundantly" (John 10:10). The events of life—ordinary and extraordinary—are to be thoroughly enjoyed. The primary relationships of life are to be celebrated, not taken for granted.

A meal is an ordinary event. Most of us have three of them a day, and over a thousand in the course of a year. But I wonder how many of those meals we will actually enjoy? Americans are notorious for eating on the run—either grabbing a burger in the car on the way to an appointment or plowing through a plate of food with a cellular phone in one hand and a newspaper nearby.

There was a time in the not-so-distant past when family meals were the day's emotional touchstone—when spouses and children gathered not simply to eat but to enjoy one another. In Solomon's age it was typical for families to share their evening meal together, but he may have had a few meals-on-wheels himself and missed the fellowship of family and friends around his table. "Go then, eat your bread in happiness," he advised, "and drink your wine with a cheerful heart; for God has already approved your works" (Eccles. 9:7).

It is better to have a few vegetables and herbs, he said in Proverbs, than the fat of a roasted pig if there is hatred around your table instead of love. Your home may not resemble that of "The Waltons" with three generations of family gathered around a steaming home-cooked meal every night, but a husband and wife, "take-out Chinese" and a few stolen moments of quiet can be just as precious. We can seize the ordinary occasions in our day, and give ourselves over to them wholeheartedly.

Life's special occasions are to be celebrated, as well. "Let your clothes be white all the time, and let not oil be lacking on your head" (v. 8). Enjoy weddings. We can enjoy family reunions and vacations and trips and holidays. Let every day be a special day where we wear white clothes, and put perfumed oil on our heads. White may have been symbolic of living a clean life, and oil, in the Bible, is frequently a symbol of the Holy Spirit. When we live clean lives empowered by the Holy Spirit, every day is a "festival day."

Then, he said to enjoy the special relationships of life: "Enjoy life with the woman whom you love all the days of your fleeting life which He has given you under the sun; for this is your reward in life, and in your toil in which you have labored under the sun" (v. 9). It's strange, isn't it, that Solomon—who had at least a thousand women in his life—would recommend loving but one faithfully? I believe Solomon had one great love in his youth and then took that gift for granted and allowed his relentless pursuit of pleasure to destroy the earthly relationship that could have been most satisfying.

The primary relationships of life should be a source of deep pleasure and satisfaction.

Husbands, God has given you your wife. Enjoy her! Wives, God has given you your husband. Enjoy him! Parents, your children are a gift from God, not an added expense or a hindrance to spontaneity. Enjoy them. I have met hundreds of men and women who regretted the lack of time spent with their loved ones but never anyone who said they took too much delight in their family. The primary relationships of life should be a source of deep pleasure and satisfaction.

Finally, the king advises his listeners to enjoy their work: "Whatever your hand finds to do, verily, do it with all your might; for there is no activity or planning or wisdom in Sheol where you are going" (v. 10). Do you enjoy your work? Do you ever find yourself thinking in the middle of a busy day, "This is so great—I can't believe they pay me to do this?" I have never had a job into which I did not put everything I had. No matter what it was, I tried to give myself to the task completely—and I've had some jobs that few would envy. I've worked in sewers and sold merchandise door-to-door —and I've enjoyed all of it.

Joy may be the missing ingredient in the lives of the men and women of the twentieth century.

I meet folks frequently who tell me they are unemployed, or under-employed, or over qualified, or that their work is not meaningful. My advice to them is the apostle Paul's advice to every working man or woman under the sun: "Whatever you do, do your work heartily, as for the Lord rather than for men; knowing that from the Lord you will receive the reward of the inheritance. It is the Lord Christ whom you serve" (Col. 3:23–24). Whatever we are doing, we should do it with all of our hearts. We should work as if every bit of our labor carried a tag that read, "Inspected by God" and offer our diligence as a sacrifice to Him. We should live to the hilt in our work lives.

Some of us have forgotten how to have fun. Life for many has become so burdensome, so negative, and so bogged down that we can no longer enjoy a good meal, a good conversation with a loved one, or a good, hard day's work. In fact, joy may be *the* missing ingredient in the lives of the men and women of the twentieth century. What has impaired our ability to truly enjoy life? A look at a first-century Christian church may provide some answers.

Identifying the "Joy Thieves"

The apostle Paul brought the news of the message of the gospel to the region of Galatia, establishing churches in the ancient cities of Antioch, Iconium, Lystra, and Derbe. Many of the early converts to Christianity in Galatia were Jews, and they received the message of salvation by grace through faith in Jesus Christ. But soon afterward, "joy thieves" began a campaign to rob these new believers of their freedom and satisfaction in Christ by demanding that they continue to fulfill Jewish ceremonial law.

Perfectionism

Many succumbed to the trap of *perfectionism*, as this letter from Paul implies: "You foolish Galatians, who has bewitched you, before whose eyes Jesus Christ was publicly portrayed as crucified? This is the only thing I want to find out from you: did you receive the Spirit by the works of the Law, or by hearing with faith? Are you so foolish? Having begun by the Spirit, are you now being perfected by the flesh?" (Gal. 3:1–3).

The new believers in Galatia were liberated, on top of the world, and full of joy. Others did not appreciate their newfound freedom, however, and insisted that these converts continue to adhere perfectly to the rites of Judaism to receive God's favor. The joy thief of perfectionism is not unique to the Church. Certainly perfectionism is deadly to Christians who mistakenly believe that their actions dictate God's acceptance. But perfectionism harms families, friendships, work environments, and a host of other dynamic relationships. The belief that the favor of others is contingent on our consistent, infallible behavior is a notorious joy thief.

Legalism

Legalism is another trap in which we become ensnared and one that robs us of joy. A friend of mine told me about a religious tract he saw being handed out in the streets of a large city. The title of the tract was "Jesus Says Don't." Is that really good news? Jesus says don't. Inside, forty "don'ts" of Jesus were listed—from wearing long hair to withholding gifts from the church. I'm sure the recipients were moved—to run in the opposite direction. The truth is that when we say yes to God in Jesus Christ, He builds into our lives the character to say no to the temptations of Satan. As we abide with Him, disobedience becomes less attractive, and obedience be-

> *The truth is that when we say yes to God in Jesus Christ, He builds into our lives the character to say no.*

comes the norm. We still sin—but by God's grace we are not in the *habit* of sinning.

We obey Him not out of a sense of legalism, but out of a grateful heart of love. We are slaves to sin only if we choose to make sin our master, as Paul pointed out: "However at that time, when you did not know God, you were slaves to those which by nature are no gods. But now that you have come to know God, or rather to be known by God, how is it that you turn your back again to the weak and worthless elemental things, to which you desire to be enslaved all over again?" (Gal. 4:8–9). Legalism is slavery, and trying to please God (or people) with a list of "don'ts" is a genuine joy-killer.

Conformity

The third joy thief we encounter frequently is *conformity*. It is a mistake to strive to conform to someone else's standard of righteousness. "You were running well," Paul wrote his friends at Galatia. "Who hindered you from obeying the truth?" (Gal. 5:7). Race horses frequently wear blinders to keep them from being distracted by the other animals on the track. Their focus should be on the race before them, not on their competitors. Paul used the same symbolism when he wrote " . . . and let us run with endurance the race that is set before us, fixing our eyes on Jesus, the author and perfecter of faith . . . " (Heb. 12:1b–2a).

The prayers of a new Christian are frequently fresh and unselfconscious. "God are you there?" he might ask. "Well, God, I'm here, and I'm not quite sure how to handle this situation. I've really messed up and I need You, if You have time, to help me a little bit." That's a reasonable prayer, is it not? But if he stays around the church for a while, he'll get the idea that his prayer is not quite "spiritual" enough, and before long he'll conform to the norm he observes. Soon his prayers will sound like this: "Our heavenly Father, Thou art almighty and all-wise. Thou knowest my needs even better than I do and art ever-ready to helpest Thy servant . . .. " Conformity.

When I first started to preach, I was unsure who God meant for Ed Young the preacher to be. But I knew that Billy Graham was a man whose deep commitment and confident, engaging style I greatly admired. I used to watch Billy Graham preach and try to be like him. I picked up his phrase, "The Bible says," and used it often. But Dr. Graham, if he had known, would have discouraged that kind of conformity. I read that George Mueller prayed for eight hours in the snow, and I was convicted by his testimony to become a man of prayer—but since it didn't snow much where I lived, I could hardly emulate his practice under such Spartan conditions. Conformity is a joy-thief, but "fixing our eyes on Jesus" is a joyful, life-giving exercise.

> *Loving Jesus more is not the answer. The answer is realizing how much He loves me.*

Jesus, in the first sermon He ever preached, declared that He came to set men free. Unfortunately, many of us are like the Galatian Christians who wanted to exchange their freedom for the chains of perfectionism, legalism, and conformity. For many years I wished I could love Jesus more. Now I understand that loving Jesus more is not the answer. The answer is realizing how much He loves me. My love for Him will always be a responsive love. First John 4:19 says it: "We love, because He first loved us." When we begin to comprehend His love, our motives are changed and our lives are infused with spontaneity, joy, liberty, and reciprocal love.

Solomon did not have the entire picture in Ecclesiastes. His understanding of the Almighty was limited to the God he observed in nature, and in nature we see only the back of God. Scripture reveals the mouth of God. But in Jesus—and in Him alone—we see the face of God. Ecclesiastes is but a silhouette—and the face of Jesus Christ fills its shadowed form. Life is uncertain, the king reported. And so it is. Death is certain, he opined, and so it is. But the preacher still recommended life—in its thrilling, terrifying, tragic fullness. He had merely glimpsed joy, but we see it full-faced in the Son of God.

Seize the Day

How can we seize each day and live this life under the sun to the fullest? Solomon suggested three areas of focus for our consideration: our private lives, our people skills, and our professional endeavors.

Our Private Lives

First, he argued convincingly for *an ordered private life.* "Dead flies make a perfumer's oil stink, so a little foolishness is weightier than wisdom and honor. A wise man's heart directs him toward the right, but the foolish man's heart directs him toward the left" (Eccles. 10:1–2). We should live a life that is internally pure—because the least bit of chicanery or indiscretion has the power to taint an otherwise spotless life.

Imagine being served a glass of iced tea in a restaurant, adding lemon and sugar, stirring it all up just right and discovering . . . a dead fly floating in the tea. Would you be satisfied, after calling your waiter over, if he simply took a spoon and removed the offending insect? Certainly not. You would want a new glass of tea, even if the fly only "swam" in a small portion of it. A little touch of evil in a man's private life can contaminate the whole.

A little touch of evil in a man's private life can contaminate the whole.

When Solomon's father, King David, is mentioned, most adults remember his disastrous affair with Bathsheba, the wife of another man. (Children, thankfully, are more likely to recall his victorious battle with the giant Goliath.) When Richard Nixon is named, what comes to mind—great strides in foreign policy or a bungled burglary known as Watergate? What is your first mental association with the name Edward Kennedy? A life-long career of public service, or a bridge near Chappaquidick?

You see, life is a lot like baseball. If Michael Jordan can get three hits every ten times at bat in his "second career," he will be considered a successful baseball player. But if he makes one error on every ten balls he attempts to field, he will almost certainly be cut from his team. One dead fly can make a bottle of perfume stink, Solomon said. It is important that we "live pure" and equally important that we "think right." The "right" in this verse represents that which is worthy of our effort and pursuit. The "left" is that which is unworthy of our effort and pursuit. Paul elaborates on this idea of right thinking in his letter to the Philippian believers: "Finally brethren, whatever is true, whatever is honorable, whatever is right, whatever is pure, whatever is lovely, whatever is of good repute, if there is any excellence and if anything worthy of praise, let your mind dwell on these things" (Phil. 4:8).

> *Ordering our private lives means striving for purity of character and cultivating the habit of right thinking.*

Left-handedness was viewed as negative in Solomon's day; in fact, the word for left-handed in Latin is sinister. When Jesus talks of the last judgment in the Gospel of Matthew, He says the Shepherd will separate the sheep from the goats, placing the sheep on the right, and the goats on the left. Ordering our private lives means striving for purity of character and cultivating the habit of right thinking.

Our People Skills

Second, we can seize the day by *improving our people skills*. "If the ruler's temper rises against you, do not abandon your position," said Solomon, "because composure allays great offenses" (Eccles. 10:4). In other words, stay calm. When the boss with a fiery temper explodes in our presence, although our first response might be to fire back, "I quit!"—don't. We remain calm, and by our serenity and coolness, we will likely defuse a volatile situation. "A gentle answer turns away wrath," the king wrote in Proverbs, "but a harsh word stirs up anger" (Prov. 15:1).

Discernment is another critical people skill. "There is an evil I have seen under the sun," Solomon said, "like an error which goes forth from the ruler—folly is set in many exalted places while rich men sit in humble places. I have seen slaves riding on horses and princes walking like slaves on the land" (Eccles. 10:5–7). We should sharpen our discernment and not take things at face value, especially where people are concerned. Position may or may not equate with power. Titles may or may not accurately reflect a person's skill. We should observe and look beneath the surface. Some very foolish individuals have been exalted and elevated beyond their level of competence, while other wise, insightful individuals who could have made tremendous contributions have been overlooked.

Professional Wisdom

Finally, King Solomon advises, we seize the day by *exercising professional wisdom*: "He who digs a pit may fall into it, and a serpent may bite him who breaks through a wall. He who quarries stones may be hurt by them, and he who splits logs may be endangered by them. If the axe is dull and he does not sharpen its edge, then he must exert more strength. Wisdom has the advantage of giving success. If the serpent bites before being charmed, there is no profit for the charmer" (vv. 8–11). Snakes, stones, logs, axes —what is this all about? It is about professionalism. Whatever we do, the king advises, we should work smarter—not simply harder. We consider the consequences of our actions. We have a plan. We take the long term look—not the short term glance. We examine all the options. We discuss the contingencies. There is always risk in opportunity, so the wise person is not blinded by dollar signs. Even the most routine task requires concentration; we do not just close our eyes and swing.

> *Anyone who decides to seize life and live it for the glory of God will face two adversaries: himself and the world.*

The Challenge to a Victorious Life

Anyone who decides to seize life and live it for the glory of God will face two adversaries: himself and the world. Himself? That's right. Listen to the gut-wrenching confession of the man whose picture should appear beneath the words "carpe diem" in the Latin dictionary, the apostle Paul: "For I know that nothing good dwells in me, that is, in my flesh; for the wishing is present in me, but the doing of the good is not. For the good that I wish, I do not do; but I practice the very evil that I do not wish. But if I am doing the very thing I do not wish, I am no longer the one doing it, but sin which dwells in me. I find then the principle that evil is present in me, the one who wishes to do good" (Rom. 7:18–21).

Paul's first obstacle in living the abundant life was himself! We somehow forget that we are all depraved. We were *born* depraved. And there is something about our inherent depravity that we need to know: It will never change as long as we live. That's right—our depraved nature will not improve. It cannot be surgically removed or tamed into obedience. It is with us for the remainder of this life. It matters not how much we love God, how much we pray, or how sorry we are for our shortcomings. Moreover, our depraved nature acts like a magnet, drawing all that is depraved in this world to it, thus beginning a vicious cycle. From our depravity we move to permissiveness. From our permissiveness we move to promiscuity. From our promiscuity we move to guilt, from guilt to rationalization, and finally from rationalization to rebellion.

If you are unconvinced ("I just have a little problem with temptation; I certainly wouldn't consider myself *depraved. . . .*"), examine further the words of Paul: "There is none righteous, not even one; there is none who understands, there is none who seeks for God; all have turned aside, together they have become useless; there is none who does good, there is not even one. Their throat is an open grave, with their tongues they keep deceiving, the poison of asps is under their lips; whose mouth is full of cursing and bitterness; their feet are swift to shed blood, destruction and misery are in their paths, and the path of peace they have not known. There is no fear of God before their eyes" (Rom. 3:10–18).

There is something about our inherent depravity that we need to know: It will never change as long as we live.

Not only is man depraved, our world is dark. We live in a "talk show" culture where every troubled, confused, lost soul is given equal billing with the semi-normal among us, and where history, truth, and experience are all under attack. Few events in history have been more thoroughly documented than the holocaust. There are

Nazi soldiers still alive who have verified the atrocities of the Third Reich. There are Allied soldiers still alive who liberated those remaining in the concentration camps. Yet this year a national poll reported that a third of Americans agree it is possible that the holocaust did not take place. Amazing! The Cherokee Indians are now claiming they invented styrofoam, and Alex Haley has said that history was written by the strong who conquered the weak. The deconstruction of history is alive and well. Day after day the sickness of the world calls out to the sickness within men's souls to confound those who would rise above the darkness.

Is there hope? Can we live a full, free, abundant life? "Wretched man that I am!" Paul cried out. "Who will set me free from the body of this death? Thanks be to God through Jesus Christ our Lord! So then, on the one hand I myself with my mind am serving the law of God, but on the other, with my flesh the law of sin" (Rom. 7:24–25). Is there hope? Oh yes. Our hope is in the Lord Jesus Christ and the Holy Spirit. There is cause for hope in the One who invaded this world from above the sun to set us free from sin and death.

When we receive Him, the Holy Spirit gives us the power to strive successfully and win our battles with ourselves and with the world. How do we win? How does the new nature conquer the old nature? How does the spirit overcome the flesh? We win in the battle of the mind. What are we feeding our mind? Who are our friends? What are we watching? What are we reading? What are we listening to? What are we thinking of? What does the landscape of our private world look like?

An old story is told of a dog sledder in Alaska who owned two dogs: one black and the other white. Once a month he would bring the dogs to town and pit them against one another, taking bets from the townspeople on which dog would win. Sometimes the white dog would be victorious; on other occasions the black dog would win. The fights were not fixed; in fact, they were quite ferocious—but the owner always bet on the winning dog. When he finally stopped fighting the animals, he was asked how he could always tell which dog would win. "That's easy," he replied. "The one I feed."

He would starve one dog for a week or two, feed the other well, then let them fight. The starving dog would lose; the well-fed dog would win—every time. If the old, depraved nature is winning consistently in your life, check your eating habits. Which "dog" are you feeding? If an abundant life free from the heart's wickedness and the world's filth is what you desire, you need a new nature. Jesus Christ can give that. His Spirit in us is our only hope of glory. We must be hungry for God—and for the goodness that a life with Him yields. "We are half-hearted creatures," said C. S. Lewis, "fooling about with drink and sex and ambition when infinite joy is offered us, like an ignorant child who wants to go on making mud pies in a slum because he cannot imagine what is meant by a holiday at the sea. We are far too easily pleased."[5]

Let us seize the day. Let us live like men and women of the King, and feed ourselves at His royal banquet table. Let us choose life and live it to God's glory and to our good. *Carpe diem.*

(Eccles. 9:1–18)

An Above-the-Sun Postscript

Watch over your heart with diligence,
For from it flow the springs of life.
                                    — Proverbs 4:23

Do you want to simply survive or do you want to really *live*?

Get Alone

Reflect. Take in a sunset by yourself. Take a deep breath. Slow down. Step out of the crazy, hectic pace and take a hard look at your life and relationship with the Lord. If you don't have time for this you only have time to survive. The choice is yours. What gods are you following? What circumstances or pain are you saying must be changed before you can really *live*?

Get Purpose

Align your purposes with His. What is His will? Put your life "on the altar" becoming alive to Him. Pray to be made holy and sanctified, to be mature, to be completely yielded to your Sovereign God.

   Resolve to spend time daily in God's word. Write down His commands and desires, and commit each day to yielding to His Spirit so that Jesus can live His life through you. Envision your future family and career in light of God's Word. Live out a specific command that day, by the power of the Holy Spirit. Ask yourself, "Is my purpose to do all I can to get a little more glory for the Lord, or to get a lot more of something else for myself?"

Forsake False Gods

Resolve to throw away the opiates of death—mind-numbing television, escapism, illicit sexual intimacy, selfish pursuit of money or status that makes the attainment of those ends a god.

Psalm 16:11says: He has made known the path of *life*. Come into His presence. Praise Him with gladness, adoration. Exalt Him, magnify His name. Read His word intently. Pray to Him. Listen to Him. Be still and allow Him to wash over you, cleansing, remaking, conforming, challenging.

Choose Joy

Remember that pain is inevitable but misery is optional. Scream to yourself that "Life is *difficult!*" and allow that truth to permeate your being. No longer expect life to be easy or idyllic.

Thank. Start looking for things to thank the Lord for, tough things and easy things. Tell others what is so awesome. Drink in *life* and spread the praise of the Author of *life*.

> Come, all you who are thirsty,
> come to the waters,
> and you who have no money,
> come, buy and eat!
> Come, buy wine and milk
> without money and without cost.
> Why spend money on what is not bread,
> and your labor on what does not satisfy?
> Listen, listen to me, and eat what is good,
> and your soul will delight in the
> ichest of fare.
> Give ear and come to me;
> hear me, that our soul may live.
> —Isaiah 55:1–3

12

Dare to Lead

We need commanders for spaceship earth
who can not only keep the atmosphere
of the spaceship liveable, but, more urgently,
can also bring the crew to the belief that
there is a future and a hope—
a star to steer by.

—Leighton Ford

DEPUTY SHERIFF BARNEY FIFE of the mythical hamlet of Mayberry, North Carolina, was running for office in an old episode of "The Andy Griffith Show." Eager to learn some necessary skills from his superior, Sheriff Andy Taylor, Barney asked Andy how he had acquired his unusually good judgment. "Well, Barn," Andy said, "I guess you could say good judgment comes from experience." Barney considered that for a moment. "Then where does experience come from?" he asked, to which Andy replied, "Experience comes from bad judgment."

Solomon's experience as a leader was unmatched. He ruled as Israel's king for forty years, and his accomplishments were great. Under his direction, Israel rose to the peak of her size and glory. His achievements, including the construction of the mighty temple in Jerusalem, brought him worldwide fame and respect. But Solomon's initial zeal for God diminished later in life as his pagan wives and concubines turned his heart away from true worship. His forty-year reign, which was marked by early success, ended in bitter disappointment. His heart was divided, and in the end so was his kingdom.

> *Leadership is assuming responsibility for building relationships with grace.*

King Solomon exhibited good judgment in the beginning of his reign, exercising the gifts of wisdom and discernment that were given to him by God. But the leadership principles he spoke of at the end of his life were those shaped from the crucible of experience and forged in the fires of bad judgment.

Our day desperately needs leaders. Any serious conversation about business, politics, world events, or popular culture will eventually turn to the subject of leadership. What is leadership? Leadership is assuming responsibility for building relationships with grace. How can we identify a leader? A leader steps out, and others follow, consistently and enthusiastically over time. Leadership has little or nothing to do with title or salary. The goods don't come with the nametag. As with many things, our perception of leadership is frequently formed by seeing *what it is not*. Looking at Solomon's writings on leadership is like viewing the negative of a photograph: The true image is reversed.

What a Leader Is *Not*

First, the king describes a non-leader's words. "Words from the mouth of a wise man are gracious, while the lips of a fool consume him; the beginning of his talking is folly, and the end of it is wicked madness. Yet the fool multiplies words. No man knows what will happen, and who can tell him what will come after him?" (Eccles. 10:12–14). Solomon recognized the dangers of putting a little person in a big position. Just let him talk, the king observed, and his own words will devour him.

Leaders-in-training at West Point begin their freshman year with a rather small vocabulary. Plebes answer questions from their superiors in only four ways: Yes sir; No sir; No excuse, sir; and Sir, I don't understand. "Yes, sir" and "No, sir" teach the value of being direct. "No excuse, sir" makes sure they learn to think in terms of teamwork and success. "Sir, I don't understand" impresses cadets with the importance of making sure instructions and expectations are crystal clear. It is a rather limited vocabulary, but it works—and any system for developing leaders that has been honed for nearly two centuries probably has as much to teach business executives as it does future four-star generals.

Non-leaders in leadership positions tend to say too much. What is only benign chatter may, in the end, become quite dangerous. I was amazed at what came from the lips of some of our own newscasters during the Persian Gulf War. The Iraqi defense efforts were reportedly aided simply by tuning in to CNN, where strategic communication was shared with a worldwide audience in the name of "breaking news." (Apparently "breaking news" beats national security interests in a ratings show-down.)

A non-leader's words are reckless. Leaders understand the impact and the power of words. They choose them carefully and handle them as if they might detonate—because sometimes they do. "When there are many words," King Solomon wrote in Proverbs, "transgression is unavoidable, but he who restrains his lips is wise" (Prov. 10:19). I learned many years ago that before I broadcast my profound opinion based on excellent insight, I had better get all the facts that are available and seek the whole truth, not just a piece of it. The fool is indiscreet, but a leader carefully measures his words.

Leaders understand the impact and the power of words.

What about a non-leader's works? Often his energy is misdirected due to lack of experience. "The toil of a fool so wearies him that he does not even know how to go to a city," said Solomon (Eccles. 10:15). This is a picture of someone who needs to work smarter, not just harder. It is possible to arrive at work at 5:00 A.M. and leave fifteen hours later, having accomplished very little. The ineffective leader is worn out but completely unproductive. His labor does not benefit him or those whom he directs.

Leaders have to discover and use their own personal style. Borrowing from a mentor or blindly adopting the methods of a successful predecessor will not work. Composer Irving Berlin once offered the then-undiscovered George Gershwin a job at triple his own salary and then advised him to turn it down. "If you take it," he told him, "you may develop into a second-rate Berlin. But if you insist on being yourself, someday you will become a first-rate Gershwin." There is nothing more wearying and unproductive than imitating someone else.

A non-leader's inexperience may also be reflected in his ways—his work ethic. "Woe to you, O land, whose king is a lad and whose princes feast in the morning. Blessed are you, O land, whose king is of nobility and whose princes eat at the appropriate time—for strength and not for drunkenness. Through indolence the rafters sag, and through slackness the house leaks" (Eccles. 10:16–18). The picture Solomon paints here is of a young king who "plays" at the game of royalty and surrounds himself with equally inexperienced friends, literally intoxicated by the power of their newly-acquired positions.

Do not misunderstand. There is nothing wrong with being young, only with being young and dangerously irresponsible. Paul encouraged his youthful disciple Timothy to offset his limited years with sound action: "Let no one look down on your youthfulness, but rather in speech, conduct, love, faith and purity, show yourself an example of those who believe" (1 Tim. 4:12). The young leader who is wise will surround himself with seasoned counsel, as Proverbs 11:14 recommends: "Where there is no guidance, the people will fall, but in an abundance of counselors there is victory."

Some will never believe this, but the input of two or three or four sharp counselors will put any decision-maker way ahead of the game. William G. Pagonis, the lieutenant general and logistics wizard responsible for moving the equivalent of the population of Alaska (and their personal belongings) to the other side of the world in Operation Desert Storm, formed a team of advisors he called the "log cell." Members of the log cell reported directly to Pagonis and acted as an ad-hoc "think tank," communicating honestly to their superior when asked for advice. They were expected to provide fast, no-nonsense feedback and were given the freedom to point out what they deemed to be ill-advised plans.

Every leader needs to create an atmosphere where trusted advisors can speak the truth in love. Sound decisions generally flourish where there is free and open dialogue and a healthy sense of give and take. The leader who is inexperienced but insists on doing it alone is making a self-indulgent (and serious) mistake.

Inexperienced leaders may also be tempted to view their position not as a serious responsibility, but as something of a party. The idea that a position of leadership is a "perk" is demonstrated by those who are non-leaders. Max DePree, in his book *Leadership Is an Art*, says, "The first responsibility of a leader is to define reality. The last is to say thank you. In between the two, the leader must become a servant and a debtor. That sums up the progress of an artful leader."[1] The essence of leadership is servanthood, a truth that seems especially foreign to politicians, who are also known, oddly enough, as "public servants."

> *Every leader needs to create an atmosphere where trusted advisors can speak the truth in love.*

Political writer Peggy Noonan imagines the following conversation between a congressman and one of the voters who elected him:

> Voter: "Do what is right!"
> Politician: "But you'll kill me!"
> Voter: "Maybe, but do it anyway! I hired you to go to Congress to make hard decisions to help our country. Take your term, do it, and go home. Kill yourself!"
> Politician: "But I have seniority and expertise and I'm up to speed on the issues. Replace me and it'll be six years before he knows what I know."
> Voter: "Well maybe we don't want him to know what you know. Maybe we want someone dumb enough not to know what's impos-

sible and brave enough to want to do what's right."
Politician: "But I love this job."[2]

Too much, perhaps.

The finest illustration of servant leadership that I know does not come from the pages of *The Harvard Business Review*, but from the pages of the Bible. The Son of God was the ultimate servant-leader: "But Jesus called them to Himself and said, 'You know that the rulers of the Gentiles lord it over them, and their great men exercise authority over them. It is not so among you, but whoever wishes to become great among you shall be your servant, and whoever wishes to be first among you shall be your slave; just as the Son of Man did not come to be served, but to serve, and to give His life a ransom for many" (Matt. 20:25–28).

True leaders are quite willing to live in obscurity, but they seldom do. Non-leaders are likely to become infatuated with their own image and to believe their own press releases. A young member of our staff reports that his first boss shared these words from the prophet Obadiah with him in his early days of ministry: "Behold, I will make you small among the nations; you are greatly despised. The arrogance of your heart has deceived you, you who live in the clefts of the rock, in the loftiness of your dwelling place, who say in your heart, 'Who will bring me down to earth?' Though you build high like the eagle, though you set your nest among the stars, from there I will bring you down, declares the LORD" (Obad. 2–4). He says hearing those words was like an inoculation against self-importance.

> *The Son of God was the ultimate servant-leader.*

I'm reminded of the humorous story of a visit by the president of the United States to a nursing home. The president entered the facility with his entourage and was received with delight by the elderly residents. As he went from person to person in the living area, he noticed a woman in a wheelchair who seemed rather disinterested. Months of campaigning for election had taught him how to "work the room," and he did not want to offend someone who might be around to vote in the next race. He approached her, smiled, patted her shoulder, and gently squeezed her frail hand. She smiled back but said nothing. "Do you know who I am?" the president asked. "No," she replied, "but if you'll ask the lady at the nurses' station over there, she'll tell you." So much for fame.

Finally, a non-leader looks for the quick fix, but a leader sees the long-term. One of the tremendous problems in American industry today is the tendency of its leaders to take a short-sighted look at the bottom line. Solomon aptly described this approach: "Men prepare a meal for enjoyment, and wine makes life merry, and money is the answer to everything" (Eccles. 10:19). Wise corporations put things in perspective, and their leaders are often willing to sacrifice short-term profits for long-term growth. West Pointers learn this as the concept of the "hard right." Taking the "hard right" means learning to make decisions that affect the widest number of people positively, even if it hurts. Johnson & Johnson executives illustrated this in the 1980s when they recalled the entire inventory of Tylenol after a few poisoned bottles were found—a move that put the company at great short-term financial risk but ensured the safety of its customers.

> *A non-leader looks for the quick fix, but a leader sees the long-term.*

A real leader is normally generous, conscientious, caring, self-sacrificing, and industrious. A non-leader is tight-fisted, lazy, arrogant, and irresponsible. Under his authority, Solomon says, the rafters sag and the house leaks. But perhaps the non-leader's greatest hindrance is that he is always on the defensive. There is usually someone ready to step in and do a better job. Non-leaders are often threatened by the abilities of others. A non-leader in a position of leadership is second-guessed constantly—and frequently has a problem with loyalty.

The Laboratory of Leadership

I believe the laboratory of leadership should be the home. A laboratory is a place where you can experiment in reasonable safety. Adam and Eve provided the first laboratory of leadership, since theirs was the first home, but the experiment quickly went awry.

First Eve was deceived and then Adam was disobedient—and there is a difference between the two. Adam, you see, was the one with spiritual responsibility and accountability for their home. Had he assumed that responsibility for building relationships with grace, he would not have listened to Eve when she suggested their change in diet. Instead, Eve's deception and Adam's disobedience caused us to inherit our sin nature at birth.

Adam failed to exercise *spiritual leadership*. Much has been written and said about the concept of spiritual leadership in the home and the man's role as the spiritual leader. But many misconceptions exist. A spiritual leader, for example, is not a preacher, proclaiming "so shall it be," or "thus sayeth the man." Not at all. Spiritual leaders lead more often by graceful example than by autocratic dictum. It is not necessary that a spiritual leader be eloquent or prone to speeches, either. He does not need to possess the salesman's gift of gab or the politician's smooth rhetoric.

The person who has to tell you he's the boss, probably isn't.

A spiritual leader is not a field general, lining up the troops and giving orders: "Allright, Susie, you do this. Billy, you do this. I expect everyone to complete his task by 0700 hours. Count off!" Nor is he assuming. The person who has to tell you he's the boss, probably isn't. The true spiritual leader may actually be a man of few words.

A spiritual leader is not God. God does not need a stand-in. He is capable of convicting, correcting, and judging the motives of the heart on His own. A spiritual leader is not an idealist. He does not cling to an unrealistic, holier-than-thou view that keeps everyone around him on a constant guilt trip. He does not insist on perfectionistic standards or demand an unattainable level of efficiency. But a spiritual leader *is* a lover. He is a lover of God and a lover of his family. This is commanded in Ephesians, chapter 5, when Paul writes, "For the husband is the head of the wife, as Christ also is the head of the church, He Himself being the Savior of the body. But as the church is subject to Christ, so also the wives ought to be subject to the husbands in everything." Hold on. Watch this. "Husbands, love your wives, just as Christ also loved the church and gave Himself up for her; that

He might sanctify her, having cleansed her by the washing of water with the word, that He might present to Himself the church in all her glory, having no spot or wrinkle or any such thing; but that she should be holy and blameless. So husbands ought also to love their own wives as their own bodies. He who loves his own wife loves himself . . . ." (Eph. 5:23–28).

A spiritual leader has integrity. His public world and his private world are in harmony with each other.

That's what spiritual leadership is about. A spiritual leader initiates. Too many leadership laboratories today are run by passive men. Real leaders initiate—touching, affirming, dealing with difficulties. A spiritual leader cultivates intimacy. He shares his failures and his worries and encourages his loved ones to do likewise. He allows them to walk inside his life and seeks to maintain a transparency that is inviting and warm. A spiritual leader exercises influence. He is a natural teacher and is not afraid to say, "This is what I believe . . ." A spiritual leader identifies with others. He does not hold himself aloof. He relates to others where they are and says, "I've been there, too, and I understand." And a spiritual leader has integrity. His public world and his private world are in harmony with each other.

This is a picture of a spiritual leader. It is possible for men to be such leaders. But they have to see their goal clearly, and pursue it with single-minded passion, like the mother in the following story. A young mother of four small children loaded the kids in the car on a Saturday to do some shopping. She herded them successfully through the grocery store without incident. She took them to a shoe store and had them all fitted for new shoes. A stop at the dry cleaners and the gas station followed. By this time, the children were "at that point." If you are a parent, you know what I mean. The younger ones were crying; the older ones were fighting. She was driving and trying to referee the free-for-all at the same time.

She knew the problem. They were hungry. Since it was almost lunchtime, she drove into Wendy's and ordered all the kids a

Fun-Meal. (For the uninitiated, a Fun-Meal is a hamburger, fries, a drink, and a toy.) She paid at the window, distributed the meals among the children, and headed back down the freeway to run a final errand. In just a matter of moments, chaos erupted again when one child discovered her Fun-Meal had no hamburger. Mom was tired and frustrated. She whipped the car around and drove back to the restaurant.

With the incomplete Wendy's Fun-Meal in hand, she marched up to the counter and demanded her rights: "My daughter didn't get a burger. Could you put a burger in this bag, please?" The counter attendant stared blankly at her. "Did you hear what I said?" she asked, her voice rising. "My daughter didn't get a hamburger with her Fun-Meal. I'm in a hurry and I've got to go. Put one in now!" Still no response. "Look," she said, "my kids are all in the car. I've had it. Give me the burger, or I'll call the manager." The magic words. The girl behind the counter got a burger, placed it in the bag, and handed it back. "Thank you very much," the mother said, and she turned and walked out of. . . McDonald's.

It's amazing what can be accomplished with persistence and a clear cut objective.

The Slippery Slope of Spiritual Erosion

Although Solomon knew the principles of leadership, he failed to practice them in his own life. The book of 1 Kings records his descent down the slippery slope of spiritual erosion as he gradually moved away from God and began to live his life solely under the sun. Unfortunately, what happened to Solomon can happen to us, and *is* happening to many today. But there are warning signs along the way.

When I was in my last semester as a seminary student, I drove seventy-five miles to Wake Forest to attend class every day and another seventy-five miles home at night to Erwin, North Carolina, where I was pastoring a church. I drove that route twice a day, five days a week, for four or five months and, needless to say, I became pretty familiar with it. Out of boredom, I began to time myself to see how quickly I could make the trip. (I do not recommend this.)

One day I was passing through a small town called Coats, North Carolina, when a patrolman pulled me over. I could not believe it. A speed trap. It was just before seven o'clock in the morning, and I was in a hurry to get to class. I was in such a hurry, the officer informed me, that I had passed a twenty-five mile-an-hour zone going fifty-one! He wrote a ticket, and said some stern words that I completely deserved. When he got back to his car, I began talking to myself. "This is ridiculous! How would anybody know to slow down?"

> *Rationalization is the first step in spiritual erosion.*

But when I went back through Coats that evening, I started really looking. And there were the signs. One said, "Speed Zone Ahead." I had never noticed it. Then, "City Limits." I wondered if they were new. "Speed Limit 25" another one read. Then just outside of Coats, "Speed Limit 45." Four signs I had never noticed. Four reminders to slow down, take heed, pay attention. I think I understand what happened to Solomon. He passed by the warning signs—sign after sign after sign, and never noticed—but they were there.

The first step in Solomon's spiritual erosion was *rationalization*. He married outside his faith, although God had clearly instructed him not to. "Then Solomon formed a marriage alliance with Pharaoh king of Egypt, and took Pharaoh's daughter and brought her to the city of David, until he had finished building his own house and the house of the LORD and the wall around Jerusalem" (1 Kings 3:1). Egypt had always been Israel's enemy, but he must have rationalized, that the marriage would ensure peace for God's people. What was one little marriage to the Almighty? This was politics—not religion. It would be a blessing for the nation.

How can we tell whether or not we are guilty of rationalization? Do we deliberately sin and tell God we are doing it for Him? That's rationalization. Sin is never for God—it is for us. Rationalization is the first step in spiritual erosion.

The second step in the king's spiritual decline was *justification*. "Now Solomon loved the LORD, walking in the statutes of his father David, except he sacrificed and burned incense on the high places" (1 Kings 3:3). God was equally clear in His instruction to Solomon about the worship of pagan gods. How did he explain his actions? He loved God, and he reasoned that his love for God (which God certainly must know) justified his disobedient worship. Justification is the explaining to others of our own rationalizations. He sacrificed and burned incense . . . but he loved God—and, besides, it was only done to please his wife and to be agreeable with the neighbors. Rationalization leads to justification.

Then Solomon became comfortable with *unresolved conflict*. He treated a good friend of his father David's unfairly, but he felt no remorse and did nothing to make things right between them. The man's name was Hiram, and he had supplied all the cedar, gold, and silver used in the construction of the temple. He had been the procurement engineer for Solomon's ambitious building project, and, as a reward, the king gifted him with twenty cities in Galilee. But they were worthless. Solomon knew it and when he saw them, Hiram knew it. He had been deceived by his old friend's son—who apparently had none of his father's integrity: "So Hiram came out from Tyre to see the cities which Solomon had given him, and they did not please him. And he said, 'What are these cities which you have given me, my brother?'" (1 Kings 9:12–13a).

> Today's "Lifestyles of the Rich and Famous" look paltry compared to Solomon's extravagance.

Solomon disregarded Hiram's feelings and refused to make him a meaningful gift for all that he had done in the building of the temple. Evidently, the king did not let Hiram's disappointment bother him. He was able to live with the unresolved conflict indefinitely.

Then Solomon began to indulge in *exhorbitance* and *extravagance*. He became a collector of horses and chariots in direct disobedience to the commands of God. In fact, he had so many of both that whole cities were built to store them. Today's "Lifestyles of the Rich and Famous" look paltry compared to Solomon's extravagance. He failed to understand that when God blesses a person, he intends for them to be a blessing to others.

The result of Solomon's spiritual erosion was the victory of his own flesh over his spirit. "Now King Solomon loved many foreign women along with the daughter of Pharaoh: Moabite, Amonite, Edomite, Sidonian and Hittite women, from the nations concerning which the LORD had said to the sons of Israel, 'You shall not associate with them, neither shall they associate with you, for they will surely turn your heart away after their gods.' Solomon held fast to these in love . . . and his wives turned his heart away" (1 Kings 11:1–2, 3b).

Finally, the Bible says that Solomon "did what was evil in the sight of the LORD" (v. 6) and failed to follow Him fully. How could the wisest man in the world fall victim to the sins of the flesh? Simple. Wisdom had nothing to do with his passion. He knew what he should do and should not do—but he did not *will* to do what was right. When a man has rationalized, justified, endured interpersonal conflict, and engaged in extravagance, his flesh is poised to win out over his weaker will when decision time comes.

Satan is not stupid. He knows we will brace ourselves for a full frontal attack, but that we may be oblivious to a series of small skirmishes. He is pleased with a little bit of justification: "I'm just marrying this woman to improve our situation with Egypt; surely God will understand." He is even more encouraged when rationalization begins: "A little incense on the altar— what could it hurt? God knows my heart." Conflict elates him: "Hiram—big deal. He's a pagan anyway. I'm the man—and I am not indebted to anyone. If he's not satisfied with his twenty cities, then forget him!" A tendency toward extravagance is welcomed: "I need this city to store my horses. I need another one for my chariots. And while I'm at it, how about a flat in Rome, a summer palace on the Euphrates, and an army of servants to take care of it all?"

Now Satan has us where he wants us. Slowly, imperceptibly, unbelievably, the flesh wins over the Spirit. "Well, that was Solomon," we might say. "What's that got to do with us?" Just this: "Now these things happened to them as an example, and they were written for our instruction, upon whom the ends of the ages have come. Therefore let him who thinks he stands take heed lest he fall" (1 Cor. 10:11–12). To take heed means to listen.

It means to pay attention to the signs, to act, to slow down to a reasonable speed, and to ask ourselves, "Where am I? Is there erosion in my life? Am I on the slippery slope right now—and if I continue will I end up a leader with more regrets than victories, like Solomon?" The choice is ours.

A Seasoned Leader's Retrospective

Solomon was an old man when he wrote the words of Ecclesiastes. He had become jaded, disillusioned. He was a man who had everything, but missed life. As this seasoned leader looked back, he offered three words of advice to those who would follow him: Rejoice. Remove. Remember.

Rejoice

The first imperative the king gave was to *rejoice*. "The light is pleasant, and it is good for the eyes to see the sun. Indeed, if a man should live many years, let him rejoice in them all, and let him remember the days of darkness for they shall be many. Everything that is to come will be futility" (Eccles. 11:7–8). I believe he was saying, "It's great to get up in the morning!" It certainly beats the alternative, does it not? Each new morning in this world is an opportunity to say, "Bless the Lord, O my soul, and all that is within me bless His Holy Name." Remember, Solomon had lived most of his life without God. Looking back, he saw that there were opportunities for rejoicing that he had missed. Looking ahead, he understood that his days were numbered, and he said, "Rejoice!"

Let us enjoy our youth, follow our dreams, explore, get interested.

Even better, the king advised, we should rejoice while we are young. "Rejoice, young man, during your childhood; and let your heart be pleasant during the days of your manhood. And follow the impulses of your heart and the desires of your eyes. Yet know that God will bring you to judgment for all these things" (v. 9). Let us enjoy our youth, follow our dreams, explore, get interested. I am always concerned about adults who say to children,

"I wish you'd grow up!" Pray, tell me why! Childhood is a blessing. "Man's youth is a wonderful thing," said Thomas Wolfe. "It is so full of anguish and magic and he never comes to know it as it is, until it has gone from him forever."

Someone has said that childhood is for fun, middle age is for work, and old age is for God. Nothing could be farther from the truth. Solomon followed the impulses of his heart and the desires of his eyes as a younger man, forgetting that payday would eventually come. He understood in his advancing years the price he had paid, however. We should know that a reckoning will come, as he warned, and play the game of life by the rules.

I was a pretty good table tennis player growing up. In fact, I was better than pretty good. I worked at it and even won a few tournaments here and there. Table tennis is a great sport. I remember trying to teach a friend who insisted on slamming the ball. He had a hard time understanding that the ball has to hit the *table* before it hits the opponent. He became irritated when I told him his shots were out and finally threw the paddle down in disgust and said, "I don't like this game." Why not? Because he didn't play according to the rules. Table tennis is a great game if we play by the rules. If we don't—there's not much to it. Any age is an age to rejoice when we play the game of life by God's rules. They are not limiting—but liberating!

Remove

The king's second imperative was *remove*. "So remove vexation from your heart and put away pain from your body, because childhood and the prime of life are fleeting" (v. 10). "Vexation" is a strange word in our day, but in the Hebrew language it was actually a combination of two words: anger and resentment. Remove anger and resentment, he advised, because anger plus resentment equals rebellion. Paul understood the importance of this concept when he wrote to the Philippian believers: "Be anxious for nothing, but in everything by prayer and supplication with thanksgiving let your requests be made known to God. And the peace of God, which surpasses all comprehension, shall guard your hearts and your minds in Christ Jesus" (Phil. 4:5–6).

It is impossible to be angry and resentful and experience peace. Francis Schaeffer has said that we lack proper contentment because we cease to believe that God is God or we cease to be submissive to Him. Removing vexation means resting in God's sovereignty and submitting to His plan. Sometimes we can remove pain from our bodies by removing the rebellious attitudes in our hearts, because, generally speaking, rebellion causes pain. Ask an alcoholic or a drug user about physical pain. Ask someone who is sexually promiscuous about the effects of such a lifestyle on the body. Remove the poison of anger and resentment, Solomon said, and our life (and our leadership) will be improved.

> *It is impossible to be angry and resentful and experience peace.*

Remember

Finally, the king said *remember.* "Remember also your Creator in the days of your youth, before the evil days come and the years draw near when you will say, 'I have no delight in them'" (Eccles. 12:1). The word Solomon used for "remember" is stronger than our "don't forget." It is used throughout the Old Testament. When Hannah was unable to conceive and prayed for a child, the Bible says "God *remembered* Hannah." He did not merely consider her or think kindly of her—he acted decisively on her behalf. When God remembered Hannah, she became pregnant and bore a son named Samuel—the priest who would one day anoint Solomon's father David as King of Israel.

So Solomon urged, "Act decisively on God's behalf." He cut God out of the early years of his life but later advocated strong, decisive action for God, especially for the young. Have we remembered God? Have we ever acted decisively on His behalf? Solomon would say, "Just do it!"

Our lives are constantly changing. Very little about your world or mine is the same as it was even a decade ago. The average American changes jobs every five years, changes friends every four years, changes cars every three years, churches every two years, fashion styles every year, and his mind every month—or more. About forty million of us move each year. Between 50 and 60 percent of an average city's population changes every ten years. Our world is "mutable"—fickle.

But God is not. Solomon had been there. Done that. He'd seen many things change over the course of his lifetime, but God remained the same. He proved Himself immutable. I'm convinced that if Solomon had it all to do over again, this world-class leader would stake his life on the One whose nature and character does not change. I believe the sensual and the strange would hold very little charm for him the second time around. I want to believe that he would choose instead to act decisively for God and for His kingdom, forsaking all else.

Leaders are those who help the rest of the world navigate—but a true leader sets his course by a fixed star. Are we ready to lead? At this critical time in history, are we ready to take a stand for God and act decisively on His behalf, knowing that to do so is to fling open the door to a life that is anything but "vanity"?

My good friend Cliff Barrows told me that years ago his dad took him to Yosemite National Park. They toured the park all day, in awe of the majestic valley and its surroundings. At the end of the day, the forest ranger who was leading their group took them to the ridge called Glacier Point. Darkness was falling. Across from them stood a sheer face of rock over a thousand feet high. The ranger said that since early morning men had been burning timber above the cliff, and they could see huge piles of white-hot coals all along the rim.

> *A true leader sets his course by a fixed star.*

As the last rays of light receded from the horizon, a ranger at the top of the cliff called to the small group down on Glacier Point, "Are you ready?" Cliff said the ranger's voice echoed through the valley in a way that sent chills down his spine. The guide near him looked up and answered, "We are ready! *Let the fire fall!*"

At that moment, the men high on the cliff began to shovel the hot coals over the side, the coals bursting into flames as they hit the cool night air. For several minutes this continued, and the group watched in wonder as a fiery wall over a thousand feet high and a hundred yards wide lit the night sky. No one moved. No one spoke. Mesmerized, they watched the fire fall.

Are we ready? Rejoice in Him. Let us remove rebellion and resentment from our lives. Remember God all of our days . . . and let the fire fall!

(Eccles. 8:1–9; 10:12–20)

An Above-the- Sun Postscript

Unless the LORD build the house,
They labor in vain who build it,
Unless the LORD guards the city,
The watchman keeps awake in vain.
—Psalm 127:1

How do you lead effectively? How do you even know if you are a leader? Simply put, step out and if others follow you are leading. What can you do to increase your effectiveness as a leader?

Get a Vision

All leaders begin with a vision—an ultimate goal. Get alone with the Lord to think and pray. Ask Him for His vision for you, your family, your church, or your company. Dream big dreams, asking God what He can accomplish through your life.

Communicate the Vision

Vision can never be over-communicated. People cry out for leadership, desiring to know where they are going. The leader tells them in a variety of ways, appealing to visual and auditory learners. As he does, others begin to see, hear, and even touch the vision. If you strive to be a leader, challenge, exhort, and illustrate the grand possibilities. In so doing, you will appeal to others' desire to leave a legacy.

Give the Vision Away

Ask for input and opinion, allowing others to help in determining the scope of your dream. Communicate the expectations and the available resources, and give them a personal stake in making your dream a reality. As they catch the vision, they will sacrifice to make it happen, sell others on it, and recruit even more workers to move it forward. Your vision eventually becomes everyone's vision as it moves beyond your original idea.

Exercise Discernment

Put the right person in the right place to accomplish each aspect of your vision. This is not as easy as it sounds. Many people believe they are gifted in one area, when in reality, their gifts lie elsewhere. The leader must effectively place people where they will be most productive, while instilling in them confidence and self-esteem. People are the leader's greatest resource.

Be Tenacious

Do not allow small problems to delay or discourage you from your goal. Leaders hear a constant barrage of statements like, "It will never work," or "It's ruined," or "I quit." But a leader refuses to accept failure. Set-backs perhaps, or re-designs, but never failure. Be steadfast and persistent in your follow-through, and when you step out to lead, there will always be those who will follow.

13

Love God

The surest sign that God has done
a work of grace in my heart is that
I love Jesus Christ best; not weakly and
faintly, not intellectually, but
passionately, personally and devotedly,
overwhelming every other love of my life.
                                   —Oswald Chambers

THE HEADLINE READ "Court Tape Is Selling Fast," and above it was a photograph of pop superstar Michael Jackson. "Pearl Jam is passé," the accompanying article began, "Mariah Carey is blown away. It's Michael Jackson's testimony from Federal Court that is selling strong. A fifty minute cassette of Jackson, the witness in a recent copyright fight, has him snapping his fingers and singing bits of 'Dangerous' and 'Billie Jean.'"[1] Court clerk James Mannspeaker was quoted as saying that orders for the cassettes, which were being sold for $15 each, were "streaming in." How many tapes do you suppose were sold? Five hundred? A thousand? A hundred thousand? Would you believe *fifty*? That's right. Fifty.

When stories like this one are considered "news," I wonder what truly newsworthy events must go unreported. Too often the contemporary media either over- or under-plays what is really occurring in our world. The twenty-fifth anniversary of the Stonewall uprising happened to coincide with the world-wide March for Jesus—an ecumenical event staged annually to show support for the central figure in Christianity. (The Stonewall was the name of a New York City nightclub where homosexuals and drag queens confronted police and were arrested during a raid on the club. The incident was later heralded as the beginning of the gay pride movement.) Do I need to tell you which event the press treated more thoroughly and sympathetically?

Far too many of us would have to agree with Solomon that we have played the world's game and lost.

It seems we have lost our perspective—but our dilemma is a far from modern phenomenon. Nearly three thousand years ago, Solomon, too, accepted the world's system. He had been everywhere, done everything, and followed every dream to which a person could aspire under the sun. Now an old man, the king dispensed with philosophical meanderings and rhetorical questions. He was through with the "how to" approach to life: "How can I make my mark in this world?" "How can I achieve success?" "How can I find love?" "How can I know happiness?" It was now time for another approach: "How come?" "What did it all mean?" "Did any of the things I learned/saw/acquired/experienced really matter?" "What good came of my life?"

Far too many of us would have to agree with Solomon that we have played the world's game and lost. We have experienced broken hearts and broken families. We have been disappointed in our vocations. We have made and lost fortunes or made hardly anything at all. God, if we have taken the time to acknowledge Him, has been relegated to an ace-in-the-hole or fall back position. He is there if nothing else works. But that's not the best way, Solomon concluded. Better to remember God when we are young, "before the evil days come and the years draw near when you will say, 'I have no delight in them'" (Eccles. 12:1b).

What the ancient king said is utterly contemporary: Eventually, we burn out. Anyone who lives hard enough and long enough with the world's perspective will get more than enough of life. The zest for living will be lost before he or she dies. I'm reminded of a friend of mine who visited a ninety-eight-year-old man named Uncle Billy who lived in the Smoky Mountains. Uncle Billy asked everyone he met the same thing: "Why doesn't the Lord take me? All my friends are dead. All my family is dead. Most of my children are dead. Why am I still alive? I don't even want to be here anymore." My friend looked him squarely in the eye and said, "Uncle Billy, have you ever thought maybe the Lord still has something for you to do?" To which Uncle Billy replied, "Well, I ain't gonna do it!"

"You Look Wonderful!"

It has been said that there are four stages of life: infancy, childhood, adulthood, and "You look wonderful!" Modern technology is ensuring that "You look wonderful" can last a long time. Solomon must have glanced in the mirror one day and discovered that friends who say, "You look wonderful," cannot always be trusted. I believe His observations comprise the most magnificent allegory on aging that can be found anywhere in literature.

Listen as Solomon chronicles the anatomy of old age: "Before the sun, the light, the moon, and the stars are darkened, and clouds return after the rain; in the day that the watchmen of the house tremble, and the mighty men stoop, the grinding ones stand idle because they are few, and those who look through windows grow dim; and the doors on the street are shut as the sound of the grinding mill is low, and one will arise at the sound of the bird, and all the daughters of song will sing softly" (Eccles. 12:2–4).

Old age frequently brings one ailment after another: Fragile bones, senility, trembling hands, weak knees. When my boys come home we still play basketball in the backyard but those are the times I know that the legs—the mighty men—are the first things to go! I still have a sense of touch, and I can dribble fairly well—but I can't jump! I used to be able to jump and touch the rim of the goal; now I can't touch the net! Then the teeth—the grinding ones—begin to wear. The eyes grow dim. Hearing is impaired. Sleep becomes more critical. Voices that were once strong and robust grow warbly and weak.

And there's more. "Furthermore, men are afraid of a high place and terrors on the road; the almond tree blossoms, the grasshopper drags himself along, and the caperberry is ineffective. For man goes to his eternal home while mourners go about in the street" (v. 5). We become more cautious as the years go on. We take fewer physical risks. Our sense of danger is heightened, and our taste for adventure is dulled. Our hair turns gray like the almond tree's blossoms (if we're lucky enough to still have hair!) Our sexual drive wanes and our ability to reproduce decreases. Then what? Well, then we die, and the world keeps turning. In fact, few seem to notice that we no longer occupy space on the planet. We go, Solomon says, "to our eternal home."

I know many people who plan their retirement in great detail. They anticipate their exact financial needs, coordinate their resources, plan how they will use their time, and prepare for all of life's contingencies. But retirement, even though it is likely, is not inevitable. Death is. Our retirement is "iffy"—our graduation to our eternal home is a sure thing. The end of old age is death: "Then the dust will return to the earth as it was, and the spirit will return to God who gave it. 'Vanity of vanities,' says the Preacher, 'all is vanity'" (vv. 7–8). Solomon seems to imply that the truly wise will plan for the time when God calls us home.

"Remember Him"

No life has meaning without God. The choice to disregard Him always leads to the same conclusion: "Vanity of vanities, all is vanity." Solomon believed there was a God, but he cultivated no relationship with Him. His God was a concept—not a Person. I know men who say "I believe in the God of nature," but nature can only reveal so much of God and no more. We can learn from nature that God is powerful and creative and orderly, but we cannot learn from nature that God is love. Nature cannot confirm that God longs for fellowship with us, or that He cares for us more than anything. Nature speaks of origin—but is silent on the subject of relationship.

Twice in his discourse on the end of life, Solomon used the word "remember" in relationship to God. "Remember . . . your Creator," he said (v. 1). "Remember Him . . . " (v. 6). Every life must have a focal point—a center. When we are the center of our own lives, the end is vanity. But when we make God, in Jesus Christ, the center point of our lives, there is meaning. In Him, Paul said, we have redemption and the forgiveness of sins: "And He is the image of the invisible God, the first-born of all creation. For by Him all things were created, both in the heavens and on earth, visible and invisible, whether thrones or dominions or rulers or authorities—all things have been created by Him and for Him. And He is before all things, and in Him all things hold together" (Col. 1:14–17).

Solomon believed there was a God, but he cultivated no relationship with Him.

When the worship center of the church I pastor was being constructed, the contractor drove a peg down into the dirt in the place where the pulpit would one day stand. That peg was the center point from which every other measurement in the structure was taken. More than once I knelt in the dirt close to the spot where the peg was driven and prayed that God would keep us faithful to Him and to His Word in our worship and in our work, and that many would come to know Him in that place. It was the center point—the reference for all that has happened since.

When we give God the very center, the throne of our lives, He takes up residence in our hearts and becomes our standard by which everything else is measured. Solomon said "Remember God," and I believe at the end of his life he would have traded every place he had been and everything he had accomplished to have made the journey with Him. Then when the years had passed, and the end drew near, he would have known that God was waiting to welcome him home.

Charles Allen, my friend and former pastor of the First United Methodist Church of Houston, Texas, tells a tremendous story of such a homecoming. John Todd was born in Vermont in the early 1800s. He was six years old when his parents died, and an aunt who lived nearby offered to take him into her home. He spent fifteen wonderful years with her, and grew to love her as if she were his own mother. Thirty-five years passed. John Todd became a minister and settled comfortably into middle age. Then word came that his dear aunt was dying. She wrote him a fearful letter, asking what death might be like. "Would it be the end of everything or would there be, beyond death, a chance to continue living, growing, loving?"[2]

Her nephew sent the following reply:

> It is now thirty-five years since I, a little boy of six, was left quite alone in the world. You sent me word you would give me a home and be a kind mother to me. I have never forgotten the day when I made the long journey of ten miles to your house in North Killingsworth. I can still recall my disappointment when, instead of coming for me yourself, you sent your colored man, Caesar, to fetch me. I well remember my tears and my anxiety as, perched high on your horse and clinging tight to Caesar, I rode off to my new home. Night fell before we finished the journey and as it grew dark I became lonely and afraid.
>
> "Do you think she'll go to bed before I get there?" I asked Caesar anxiously. "Oh no," he said reassuringly, "she'll sure stay up for you. When we get out of these here woods you'll see her candle shining in the window." Presently we did ride out in the clearing and there, sure enough, was your candle. I remember you were waiting at the door, that you put your arms close about me and that you lifted me—a tired and bewildered little boy—down from the horse. You had a big fire burning in the hearth, a hot supper waiting for me on the stove. After supper, you took me to my new room, you heard me say my prayers and then you sat beside me until I fell asleep.
>
> You probably realize why I am recalling all of this to your memory. Some day soon, God will send for you, to take you to a new home. Don't fear the summons—the strange journey—or the dark messenger of death. God can be trusted to do as much for you as you were kind enough to do for me so many years ago. At the end of the road you will find love and welcome waiting, and you will be safe in God's care. I shall watch you and pray for you until you are out of sight, and then wait for the day when I shall make the journey myself and find you waiting at the end of the road to greet me.[3]

Remember God, Solomon said, and He will remember you.

"Read My Book"

Ecclesiastes, if it proves nothing else, proves that King Solomon possessed an incredible command of language. He was a man of many wonderful words. He could express the wisdom he possessed through words. He could teach the knowledge he acquired through words. He collected and arranged words in the form of proverbs, epigrams, pithy sayings. He could communicate truth through the writing of words. He was a wordsmith . . . an author . . . and his closing appeal was typical of any author: "Read my book," he said. Then he described what I believe is the "anatomy of a bestseller." If Ecclesiastes had sported a slick, colorfully-designed book jacket, the Preacher's closing words would surely appear on it. First, the title: *Vanity of Vanities, or Been There. Done That. Now What?* Then the subtitle: *All is vanity.* The author: *The Preacher.*

When I'm browsing in a bookstore, I sometimes buy a book based on the title or the author. If I'm unsure, I read the jacket flaps, which usually tell more about the author and list other works he may have written. Solomon's credentials were hefty: "In addition to being a wise man, the Preacher also taught the people knowledge; and he pondered, searched out and arranged many proverbs" (Eccles. 12:9). He was a noted academician and the author of some well-known, shorter works. So far so good.

> *Solomon offered his readers sound principles to live by, hammered through real-life experience, and anchored in a single source.*

I especially like to read about an author's intent—his reason for writing. Why this book? What methodology was used? The king was forthright: "The Preacher sought to find delightful words and to write words of truth correctly" (v. 10). Solomon wanted to find living words, practical words, picturesque words with which to present deep truth. His was a book that valued style *and* substance—and he was unwilling to sacrifice one for the other. The very best writers are passionate about this.

Lately I have noticed that many books carry selling points on their covers. Readers apparently want to know, "What will this book do for *me*?" Solomon did not leave his would-be audience guessing: "The words of wise men are like goads," he said, "and masters of these collections are like well-driven nails; they are given by one Shepherd" (v. 11). "I'm writing words that will prod men to action," he said, "and words that will nail things down, and secure them in place." Solomon offered his readers sound principles to live by, hammered through real-life experience, and anchored in a single source. He had been there, remember? He had done that. And his conclusions were not vague or unformed. They represented dead-on truth—given by one Shepherd.

> *The mark of a well-educated person today is actually open-mindedness.*

In other words—he had a message from God.

Then this author-king issued a warning, a disclaimer of sorts. "But beyond this, my son, be warned: the writing of many books is endless, and excessive devotion to books is wearying to the body" (v. 12). Solomon knew from experience that it was possible to study forever and never say, "This I know." If being a student appeals to us, it is possible to be a student forever. It is possible to contemplate and argue and refine our repertoire of knowledge endlessly, never reaching any firmly-held beliefs. The mark of a well-educated person today is actually open-mindedness. To say, "I believe this beyond a shadow of doubt," is to be held suspect in terms of intellect.

More books exist than could ever be read, and Solomon knew it. Today the Library of Congress of the United States of America has surpassed the 100,000,000 mark in its collection of writings and pieces of information. In the spring of 1994, there were 104,834,652 catalogued pieces in the Library's collection.

Each year over 50,000 new books are printed in the United States, according to *Publishers' Weekly*. That is nearly 150 new titles in print *each day*. If an average reader decided to read every new book published on a given day of 1994, it would take him three years, reading eight hours a day, to finish them!

A book super-store that recently opened in my neighborhood receives and sells so many books from day to day that its computer cannot keep an up-to-date accounting of the number of titles stocked, but employees estimate that there are presently over 100,000 books in the store.

Excessive devotion to books can indeed be wearying, but even more wearying is study that never proves anything and learning that never answers any questions. Solomon tried intellectualism as a road to meaning, remember? And he found it empty and frustrating. In fact, he reported that knowing more—gathering more data—can actually make life *less* satisfying. It is essential that we "land" somewhere in our belief, and not simply circle the flight patterns of learning indefinitely. It is essential to reach a conclusion—and Solomon did.

Advice from a Seasoned Veteran

Life's bottom line, according to Solomon, was simply this: Fear God, and keep His commandments. These two imperatives were the "Cliff Notes" to his autobiography. I believe three things hindered him from loving and obeying God earlier in life.

First, Solomon took God's Word casually. He disobeyed direct instructions from God with regard to marriage and the accumulation of possessions. God commanded him to refrain from multiplying wives or riches; Solomon collected both with a passion. History allows us a comfortable distance from which to view the king's mistakes— but in truth, they are not far from us. Solomon simply responded to God the way a willful child responds to a parent: "I hear you—but I know better."

Rarely does a six year old know better than his father or mother. Are you a Christian who is seriously considering marriage to an unbeliever? God says no. Do you know better? Are you challenging God's authority in your financial dealings? God has some specific instructions with regard to money. Do you know better? Are you pursuing sexual intimacy outside the bounds of marriage? God says no. Do you know better? Solomon believed for many years that he did know better

Solomon simply responded to God the way a willful child responds to a parent: "I hear you—but I know better."

> Solomon turned
> his focus from
> God Himself to
> the gifts of God.

than God, but he summed up his life-search with the words "Fear God," not "Ignore Him and do whatever feels right."

Not only did Solomon fail to take God's instructions seriously—he refused human accountability. Deuteronomy 17:18 records that all kings, including Solomon, were instructed to write God's commands on a scroll before the priests and read them in the presence of these men all the days of his life. If he had done this, perhaps the priests could have held him accountable:

"Don't you think 12,000 horses is a tad excessive, my king?"

"Won't 1,400 chariots be more than enough for the New Year's parade?"

But there was no accountability—and no record that he wrote down God's specific prohibitions, or referred to them again—even in private.

Solomon's father David knew the importance of human accountability. In David's court a prophet named Nathan was a fearless truth-teller. Nathan called David to task over his sin of adultery with Bathsheba and the subsequent murder of her husband.

Any man or woman who would desire to walk with God needs a Nathan. If you do not have such a person in your life, find one! Seek out a trustworthy confidant who will love you, look you in the eye, and ask, "Have you considered this?" No one held Solomon accountable, even though many knew he was disobeying the commands of God. He was accumulating wives, wealth, and horses; Solomon needed a Nathan.

Finally, Solomon turned his focus from God Himself to the gifts of God. God gave him wisdom and honor and prestige and wealth to an unprecedented degree. Instead of drawing near to the Giver, however, he began to believe that the gifts were deserved as an extension of his own natural abilities. "This is who I am," he must have said. "And this is what I have done." In his old age he offered incense to the pagan goddesses and sacrifices to pagan idols. He built storage cities for his royal toys.

He abandoned fellowship with the Giver in order to play with the gifts.

We have seen it happen many times. A twenty-five year old says, "I want to make a difference for God. I want to count for Him in this world." The same man at forty-five says, "I want to get some of the world's stuff. I want good things to enjoy." At sixty-five he says, "I just want to reap the fruits of my labor. I've made my contribution. Now it's my turn to coast." We do not take God's Word seriously. We refuse human accountability. We focus on the gifts—not the Giver. And when we do, we're guaranteed to become participants with Solomon in the existentialist's worthless legacy: Been there. Done that. Now what?

Life's Bottom Line

Look at the final words of Solomon's diary one last time: "The conclusion, when all has been heard, is: fear God and keep His commandments, because this applies to every person. For God will bring every act to judgment, everything which is hidden, whether it is good or evil" (Eccles. 12:13–14). Fear God. Stand in awe of the Holy One who created heaven and earth and made man with a purpose. Know that His commandments are just, and that to break them is to ultimately be broken by them. You are built for relationship with the Eternal and you will be lost until you are united with Him who came from above the sun.

Solomon was right. Words are wearying. But there is a *Word* that is life-giving. His name is Jesus. You see, Solomon's word was not the last word. God had the final word: "In the beginning was the Word, and the Word was with God, and the Word was God. He was in the beginning with God. All things came into being by Him, and apart from Him nothing came into being that has come into being. In Him was life, and the life was the light of men" (John 1:1–4).

He came from above the sun and invaded our under-the-sun world at precisely the right time. He was beau-

> *You are built for relationship with the Eternal and you will be lost until you are united with Him.*

tiful. There was none like Him: "And the Word became flesh and dwelt among us, and we beheld His glory, glory as of the only begotten of the Father, full of grace and truth" (John 1:14).

He was the *spoken* Word of God, and He *spoke* the words of God:

> "God, after he spoke long ago to the fathers in the prophets in many portions and in many ways, in these last days has spoken to us in His Son . . ." (Heb. 1:1). "But He answered and said, 'It is written, "Man shall not live on bread alone, but on every word that proceeds out of the mouth of God."'" (Matt. 4:12)

His name is the password to eternity and the doorway to abundant life: ". . . if you confess with your mouth Jesus as Lord, and believe in your heart that God raised Him from the dead, you shall be saved . . . ." (Rom. 10:9). "Jesus said to him, 'I am the way, and the truth, and the life; no one comes to the Father, but through Me'" (John 14:6).

He is the righteous One who will come again one day in judgment: "And I saw heaven opened; and behold, a white horse, and He who sat upon it is called Faithful and True; and in righteousness He judges and wages war. And His eyes are a flame of fire, and upon His head are many diadems; and He has a name written upon Him which no one knows except Himself. And He is clothed with a robe dipped in blood; and His name is called . . . The Word of God." (Rev. 19:11–13).

Jesus is God's final word. With Him, life is a love affair with God. Without Him, it is meaningless. He is knowable—and He wants to be known, as Peter Marshall reasoned in *Mr. Jones, Meet the Master:* "Let's put the question bluntly . . . can you and I really have communion with Christ as we would with earthly friends? Can we know personally that same Jesus whose words are recorded in the New Testament, who walked the dusty trails of Galilee two thousand years ago? I don't mean can we treasure His words or try to follow His example or imagine Him. I mean is He really alive? Can we actually meet Him, commune with Him, ask His help for everyday affairs? The Gospel writers say yes. A host of men and women down the ages say yes. The church says yes."[4]

Meet the meaning of life. His Name is Jesus. And say yes.

An Above-the- Sun Postscript

The LORD possessed me at the beginning of His way,
Before His works of old.
From everlasting I was established,
From the beginning, from the earliest times of the earth.
— Proverbs 8:22–23

At last, Solomon arrives at the under-the-sun answer to the ultimate question: What is the meaning of life? The long and winding roads yield the surprising conclusion of "Fear God and keep His commandments."

What does it mean to fear God? What should we do? A simple acrostic will help us remember.

1. *Faith* begins the relationship of a proper fear of God. Trust Him and cultivate your faith by stepping out of your comfort zone into unchartered areas, forcing yourself to trust Him alone to achieve success. Believe that God sits on His throne and keeps sovereign watch over His creation.

2. *Experience* His Grace. Revel in His magnificent gift that saves and sanctifies, deepening your reverence for Him. Continue to meditate on God's Word that proclaims you clean, utterly, and eternally clean before Him. The Lord accepts you, the Lord loves you and nothing in you will ever change that. Indeed, nothing in you can ever change that. His grace conquers all.

3. *Awe* flows out of a deep respect for the majesty of the Lord. Behold your King! Isaiah beheld the Lord and cried out, "Woe is me, I am ruined, for I am a man of unclean lips!" R. C. Sproul aptly calls this the "trauma of holiness," as we humble our hearts, our agendas, and our desires in surrender to the blinding brilliance of the great I AM.

237

4. *Resolve* to stay within the boundaries. Sometimes we can slip into delighting in cheap grace, seeing how much we can get away with before God. That's not what Solomon has in mind when he says, "Fear God." On the contrary, fearing God induces us to firmer resolution. Out of reverence for our King, out of love for our Savior, we commit to honoring Him and pleasing Him.

Conclusion

H ERE WAS SOLOMON'S UNSTATED THESIS: Somewhere, somehow, some way under the sun, I will do something, discover something, get something, achieve something, or become something that will give life meaning.

He doggedly and exhaustively pursued all the wordly ways that have been tried to make sense of life. Remember—there are only five possibilities. He explored Hedonism. Materialism. Philosophy. Intellectualism. Religion. Ecclesiastes is his uncensored report from the front lines—complete with its staggering conclusion: "Vanity of vanities. All is vanity." Or in the language of our generation, "Been there. Done that. Now what?"

Like all under-the-sun explorers before and since, Solomon came up empty. He continued to expect different results, and only came to his senses later in life. Too late, really. His was not a bad life by worldly standards. He was wealthy, wise, well-traveled, well-read, respected, and revered. We could ask ourselves the same questions we would ask of this ancient king: How could a wise man be so blind? Why not just learn from the past? Why continue to repeat the same mistakes over and over again?

The Lord Jesus Christ breaks through these frustrating questions with some good news: We don't have to replicate Solomon's insane search for meaning, peace, and joy. We can learn from him and avoid his mistakes. How do we avoid Solomon's life of "vanity" and get on with one of our own that is full and satisfying?

First every person must answer correctly the ultimate question: What is the meaning of life? What is the *summum bonum*—the greatest good? If this question is answered correctly at the outset, it is possible to bypass all the destructive roads that Solomon followed to their end. Perhaps you have tried a few of these roads already, and are a good way down another one right now. That is quite allright. I assume the dissatisfaction of your search so far will motivate you far more than the prospect of learning from someone else's mistakes. Stop where you are and return to that intersection where all roads converge. Then, correctly answer the question.

What is the answer? Remember, at the end of his search, Solomon said, "Fear God and keep His commandments" (Eccles. 12:13). To fear God basically means to worship Him. Fearing Him is not cringing in fright—it is a reverent, child-like awe of Him. To keep His commandments simply means to obey God. Do what He says.

Solomon's conclusion was true, but he was also trying to get an above-the-sun perspective before *the Son* came. The phrase, "fear God and keep His commandments" is the best pre-incarnational answer that can be given to the question, "What is the meaning of life?" But now we must connect it to the above-the-sun reality. Solomon searched, discovered, and wrote without knowledge of Jesus Christ—but we have access to the very Son of God!

The meaning of life is the Lord Jesus Christ. He is the answer. He is the *summum bonum*. He is the end all, be all. He is the Highest, the Greatest, the First, the Last, the Beginning and the End. He is the Living Water that quenches our terrible thirst and the Bread of Life that satisfies our deep hunger and in Him and Him alone do we find meaning. As the apostle Paul wrote:

> He is the image of the invisible God, the first born of all creation. For by Him all things were created, both in the heavens and on earth, visible and invisible, whether thrones or dominions or rulers or authorities—all things have been created by Him and for Him. And He is before all things, and in Him all things hold together. He is also the head of the body, the church; and He is the beginning, the first-born from the dead; so that He Himself might come to have first

place in everything. For it was the Father's good pleasure for all the fullness to dwell in Him. (Col. 1:15–19)

The first step in skipping Solomon's wearying quest is realizing that Jesus Christ gives meaning to life. The second step is to receive Him into your life. Receiving Christ involves opening the door of your life and inviting Christ to come in. You may do this by simply praying to Him. When a man receives Jesus Christ, he surrenders all that he is and all that he does to Christ, actively placing his trust in Him and accepting Jesus' death for the forgiveness of sin.

Step three is to worship Him. "Worship," it has been said, "is our response, both corporately and privately, to God, for who He is—and what He has done—expressed in and by the way we live and the things we do and say." [1] Show me someone who knows God and fears Him, and I will show you a worshiper. To love God is to worship Him.

God commands us to obey Him and to live out His precepts. However, our first impulse must be to worship Him. Worship always comes first. I love evangelism. I have dedicated this book to seven friends and men of God who have, at every church I have pastored, energetically proclaimed the Gospel to lost people. In my opinion, there aren't many priorities higher than evangelism. What can match the thrill of being God's ambassador, or leading men and women out of darkness and into light? What privilege could be greater than to be God's instrument for reconciling His people to Himself?

The answer to both of these questions is worship. Worship exceeds the thrill of evangelism and worship is the highest privilege of the Christian's life—because God created us first and foremost to glorify and adore Him.

Obedience to God's commands flows out of worship. Again, our first impulse must be to worship; our second to obey Him. Sanctification, one of those fancy church words, means to become holy, to become righteous. Righteous literally means to be "right-wised." God commands us to be holy, and obeying Him spurs us toward sanctification, or becoming "right-wised."

God saves us and sanctifies us by His grace. "Scripture speaks of both a holiness we already possess in Christ before God and a holiness in which we are to grow more and more. The first is the result of the work of Christ for us; the second is the result of the Holy Spirit in us. . . The objective holiness we have in Christ and the subjective holiness produced by the Holy Spirit are both gifts of God's grace and both are appropriated by faith."[2]

Both our position in Christ and our experience in Christ originate with God's grace. When God looks at you, at your position in Christ, He sees holiness. "And by that will (of God) we have been made holy through the sacrifice of the body of Jesus Christ, once for all" (Heb. 10:10). "Have been made holy" is past tense. It is done. Your legal position in Christ is as one whose sin debt has been paid in full, therefore you are holy in God's sight.

"I still sin a lot, even though I have received Christ," someone might say. "It is one thing for God to see me as positionally holy, but it's quite another to be experientially holy. I still sin. What about that?" God says, "This is the covenant I will make with them after that time, says the Lord. I will put my laws in their hearts, and I will write them on their minds" (Heb. 10:16). Ezekial 36:26–27 says, "I will remove from you your heart of stone and give you a heart of flesh. And I will put my Spirit in you and move you to follow my decrees and be careful to keep my laws." God not only saves us from sin's penalty—He also saves us from sin's power. He doesn't save us merely to leave us tossed to and fro by winds of evil. He personally gives us the ability, the strength, to walk in His ways. [3]

Does that mean we can just "let go and let God," or wait for Him to work some kind of magic in our lives? No. God works alone in saving grace—but commands us to cooperate with Him in sanctifying grace.

Solomon had the answer all along: "For a man's ways are in full view of the Lord, and He examines all his paths. The evil deeds of a wicked man ensnare him; the cords of sin hold him fast. He will die for lack of discipline, led astray by his own great folly" (Prov. 5:21–23). How does a man deal with the gap between his position of holiness and his experience of repeated sin? Discipline, discipline, discipline.

Only the regular practice of the spiritual disciplines can impel him along the road to experiential holiness. Cooperate with God in this manner: prepare the soil of your heart through prayer and fasting, sow seeds of His word through study and meditation, grow as He works in you, and reap what you sow. Abandon the spiritual disciplines and you may lead a life of frustrated carnality, like Solomon. Practice them and you will be "like a tree firmly planted by streams of water, which yields its fruit in season, and its leaf does not wither" (Ps. 1:3). Such a man prospers, the Bible says, in whatever he does.

As you live in the disciplines daily, you will experience the miracle of fruit. Love, joy, peace, and patience—the very things Solomon always wanted—will overflow from your disciplined heart. Solomon had all this at one time, but he let his disciplined life erode. Abandoning prayer and study of the Scriptures, Solomon "cut the cord" that connected Him to God and began instead to collect foreign wives, Egyptian horses, and excessive wealth. And, as always, he reaped the destruction that he sowed.

Here is the good news: You now know the meaning of life—Jesus Christ. You have taken step two, receiving Him into your life. Step three is worship. Step four is obedience, through the practice of the spiritual disciplines of prayer, fasting, Bible study, and meditation. Have you been there—and done that? Now what? Just this. Enter into your Master's rest. He is worthy to be praised! "To Him that sits on the throne, and to the Lamb, be blessing and honor and glory and dominion forever and ever!"

To An Open-Minded Skeptic

D o not ask questions. It is all faith. You just have to believe! Ever hear that? Christianity is full of holes. Educated people do not buy that stuff anymore. The Bible has lots of contradictions and myths. Science has proved it all false. Besides, Christians are so intolerant. Ever think that? If you are a skeptic—Ecclesiastes is a book for you. I hope it will cause you to re-examine your life.

First: Ask all the questions you want. Feel free. If something seems strange, untrue, or inconsistent, say so. You don not have to leave your inquiring mind at the door. Jesus said, "Come let us reason."

When people tell you to "just believe, it's all faith" they generally speak out of both good intentions and insecurity. The problem is, it's not all faith. I never advocate a blind, a stick-your-head-in-the-sand variety of faith. That is foolish. I do advocate a *reasoned* faith, a trust built on solid, unimpeachable reason and facts. Christianity is rooted in time. . . space. . . and history. It certainly requires a measure of faith, but reason and fact create a tremendous foundation on which to build that edifice of faith.

Second: Critics come and critics go, but Christianity outlasts them all. Attacks come from scientists, historians, leaders of other religions, textual critics, and philosophers, but Christians repeatedly repel the attacks for one reason—Christianity is true. Because it really is true, Christianity affords an awesome arsenal of intellectual firepower to its defenders.

Far from being solely the domain of the ignorant and downtrodden, Christianity claims erudite scholars from every major discipline. Astrophysicists, archaeologists, historians, lawyers, biologists, linguists, philosophers, and more staunchly proclaim the truth of Christianity based on evidence from their own scholarly disciplines.

Contradictions and myths? The stuff of modern misconceptions of the masses, perhaps, but no part of the Scripture written by the original authors of the Bible. Yes, "Christian" theologians exist that espouse such thinking, but their celebrated conclusions merely flow logically from the biased presuppositions that myth and error comprise the Bible.

Let me illustrate. A well-known professor at one of America's most prestigious colleges, the chairman of the religion department, informs his impressionable students that Matthew was written after A.D. 71. He pauses. Students naturally raise hands and ask, "Why do you say that, Prof.?"

"Because," he proclaims, "Jesus 'prophesies' the destruction of the Temple in the 24th chapter of Matthew. In A.D. 71 the Romans laid siege to Jerusalem and utterly destroyed the city and Temple. We know there is no such thing as predictive prophecy, because that would suggest the existence of supernatural power. Since we rule that out, we must therefore conclude that Matthew was written after A.D. 71."

"We know there is no such thing. . . .?" Since we rule that out. . . .?" Do you see the bias? Prejudiced, the professor pre-supposes that no supernatural Being exists. He employs flawless logic after that, to his credit, resulting in a conclusion which stands opposed to the claim of Matthew and church history. To the impressionable student, the professor seemingly had enlightened his or her mind by debunking the silly old Christian superstition. However, as we now see, it's merely a case of prior bias against Christianity.

So, again, please ask all the questions you have. I commend you for seeking truth and for being unwilling to give your life to suspect notions. But—be forewarned that education and knowledge, far from being the enemies of Christ, are the allies of Christ. If you are honest and rigorous in your quest for truth, you will discover that Christianity is the foundation that supports the only world view with eternal validity.

Truth- Seeker or Intellectual Coward?

This raises one last issue before we begin to look at reasons to believe—do you have the guts and the integrity to make an honest search? Skepticism properly applied (in the manner of Socrates) remains a noble and necessary tool for the truth seeker. Unfortunately, skeptics come in two varieties, the Open-Minded Skeptic (a truth-seeker) and the Close-Minded Skeptic (an intellectual coward).

The Open-Minded Skeptic resolves to admit he doesn't know everything (a wise move), and is willing to discover truth and live by it. The Close-Minded Skeptic merely casts stones from a distance. He wants an intellectual rationale that justifies his lifestyle. Evidence that supports an opposing view he flees like the plague.

The Close-Minded Skeptic, while speaking the language of the intellectual and wrapping himself in the mantle of Socrates, reveals himself to be nothing more than an intellectual coward. He cares little for truth, caring instead for comfort in his current views. An Open-Minded Skeptic embarks on the quest for truth with abandon, for he knows of nothing more noble than discovering and living out truth. Preconceived notions cannot shackle his search for he knows that he'll return to them if they withstand the searing searchlight of Truth. And if the preconceived notions can't withstand the test, why would he hold them anyway? History, tradition, comfort, culture, family heritage, and the like hold value for the truth-seeker only if they consist of demonstrable truth. The intellectual coward clings to "my opinion" no matter what, living in that gray twilight of timid ignominy.

Do you have the guts and intellectual integrity to make an honest search? I challenge you to weigh the following evidence on the scales of Truth and make an informed decision. The following introduction reasons to believe serve only to point the Open-Minded Skeptic down the road toward more developed defenses of Christianity provided by others. I do not intend to provide "conclusive proof" or "proof beyond a shadow of doubt," but hopefully will show that Christianity at least boasts a solid foundation.

Reasons To Believe

Does God Even Exist?

Science, philosophy, history, archaeology, textual evidence, and reason all support the truth of Christianity. But, first, how do we even know if there is a God? Atheists (*a-* against, *theism-* belief in *theos* or God) argue that God does not exist and agnostics (*a-* against, *gnosis-* knowledge) contend they don't know either way. Christians are theists (believing in *theos*, God). Who's right?

This may seem rather stark, but frankly, atheism is untenable. It's one thing to be unsure whether God exists, like the agnostic, but it's quite another to say that you know that God exists nowhere. To make a statement of absolute negation one must have absolute knowledge. A simple exercise will suffice . . .

Suppose I draw a box and say this box represents all that exists in the entire universe, all possible knowledge. Then I hand my pen to you and ask you to draw a box inside of the first box which represents how much of the total knowledge box that you personally know. Everything you know is summed up in the box or mark you make. Most people wisely make a little dot. For the sake of illustration I follow up their dot with another box roughly a fourth the size of the first box. I now ask you this question: Is it possible that outside of this smaller box which represents all that you know, but inside the larger box of all knowledge of the universe, there exists a God? Is it possible?

All the Knowledge in the Universe

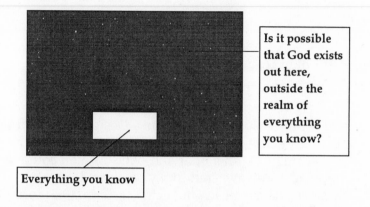

Is it possible that God exists out here, outside the realm of everything you know?

Everything you know

Of course it's possible! In other words, how can you deny *absolutely* the existence of something when you don't know absolutely everything? You can be as smart and knowledgeable as Solomon and Albert Einstein put together, but you cannot deny absolutely His existence outside of your box, because you don't know what goes on outside your box.

Thus, not only is atheism unsound, it is extraordinarily arrogant. Atheists claim to know about the non-existence of things in realms where they admit they have no knowledge.

Well, if there is no confirmable place to rest in atheism, perhaps one exists in agnosticism. Not only are the views of the agnostic humble, but they are defensible. One can certainly know that he does not possess knowledge of something else.

Argument from Cause and Effect

However, two arguments evenly weighed incline the honest agnostic towards theism. First, the Cosmological Argument. Cause-and-effect comprise the substance of the cosmological (study of the cosmos or universe) argument; if you see something (the effect) you know it was caused by something else. No effect exists apart from a cause. Is there evil in the world? Yes.

Logically, there is good, too. If there is good and evil, there must be a moral law—and therefore a moral law-giver. Let's call Him God. Trace this back all the way and you have the beginning of the universe. If the beginning of the universe is an effect, what is its cause? Christians say God is the cause, the Creator.

Argument from Design

Second, the Teleological Argument, also known as the argument from Design. *Telos* has to do with "end" or "goal," and the end result of existence points to a Designer. For example, if you noticed twenty stones on the beach arrayed in the form of a miniature hut with a door and window, you could assume that the wind and waves randomly combined their force to hurl the stones upon the beach in such a fashion. Or, more reasonably, you could assume that someone special assembled the stones. Sheer mathematical probability allows for the freak occurrence of the twenty stone hut by wind and waves, but the idea of a designer is more logical.

Take the famous illustration of finding a watch. As you walk along you discover a watch, and as you examine it's intricate inner workings you notice an impressive array of wheels, springs, bolts and watch hands, all whirring together in perfect symmetry. Assembled by random chance? Not likely. Logically, you conclude that this device points to a Watchmaker.

Now magnify the illustrations. A universe is a far cry from a twenty stone hut or even an excellent Swiss watch. Or consider the human body. Reflect for a moment on the exceedingly detailed and stunning characteristics of the human brain. If a watch points to a Watchmaker, what must the mind of man point to? If random chance could not assemble the springs, wheels, screws, and watch hands, how could it be responsible for making a human brain? No, the order and symmetry and specialized capabilities of creation point to a Designer who made it all.

The agnostic must wrestle with the cosmological and teleological arguments, while the Christian rests secure, knowing that science and philosophy lend credence to his faith, not impugn it.

What About the Bible?

The Bible constitutes the foundation of Christianity, so if the Bible is true then so is Christianity. Likewise, if the Bible is false, so is Christianity. Many times people exclaim, "The Bible is so old! How can you believe in something two thousand years old?" They speak as though the winds of time begin to blow truthfulness off of a document. Somehow the winds of time strip the Bible of merit and as the time increases the amount of truth decreases. What was apparently fine to believe in around A.D. 500 no longer holds water in 1994.

Because of the antiquity of the New Testament, people love to doubt the historical events of Scripture, like Jesus' crucifixion, but do you know anyone who doubts that Julius Caesar crossed the Rubicon River on January 10, 49 B.C.? According to documents older than the New Testament, Caesar took his army across the Rubicon in a momentous decision that led to the end of the Roman Republic and the institution of the Roman Empire.

No one doubts Caesar's action, but many doubt the Crucifixion, supposedly because of the time span between the Crucifixion and now. But if you will doubt one event because of age, why not also doubt the older event because of age? The reason? Caesar doesn't ask you to change your life and Jesus does. All of which brings back the whole issue of Truth-Seeker vs. Intellectual Coward. If you can honestly believe that Caesar crossed the Rubicon based on ancient documents, you have little choice but to believe in the Crucifixion based on historical documents— unless of course you don't mind being willfully inconsistent.

If you want to investigate the trustworthiness of the Bible, where do you begin? Is there any evidence that indicates that the Bible is true and accurate?

There is. We will look at the reliability of the Bible manuscripts that we possess, we will look at the corroboration of secular historians and archaeology, and we will look at the number and details of prophecies fulfilled centuries after their initial utterance.

Bibliographic Test

Historians employ several tests to determine whether a document is reliable. First, how many copies do we possess of the original? Second, how close in age to the original manuscript is the earliest copy we have? For example, Document A, written in 1,000 B.C. may have twenty-five copies today, but there may have been dozens or even hundreds more copies that have disappeared. Of the twenty-five copies we have, some may have been made around 500 B.C., others 300 B.C., etc. The second test has to do with the earliest copy that still exists; how recently after the original was this copy made.

Number of copies and age of earliest copy still existing indicate how reliable a text is. Let's look at a chart of other works of ancient history to see how the New Testament stacks up.

Author	When Written	Earliest Copy	Time Span	No. of Copies
Caesar	100–44 B.C.	A.D. 900	1,000 years	10
Tacitus	A.D. 100	A.D. 1100	1,000 years	20
Thucydides	460–400 B.C.	A.D. 900	1,300 years	8
Suetonius	A.D. 75–160	A.D. 950	800 years	8
Herodotus	480–425 B.C.	A.D. 900	1,300 years	8
New Testament	A.D. 40–100	A.D. 125	25 years	24,000

The ancient histories that modern people believe have twenty copies at the most, and the shortest time span between copy and original is eight hundred years. The New Testament they disparage boasts twenty-four thousand copies, the earliest within a mere twenty-five years. The Open-Minded Skeptic realizes that the Bible trounces all other manuscripts as the most reliable document in the ancient world.[1]

Secular History and Archaeology

Significant secular sources (some who were hostile to Christianity) mention Jesus Christ and other New Testament figures, confirming the historicity of people and events. For example, Tacitus, the Roman historian, writing in A.D. 112, remarks:

Hence to suppress the rumor, he (Nero) falsely charged with the guilt, and punished with the most exquisite tortures, the persons commonly called Christians, who were hated for their enormities. Christus, the founder of the name, was put to death by Pontius Pilate, procurator of Judea in the reign of Tiberius: but the pernicious superstition, repressed for a time broke out again, not only in Judea, where the mischief originated, but through the city of Rome also.[2]

Josephus, a Jewish historian, details Christ's death and resurrection, as does Suetonius and many others. But secular historians comprise only a part of the external evidence for the truth of the Bible. Because the Bible is replete with names of places, buildings, events, and people, archaeology can confirm its veracity. William F. Albright, renown archaeologist, says, "There can be no doubt that archaeology has confirmed the substantial historicity of the Old Testament."[3] Norman Glueck, a Jewish scholar adds, "It is worth emphasizing that in all this work no archaeological discovery has ever controverted a single, properly understood biblical statement."[4]

Lastly, we will look at fulfilled prophecies in the Bible as evidence of it's truth. Regarding the Messiah, over three hundred specific prophecies about His birth, preaching and ministry, suffering, and resurrection find fulfillment in the person of Jesus Christ. According to Josh McDowell, the probability of even 48 of those specifics being perfectly fulfilled in a single individual is one in 10^{157}.

Fulfilled prophecies from Ezekiel 26 regarding the destruction of Tyre paint a remarkable picture of divine foreknowledge given to Ezekiel years before the events occurred. From the prediction that Nebuchadnezzar would lay siege to the city, to the fact that the ruins of the city would be hurled into the sea; from the prediction that many nations would come against it, to the one that Tyre would be left a bare rock where fishermen would dry their nets, *every single prophecy came true.*

Many more prophecies have seen completion than space permits listing, but suffice to say that the presence of many startling and specific predictions inclines the Open-Minded Skeptic to believe that the Bible is the accurate and authentic Word of God.

Liar, Lunatic or Lord

"I don't believe all this stuff about Jesus being God. Jesus is just a great man, a guru, a sage, or an enlightened Being."

Certainly this view has the advantages of being politically correct and avante garde, but the advocates of this perspective must not excel at critical thinking.

As C. S. Lewis observes:

> I am trying here to prevent anyone saying the really foolish thing that people often say about Him: "I'm ready to accept Jesus as a great moral teacher, but I don't accept His claim to be God." That is the one thing we must not say. A man who was merely man and said the sort of things Jesus said would not be a great moral teacher. He would either be a lunatic- on a level with the man who says he is a poached egg- or else he would be the Devil of Hell. You must make your choice. Either this man was, and is, the Son of God: or else a madman or something worse. You can shut Him up for a fool, you can spit at Him and kill Him as a demon; or you can fall at His feet and call Him Lord and God. But let us not come with any patronising nonsense about His being a great human teacher. He has not left that open to us. He did not intend to. [5]

The problem with the Good Man or Guru Theory is that Jesus actually claimed to be God. Could Jesus be wrong? It's possible. But even if He were incorrect, Jesus wouldn't then be just a Good Man because He either knowingly deceived people or He insanely believed Himself to be God. Here is a pictorial rendering of what Lewis is saying.

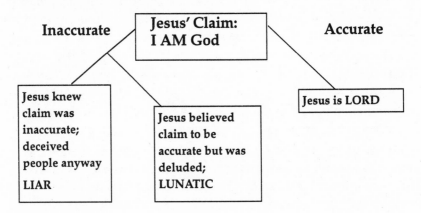

In other words, Jesus may or may not be Lord, but we can't reasonably say He was a great moral teacher, guru, sage, etc., because we would not refer to one as good who intentionally deceived people about his very nature and induced them to die for his false claim. Nor would we refer to a lunatic as a good man or a sage or guru. Almost no one wants to be guilty of intolerance, so most people don't want to say Jesus was a liar or a mentally deranged madman. Besides, the evidence of His highly ethical teachings, perfectly consistent with His flawless life, deny the idea that Jesus was a liar or lunatic.

The inescapable alternative, though, causes the Close-Minded Skeptic to cringe: Jesus is Lord. The Intellectual Coward strives mightily to discover some fourth option, but none has been uncovered. The Intellectual Coward then strives to prove Jesus never claimed to be God, but Scripture attests to His claim:

> "I and the Father are one." Again the Jews picked up stones to stone Him, but Jesus said to them, "I have shown you many great miracles from the Father. For which of these do you stone Me?"

> "We are not stoning You for any of these," replied the Jews, "but for blasphemy, because You, a mere man, claim to be God." (John 10: 30–33) "They all asked, "Are You then the Son of God?" He replied, "You are right in saying I am." (Luke 22:70-71)

> Again the High Priest asked Him, "Are You the Christ, the Son of the Blessed One?"

> "I am," said Jesus. (Mark 14: 61–62)

However, the Open-Minded Skeptic, encountering such strong thinking, realizes that this argument, too, points to the truth of Christianity.

Resurrection

All of Christianity hinges on the Resurrection. If Christ didn't rise from the dead, the apostle Paul writes, then our faith is empty and we are to be pitied as fools. With such a confession from the great apostle Paul, one would think that the enemies of Christ would have debunked the myth years ago. On the contrary, the evidence for the Resurrection remains one of the strongest arguments for the validity of Christianity.

The facts are these: Jesus was crucified with nails in the wrists and feet. A Roman spear pierced His side. Upon death, supporters wrapped His body in a linen cloth, laid Him in the tomb of Joseph of Arimathea, and rolled an enormous stone (probably weighing two tons) in front of the tomb. Jewish leaders, having heard Jesus' prediction of resurrection, persuaded the Roman governor, Pontius Pilate, both to place the Roman seal on the tomb and a guard of legionnaires around the tomb. Were anyone so foolish as to try to steal the body, he would not only have to overpower the Roman soldiers but also risk the death penalty in the future for breaking the Imperial Seal on the tomb.

Within three days, according to the disciples, Jesus rose from the dead. He showed them the holes in His hands, feet, and side, and spent some forty days with them. They went to their deaths proclaiming He was Lord and Christ because He had risen from the dead.

What is the skeptic to make of this event? While no Resurrection arguments stand conclusively over the skeptic, a commitment to reason and reasonableness will lead one to believe that Jesus did, in fact, rise from the dead.

The idea that a collection of eleven fishermen, tax collectors, and the like would overpower the Roman guard is rather silly. Besides, why risk the death penalty for breaking the seal on the tomb? What would they gain by stealing the body and proclaiming Jesus' resurrection if they actually knew the claim to be false? Proclaiming the Resurrection was hardly like winning the lottery; all the disciples received for their trouble were martyr's deaths. It is unlikely that the followers of Christ overpowered the guard, broke the seal, and stole the body, just so they could die for something they knew was false.

Consider, too, the fact that all the early Christians were in Jerusalem. Perhaps weak-minded people in a faraway city would fall for such a hoax, but not in Jerusalem, where they could easily discredit the notion. If anyone wanted to prove Christ a hoax, all he had to do was take the reporters from *The Jerusalem Times* down to the Tomb. The Roman guards would have smiled and the seal would have revealed Jesus' body was still in the tomb, decomposing. On the contrary, even with the virulent opposition of the Jewish leaders, the word got out that the Tomb was empty for all to see and thousands upon thousands were converted.

The fact that the gospel accounts portray the huge stone moved entirely away from the Tomb heightens the evidence. How could a tiny band of men have moved the stone any distance at all without encountering certain death from armed soldiers? So skeptics then assume the guards must have slept, but again this argument is unlikely. A cursory review of Roman military code reveals that falling asleep while on watch merited guards the death penalty by burning. Is it possible they fell so completely asleep that the disciples were able to move the huge stone without waking them? Yes, it's possible, but unreasonable since the guards would be afraid of sleeping on the job. Their own lives were at stake.

Many witnesses claimed to have seen the risen Christ. If you paraded not one, but fifty witnesses through the witness stand in a trial today, all testifying to the exact same event, the judge and jury would be convinced of the occurrence. What if one hundred witnesses testified? One by one, "Yes, I saw Him alive after He had been crucified." "Yes, I also saw Him alive after He had been crucified." Imagine one by one, one hundred and fifty witnesses, then two hundred and fifty, then three hundred and fifty, then four hundred, then four hundred and fifty, and then five hundred. Over five hundred witnesses claimed to have seen Jesus raised from the dead and the Open-Minded Skeptic should be inclined to believe such testimony.

Finally, consider the disciples' lives. The night of Jesus' arrest they all fled except one, John. Peter, the big and bold disciple who had boasted that he would die for Jesus, ended up denying he even knew Him. Only John stood at the Cross as Jesus died. The rest scattered and ran, certain they were about to suffer the same fate as their now vanquished Master.

What happened to these scared, trembling men? Something must have— because they were transformed from cowardly to courageous. All but John, history tells us, died horrid, tortuous deaths, simply because they would never renounce their faith. And why such faith? Because forever burned on their hearts and minds was the resurrection of Jesus Christ. The disciples needed only to say to their executioners, "Hey, I was just kidding," or,

"Boy, did I ever blow that one!" Instead, they suffered the worst pain imaginable because they were certain they had seen their Risen Savior.[6]

Conclusion

Remember, Ecclesiastes asks the question the rest of the Bible answers: "What is the meaning of life?" Jesus Christ—and Jesus alone—is the answer. What I have provided here is only a very small tip of the iceberg of apologetics. God exists, and the Bible is reliable, Jesus is Lord and He rose from the dead.

Even more wonderful is the fact that He loves you endlessly, wants to forgive you for all the mistakes you've ever made, wants to cleanse you from the sin in your heart, and desires to make you a new person in Christ. Heaven awaits at the end of life, but joy and meaning and purpose are yours for the tasting "under the sun." Why not trust your life to Jesus Christ?

Notes

Chapter 1

1. Peter Kreeft, *Back to Virtue* (San Francisco, Calif.: St. Ignatius Press, 1992), 157.
2. Ibid.
3. "The Meaning of Life," *Life* (December 1988), 76.
4. Advertisement for The Unitarian Universalists Congregations, *Texas Medical Center News* (September 1993).
5. "The Meaning of Life," *Life* (December 1988), 76.

Chapter 2

1. Leon Uris, *Trinity* (New York: Doubleday Publishers, Inc., 1976)
2. Phillip L. Berman, *The Search for Meaning, Americans Talk About What They Believe and Why* (New York: Ballantine Books, 1990), 27.

Chapter 3

1. Joy Davidman, *Smoke on the Mountain*, An Interpretation of the Ten Commandments (Louisville, KY: John Knox Press, 1985).
2. *Us* Magazine (September 1993).
3. George A. Tobin, "Moderately Religious, Desperately Sexual," *First Things* (November 1993).

4. Charles Sheldon's classic "What Would Jesus Do?" and a series of messages by Lee Stroebel entitled "What Would Jesus Say?" provided the basis for this premise.

Chapter 4

1. Charles Colson, "How to Confront a President," *Christianity Today* (April 25, 1994), 64.

2. Phillip L. Berman, *The Search for Meaning* (New York: Ballantine Books, 1990), 213–14.

3. G. K. Chesterton, *Orthodoxy* (New York: Bantam Doubleday Dell Publishing Group, Inc., 1959), 76.

Chapter 5

1. Kathleen McCleary, "Sex, Morals and AIDS," *USA Weekend* (Dec. 29, 1991), 4–6.

2. "Birth rate soars at school that dispenses condoms," *Intercessors for America Newsletter* (July/August 1992), 4.

3. Peggy Noonan, *Life, Liberty and the Pursuit of Happiness* (New York: Random House, Inc., 1994), 34.

4. Transcribed from Ted Koppel's Commencement Speech at Duke University, Sunday, May 10, 1987.

5. Peggy Noonan,"You'd cry too if it happened to you," *Forbes* (September 14, 1992), 58.

6. William J. Bennett, *The De-Valuing of America* (Colorado Springs, CO: Focus on the Family Publishing, 1992), 45.

7. Kenneth L. Woodward and Charles Fleming, "Scientology in the Schools," Newsweek (June 14, 1993), 76.

8. John Leo, "Schools to Parents: Keep out," *U.S. News and World Report* (Oct. 5, 1992), 33.

9. James D. Richardson, "A Compilation of the Messages and Papers of the Presidents, 1789-1897," vol. 1 (Published by Authority of Congress, 1899), 220.

10. William J. Bennet, The De-Valuing of America, 51.

Chapter 6

1. Beth Wagner, "Man Who Picked Up a Spilled Fortune in 1981 Kills Himself," Associated Press, 1993.

2. Ibid.

3. Helen Cordes, "How Much Dough for the Big Cheese?" *Utne Reader* (Mar/April 1992), 17–18.

4. John Ed Bradley, "Jimmy Johnson Livin' Large," *Esquire* (September 1993).

5. Porter Bibb, "Ted Turner's Wild Ride to the Top," from the book *It Ain't as Easy as It Looks: Ted Turner's Amazing Story, Success,* (November 1993), 38.

6. Rod Beaton, "Sandberg leaves field—for good," *USA Today* (June 14, 1994).

7. Ibid.

8. Ibid

9. Matt Trowbridge, "Sandberg retires from baseball," The Houston Post (June 14, 1994).

Chapter 7

1. Cal Thomas, *The Things That Matter Most* (New York: HarperCollins Publishers, Inc., 1994), 120.

2. George Barna, *The Barna Report, Volume 3, 1993-94, "Absolute Confusion"* (Ventura, CA: Regal Books, 1994) 13.

3. Marianne Williamson, *Return to Love* (New York: HarperCollins Publishers, 1993), preface.

4. Ibid.

5. Joannie Schrof,"Bookshop journeys... and beyond", *U.S. News & World Report* (April 25, 1994), 82-84.

6. Russell Chandler, *Understanding the New Age* (Grand Rapids, MI: Zondervan Publishing House, 1991), 192.

7. George Gallup, Jr. and Sarah Jones, *100 Questions and Answers: Religion in America* (Princeton, NJ: Princeton Religion Research Center, 1989), 76–77, 178–179.

8. Russell Chandler, "New Age: Menace in the Mainstream," *Current Thoughts and Trends*, vol. 10, no. 7 (July 1994), 8.

9. Peter Kreeft, *Back to Virtue* (San Francisco, CA: St. Ignatius Press, 1992), 30.

Chapter 8

1. Rance Crain, "A Defining Moment Is What You Make It," *Advertising Age (July 12, 1993).*

2. Ibid.

Chapter 9

1. Og Mandino, *The Choice*, (New York: Bantam Books, 1984), 2–3.
2. C. S. Lewis, "God in the Dock," *Essays on Theology and Ethics* (Grand Rapids, MI: William B. Eerdmans Publishing Company, 1970).
3. G. K. Chesterton, *Orthodoxy* (New York: Doubleday, 1959), 160.
4. Arlie J. Hoover, *The Case for Christian Theism*, quoted by Ravi Zacharias in *The Shattered Visage: The Real Face of Atheism* (Brentwood, TN: Wolgemuth & Hyatt, Publishers, 1990), 189–193.

Chapter 10

1. "Was It Real or Memories?" *Newsweek* (March 14, 1994), 54.
2. Philip Zaleski, "A Peculiar Little Test," *First Things*, (February, 1994), 9–12.
3. C.S. Lewis, *A Grief Observed* (New York: Doubleday, 1976), 68–69.
4. Oswald Chambers, *My Utmost for His Highest* (New York: Dodd, Mead & Company, 1935), 129.
5. Philip Yancey, *Disappointment with God: Three Questions No One Asks Aloud* (Grand Rapids, MI: Zondervan Publishing House, 1988), 253.

Chapter 11

1. William Bennett, *The Book of Virtues* (New York: Simon and Schuster, 1993), 493.
2. Ibid.
3. Emily Dickinson, Untitled, *Emily Dickinson Collected Poems* (Philadelphia, PA: Running Press Book Publishers, 1991).
4. Robert Bolt, *A Man for All Seasons* (New York: Vintage Books, Random House, Inc., 1990), 161.

5. C. S. Lewis, *The Weight of Glory and Other Addresses* (Grand Rapids, MI: Eerdmans), 1–2.

Chapter 12

1. Max DePree, *The Art of Leadership* (New York: Doubleday, 1989), 9.
2. Peggy Noonan, "You'd Cry Too If It Happened to You," *Forbes* (Sept. 14, 1992), 68.
3. Thomas Wolfe, *Of Time and the River* , Contemporary Classics Series (New York: MacMillan Publishing Co., Inc., 1980).

Chapter 13

1. "Court tape is selling fast," by..............., The Houston Chronicle, Feb. 26, 1994, Sec. A., 2.
2. Charles L. Allen, *You are Never Alone (Old Tappan, NJ: Fleming H. Revell Company, 1978)*, 77–78.
3. Ibid.
4. Peter Marshall, *Mr. Jones, Meet the Master*, (New York: Fleming H. Revell Company, 1949), 135–36.

Conclusion

1. Rev. Louie Giglio, Choice Ministries, Waco, TX.
2. Jerry Bridges, *Transforming Grace: Living Confidently in God's Unfailing Love* (Colorado Springs, CO: NavPress, 1991), 102.
3. Ibid, 107.

Appendix

1. Josh McDowell, *A Ready Defense* (San Bernadino, Calif: Here's Life Publishers, 1990), 45.
2. Cornelius Tacitus, *Annals of Imperial Rome*, XV, 44.
3. Josh McDowell, *A Ready Defense*, 92.
4. Ibid, 93.
5. C. S. Lewis, *Mere Christianity* (New York: Macmillan Publishing Co., 1960), 40–41.
6. Josh McDowell, *Evidence for the Resurrection (Dallas, TX: Josh McDowell Ministry, 1990)*.